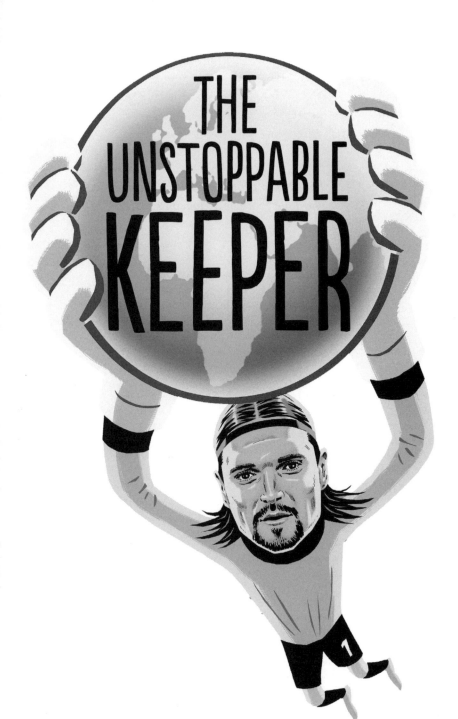

*For all the people across the world
who love football as much as I do...*

THE INCREDIBLE ADVENTURES OF...

THE UNSTOPPABLE KEEPER

BY LUTZ PFANNENSTIEL

VSP

Published by Vision Sports Publishing in 2014

Vision Sports Publishing
19-23 High Street
Kingston upon Thames
Surrey
KT1 1LL

www.visionsp.co.uk

ISBN:978-1909534-28-5

Originally published in Germany as *Unhaltbar - Meine Abenteuer als Welttorhüter* © 2009 Rowohlt Verlag GmbH, Reinbek bei Hamburg

English Language Translation: Matthew Rockey © 2014

A CIP record for this book is available from the British library

Written by: Lutz Pfannenstiel with Christian Putsch
Translated by: Matthew Rockey
English edition editor: Jim Drewett
Copy editors: John Murray and Paul Baillie-Lane
Design: Doug Cheeseman
Front cover artwork: Stephen Gulbis (*www.stephengulbis.com*)

Typeset by Palimpsest Book Production Limited, Falkirk, Stirlingshire

Printed and bound in the UK by TJ International, Padstow, Cornwall

MIX
Paper from responsible sources
FSC
www.fsc.org FSC® C013056

CONTENTS

PROLOGUE 1

1. DREAMING OF RATKO SVILAR 5

2. SWEPT OUT INTO THE BIG, WIDE WORLD 23

3. SURROUNDED BY VUVUZELAS 42

4. ALL ABOARD THE FINNISH CHILL-OUT TRAIN . . . 61

5. DROPPING THE BALL 91

6. WELCOME TO HELL 112

7. BACK TO SQUARE ONE 122

8. NIGHT AND DAY 149

9. ROAD TRIP ACROSS AMERICA 159

10. WANTED: ENTREPRENEURS IN ARMENIA 181

11. BRAZIL: SINGING ALL THE WAY HOME 199

EPILOGUE 214

ACKNOWLEDGEMENTS

There are so many people to thank for my incredible football adventure. But first and foremost I must give thanks to my parents, who have supported me and put up with the stress I have caused them throughout my career.

To my amazing wife, Amalia, who has always agreed to my crazy ideas and forgiven me when they didn't go to plan – I wouldn't be where I am without you. To my ex-girlfriend, Anita, who stuck by me while I was in prison. You saved my life with your unbelievable dedication and support during those 101 days. To Trevor Storton, who sadly died in 2011, for allowing me to rebuild my life and love for football at Bradford Park Avenue. To Bruce Macdonald, Marc Chidley and all the players and staff at Dunedin Technical – the peace and tranquility of New Zealand, and your warm, friendly attitude saved my career. To Ray Killick for saving my life three times after my heart stopped on the pitch – I'll never forget that kiss.

Finally, a special thanks goes to all the coaches, players and people I met during my globetrotting football journey – you made my career and I will never forget any of you.

PROLOGUE

Almost everything is filled with blackness. Outside it's bright, the sun is beaming, but there aren't any windows on this bus, there's no way of looking out at the outside world, nor even at the driver. Only a dim lightbulb highlights the dark silhouettes of the other passengers, who hold on tight to the bars as we drive around corners – or at least they try to, handcuffs permitting.

The stench on the prison bus is nauseating. We stand pressed against each other, barely able to move from the spot. Twelve prisoners, one cramped and stinking bus. The sticky air mixes with adrenaline and cold sweat. Some of these men have killed, some are rapists. I just played football. I wonder how long we've been on the road. It feels like an eternity, and with every passing minute I leave my old life behind me.

I feel the metal digging into my wrists. The court officer snapped the handcuffs shut so hard. At least I'm not chained to any of the bars. Only four Chinese men are, standing silently and staring into the darkness. I memorise their faces – they seem to be the ones with the most to answer for. Some of the prisoners are smoking, they must have somehow smuggled the tobacco on board. A young Asian man is standing next to me, his hair shorn to a few millimetres. He fiddles with his watch. It flips open like an old-fashioned pocket watch, revealing some white powder inside.

An emergency coke ration. His last for years – perhaps even his last ever. Calmly, he snorts it.

So here I am. On board a prison bus on my way to Singapore's Queenstown Remand Prison. Five months in one of the world's most notorious jails. Is my global journey as a professional football player really going to end here, on the afternoon of 7 January 2001? The sport has shown me half the world, and it has led me to wonderful places and to wonderful people. And now it is taking me to prison, into exile. The judge's harsh words from an hour ago still ring loudly in my ears: She said it had been proven that I had played a part in a match-fixing scheme. An absurd accusation, but what does that matter now? Nothing. Will I ever be allowed to play professional football again? My lawyers couldn't promise me that.

The bus swerves sharply to the left. I have to steady myself by holding onto one of the bars. Outside there are people who, just a few months ago, still cheered me on and voted me Singapore's goalie of the year. But recently they just pointed at me. "Kelong!" ["Fraud!"] That hurt, almost even more so than the prison sentence that awaits me. How could I ever betray something I love as much as football? How will my family survive all this time? And Anita – will she really stand by me, as she promised me teary-eyed in the courtroom?

The bus comes to an abrupt halt. Two guards wrench open the door, the sunlight hurts my eyes. We're in the middle of the prison yard, where German Shepherds have been brought out ready for our arrival. If anyone has been able to smuggle drugs on board the prison bus, they will be found out now – no matter where the drugs are hidden about their person. "Undress," bellows one man like a military drill sergeant. I know what's coming; I already spent time here while I was awaiting trial. The German Shepherds run between and around us. Then a guard comes up to me. "Open your mouth." Wearing rubber gloves, he pulls out my tongue. No drugs. "Now bend down and open your asshole." It was worse the first time I came to the prison. This time I knew what to expect, but it was still the most degrading thing I've ever been through in my life. Half an hour later, all I own are two brown pairs of shorts, two white T-shirts and see-through flip-flops. And what remains of a dream which has all but died. But first things first.

CHAPTER 1
DREAMING OF RATKO SVILAR

I never met Ratko Svilar, yet he was the inspiration for an unbelievable football journey that would take me to all four corners of the globe, not to mention landing me in a Singapore jail.

I'll never forget the moment I saw Ratko for the first time. I had turned the volume on the little colour TV in my bedroom down to a faint whisper, like I did most nights when Eurosport broadcast all the goals from the minor football leagues, my mother wrongly believing I'd been asleep for hours. The players on the tiny screen rarely appeared larger than African flying ants. I got so close to the TV that the players became nothing more than a blur. My eyes began to hurt after a couple of minutes, but I couldn't miss a single move the goalkeepers made: How they would direct their teammates, curse loudly and dive after each ball.

"... and yet again Ratko Svilar punches the ball out of danger," whispered the reporter into my little bedroom. "Without their goalkeeper, FC Antwerp would surely be five places further down the table." Ratko Svilar, what a name. I watched as the huge Serb, with his long, dirt-smeared hair and a scowl on his face, dived in slow motion to stop a shot. And at that moment I knew that one day I, too, would be a professional goalkeeper.

"I'm gonna be just like Ratko Svilar," I said as I greeted my mother at the breakfast table the next morning, as if she'd known this Svilar for years. But she was already well aware of the fact that she wasn't raising just any 12-year-old boy. "The goalkeeper?" she asked, barely looking up. I was impressed that she knew who FC Antwerp's keeper was. My mother smiled. Back then I used to harp on about famous goalkeepers on a daily basis – and at some point she'd noticed how I never praised outfield players. But that didn't occur to me. "Yes, like Svilar," I carried on. "If I don't make it in the Bundesliga, then I'll just go to a different country and become a professional there. After all, Svilar's from Serbia and he's now playing in Belgium." My mother smiled again. "Yes, Lutz. You just need to pop to school beforehand. Your first lesson starts in 15 minutes." She was great at rousing me from my daydreams. I got going exactly 12 minutes later, since I only lived a three-minute walk from school and didn't want to waste any more time than I had to.

It had snowed overnight in Zwiesel, my hometown in the Bavarian Forest in southern Germany, 100 miles from Munich. When I looked out of the house and saw nothing but white, my mood soured instantly. It was already March, and cross-country skiers keen to make the most of the late snowfall were trudging through 20 centimetres of fresh powder. In their midst was a grumpy boy tormented by just one thought: "Training's bound to be cancelled." It was the same old drama every winter. On days like those, I would take a detour on my way to school via SC Zwiesel's football ground, only to have my fears confirmed. The groundsman had already rammed that odious sign into the snow: "No trespassing on the sports field."

That afternoon it snowed so heavily that people could only drive their cars at walking pace. After school I rushed home, pulled on my wellies and set off, a ball in one hand and a snow shovel in the other. I dashed down the small hill on the other side of the road towards the football ground, climbed over the gate and began shovelling the snow out of the penalty area.

On my way I'd already seen Gerd Bielmeier's tracks in the snow. He was always there. "Bill the Indian", as we called him because of his long black hair, cut a lonely figure as he ran his laps.

He worked shifts at a big glass factory in Zwiesel, the biggest employer in the region. He would start every morning at 6am, but after 2pm his life was ruled by football – every day, every week. He obviously had the same genetic disorder as me – it didn't matter that he was already over 30. Every day he spent two hours running around the ground, more often than not on his own, occasionally stopping to launch a few balls at the empty goal before running on, further and further.

"Shall I kick a few balls at the goal for you?" asked the Indian once I'd cleared the worst of the snow from the penalty area. I chucked the shovel onto one of the huge white mounds and got in goal. Two lunatics in the snow. One shooting, the other saving. And neither of us was able to do anything else – nor did we want to.

An hour later, my father came to the ground straight from work and took over from Bill the Indian. Patiently he began kicking ball after ball at me, and I flew. Sometimes to the right, and sometimes to the left. He couldn't have made me happier if he'd tried. Some days he would just look at me and shake his head as I stood peering gloomily out of the living room window, wondering when it would finally start raining. I loved the rain, because it washed the snow away. But today on teletext it said: "Bavarian Forest: Further snowfall at high altitudes." That white coat would often lie 50 centimetres deep across the town, slowing everything in its path. I hated it.

Even so, not a day passed when I didn't play football. Not a single day. It hurt if I couldn't play football. When I celebrated my First Communion, the priest asked me what I wanted to be when I grew up. I answered that the only option for me was to become a professional footballer. Whenever I was sick I could hide it with brilliant feats of acting. When I was eight years old I once got a nasty stomach bug and spent the whole night vomiting. The next day was the Monday before Lent. We played football anyway, indoors, dressed up in our traditional Carnival costumes. So there I stood, white as a sheet, a little boy in a witch's mask defending the goal, every now and then turning round, tearing my mask off and throwing up behind the net. "Don't you want to stop?" asked my father, who was our team's coach at the time. "Not a chance," I replied and played on until the end. While the others went off to the showers, I stayed behind to clean up with paper towels and a bucket.

If my father didn't have any time or there was no training, I played out on the road against the boys from the neighbouring estate; I'd dive around until my arms and legs were absolutely covered in grazes and bruises. My emotional state depended entirely on my being able to prevent balls from crossing a goal line. When we practised crosses during training, sometimes I threw myself in among the defenders and strikers so violently that my friends would go home with their noses bleeding. That must have been how Ratko Svilar used to do it, I thought. "That young Pfannenstiel, he's mental," people would say. I took it as a compliment. You probably have to be mad to be a goalkeeper.

During the winter months the groundsman often saw me entering the ground despite the fact that he'd clearly forbidden everyone by putting up his sign. But he never stopped me, and neither did my father. And how *could* he have? In the 1960s my father had been the best keeper the little town, with its population of 12,000, had ever produced. He had been number two in Bavaria's junior league selection, second only to none other than Bayern Munich and West Germany Legend Sepp Maier. Life was to see one of them become a decent architect, and the other the best goalkeeper in the world. Even in the days of the Bavarian junior league selection, it had usually been Maier who played while Pfannenstiel sat on the bench, annoyed. My father liked to put it down to lobbying on the part of Bayern Munich, convinced of some sort of a conspiracy. Perhaps, though, you could argue that the man who would one day go on to be goalkeeper when West Germany won the 1974 World Cup was simply a bit more talented than him. Who knows? But that's not the kind of argument you can use to reason with a Pfannenstiel. On the pitch my father – who was later praised for his level-headedness as an architect – played like a madman, and even his own defenders were scared of him.

During my first official league game as keeper in the neighbouring town of Bodenmais, older people soon realised that I really was a chip off the old block. Just seven years old, I let a goal in right before the final whistle. I hadn't stood a chance of getting to the ball, but it still hurt – just like it would hurt hundreds more times throughout my life – to see our opponents cheering and to have to get the ball out of the net while my crestfallen teammates crept back to the centre circle. "You blind idiots," I shouted at our defenders, tears streaming down my face, "you need to give up football!" After the match I ran to a nearby field where nobody could see me. I cried for half an hour before finally deciding to go home.

The day when the father of my childhood friend Tobias built a wooden goal in his garden was one of my happiest ever. After we'd had enough of sliding about on the muddy lawn, Tobias and I leaned against the posts, both of us clutching a glass of lemonade, and reviewed our world-class performances. The night before, Eurosport had shown some coverage from the Brazilian league, momentarily banishing Ratko Svilar from my thoughts. "Tobi," I began, "let's make a pact." Tobi looked up and drew closer. "One day," I continued solemnly, "we'll both play for Flamengo in Brazil's top league and become filthy rich." My friend agreed it was a good plan, and when you're eight years old nothing is impossible. Neither of us was in any doubt. We raised our index and middle fingers: "I swear." Now, I never did exactly become filthy rich, but I managed to honour the part about Brazil more than 20 years later.

The better I became, the more I concentrated on my sport. I would spend hours standing around in the local sports shop trying on goalkeeper gloves. The owner, Werner Kuhndörfer, would roll his eyes whenever he saw me anywhere near his shop. During the 1990 World Cup, while my teammates were busy worshipping the likes of Lothar Matthäus and Andreas Brehme, I just talked about how Thomas N'Kono's saves were what saw

Cameroon through to the quarter-finals. Or about Luis Gabelo Conejo, Costa Rica's moustachioed goalie, and his incredible reactions on the goal line. They were my heroes, and I studied their each and every movement on video. Just like I studied everything that might bring me closer to achieving my dream. I read in a sports magazine that it was unhealthy to bathe in water above 40 degrees. From that point on I stopped taking a bath altogether on the night before we had a match. It didn't actually bother anyone, because I wouldn't go out on the day before a game anyway so that I was as rested as possible. You just need to do everything right, I told myself, and then you'll be a professional. Like Ratko.

Unfortunately though, my body didn't seem too interested in playing ball. When I was 13 years old, I was regarded as technically the best goalkeeper of my age in Bavaria. But I was just 5'3" and was playing for the little team SC Zwiesel. A club out in the sticks, where the talent scouts of the Bavarian Football Association rarely strayed. Bayern Munich's youth team keeper, on the other hand, could barely catch a ball but he was already 5'11" and got picked. While he groped in vain for one ball after another during the selection matches, I was using an old leather ball to take my frustration out on an innocent garage door in Zwiesel. It felt as if all the injustice in the world had been placed on my little shoulders.

I wasn't sure you could make yourself grow more quickly by measuring your height every day. But it was worth a try. So every day I positioned myself against the frame of the kitchen door, used a tape measure and noted down the measurements – to the nearest millimetre – neatly in a little book. Week after week, line by line. I'm not suggesting there was any connection, but in the following two years I grew by almost 20 centimetres. And that meant I was finally tall enough. So when the Bavarian selection coach gave me a ring and, after just a few games, I was even called up for the squad of the national youth team, I was finally certain that I was on my way to becoming a world-class goalkeeper.

It didn't really matter to me whether that meant playing in Brazil or the Bundesliga.

I felt as if I were in a narrow, steep tunnel that led straight ahead towards paradise. There was barely any room to look left or right, and I had to concentrate on moving up. Everyone knew that was how I thought. By then I had my first proper girlfriend, Karin. She was beautiful and funny, and even managed to open my eyes just a fraction to things beyond the world of football. We had a fantastic time together. But it soon became clear to her that I would always put football first.

After a match against the youth team of 1860 Munich, the Lions, I was stopped by the opposing team's coach. "Lutz, you're good," he said. "Come to our residential academy. You won't find better opportunities to develop anywhere else." He persuaded me in a matter of seconds, but the hard part was my mother. She was a world-class mother, but always so cautious. She had lived in Zwiesel her whole life. It was a happy life, but one that was always filled with concern about anything new and unknown. I would never have been able to convince her to let me move to Munich at the age of 16.

So I went to my father. While his former rival Sepp Maier was busy becoming one of Bavaria's first millionaire footballers, my father had decided to study architecture. Nevertheless, at heart he had remained one of those people who felt more at home, more alive, on the football pitch than anywhere else. He would have done anything to help me achieve my dream, and he understood what was going on inside me. Two decades earlier he had been tortured by the same feelings.

After days of me keeping on at him, our plan was finally in place. "We're gonna stop by the Lions today. They're playing this afternoon," we told my mother one Sunday morning as we headed for the front door and left for Munich – for a meeting with the 1860 youth coordinator. "All right," she called back to us. It was a pretty fragile plan, since the Lions weren't actually playing that day. And yet, even though my mother lived under the same roof as arguably the two most football-mad men in town, she couldn't really have cared less about the sport. She had no idea about who played when. Once everything is signed, we thought, she's bound to say yes.

It was already dark by the time we returned home. A hearty smell hung in the air; a smell that even today still instantly makes me feel at home, no matter where I am in the world. My mother had made goulash, with pasta and a sauce that only she can get just right. "Who won?" she called out from the kitchen. When we didn't reply, she came towards us with a smile on her face. "What's wrong?" We both went silent for a moment before finally confessing. The contract was signed, we told her, and I'd be moving to Munich in a few weeks.

What followed was a two-hour sermon – no, more a hurricane. By the end it was clear to me: She would never let me out of the house if I didn't first agree to finish my secondary school education. One call to Munich and my dream of living at the residential football academy was over. In the end I signed with FC Vilshofen, a club that also played at the highest youth level. That way I met the requirements of both the football association and my mother, because it meant I could stay at home. My father had to foot the bill for our failed plan. He now drove me, five times a week, the 70 kilometres to my training sessions and back. He smiled for an entire day when the authorities made a special exception and I received my driver's licence early at the age of 17.

While I was at technical college, I bought myself a bright red BMW two weeks before my driving test, thus well and truly cementing my delusions of grandeur. I parked it in the teachers' car park without a care in the world. On one cold December day, my physics teacher snapped at me when I entered the classroom. "See that sign? Teachers only?" He was one of those people with a profound hatred of anything football-related, and he wasn't exactly bursting with admiration for me either, presumably in part because of the dozens of days I had already been absent from school. I nodded with a smile, my classmates staring at me. "Are you a teacher?" he bellowed. I shook my head. My teacher nodded triumphantly, enjoying his power. "Then get out there and look at that sign until I decide you've actually understood that."

I crowed inwardly with delight. Smiling, I pushed my chair back. I loved putting on a show even then. I walked through the snow, stood in front of the sign, took my jumper off and stared topless at the words. "What do you think you're doing?" yelled Mr Wiesinger out of the window. "I think I'm coming down with something," I yelled back as I scooped up a handful of snow and put it on my head, "and I look forward to telling the headmaster all about it." Startled, he called me back into the classroom, where my classmates could barely suppress their laughter. From then on he usually left me alone.

Somehow I managed to get my diploma and was finally able to enjoy life as a footballer as I had always imagined it. In 1992 I signed with 1. FC Bad Kötzting, a successful semi-professional fourth division team that paid me enough to make ends meet. The so-called Velvet Revolution had just taken place a few kilometres away in Czechoslovakia, and the Iron Curtain had fallen without bloodshed. Our neighbour was soon to become the Czech Republic and suddenly we had eight Czechs on the team, all of them at professional level. A year earlier they had been earning the equivalent of around 100 euros a month playing for Skoda Pilsen in the top Czech league. Now they were playing in Germany's fourth division and earning several times that.

The sun beat down as I entered the training ground for the first time one July afternoon. I had an uneasy feeling; the club's number one the previous season, Vaclav Lavicka, had made a point of going out onto the pitch a couple of minutes before me. He'd once been the understudy keeper on the Czechoslovak national team. As I approached the 6'5" giant, I hid my panic beneath a face that would have impressed even the most seasoned poker player.

I had always been fascinated by famous goalkeeper rivalries. After their final training session before the first 1962 World Cup match, Hans Tilkowski trashed his hotel room on finding out that his rival, Wolfgang Farian, would be keeping goal for West

Germany. I had also eagerly followed Uli Stein's behaviour during the 1986 World Cup; he had called national coach Franz Beckenbauer a 'clown' after Toni Schumacher was selected as first-choice goalkeeper, and was sent home in disgrace. And even the chronically funny Sepp Maier was so bothered by his clash with Gladbach's Wolfgang Kleff before the 1974 World Cup, that he once joked with journalists: "I gave my dog away. Because it kept going, 'Kleff, Kleff'." Now I, too, was suddenly one side of such a duel.

I might have only been playing in the fourth division, but I fought for the no 1 jersey with just as much passion as my famous idols. There he stood, Vaclav Lavicka, with his broad frame, not deigning to even look at me. There's something absolute about the rivalry between goalkeepers – whoever loses the pre-season fight for a regular place stands little chance of playing during the season. A centre-back might also be played as a full-back, but a goalkeeper's only alternative is the substitutes' bench – and perhaps a secret hope that the other keeper will be injured or not up to scratch.

Technically speaking Lavicka and I were equals, but he was already 35. The Czech was experienced and knew not to overdo it in training. But psychology isn't quite that logical between goalkeepers. "Come on, old man," I called to him after two hours in the summer heat, "50 more shots." We took it in turns to send one ball after another flying at each other, not saying a word. Again and again, we jumped for the ball, rolled around on the dusty grass and sprang back to our feet. The other players had long since left the pitch, but neither of us wanted to show the other any sign of weakness. We barely exchanged a word with each other, not even when we were eating or in the changing rooms. He was actually a pretty nice guy – had it not been for that one thought in my mind: "If I'm not better than this old guy, then I won't be better than anyone." At some point during pre-season Lavicka's form began to drop. He had simply trained too hard, and so it was me who got to stand in goal during the first match of the season.

The days began to blur into one, which was by no means unpleasant. If I got up at 10am, my mother would have prepared my breakfast and placed the newspaper on the table, open at the sports section. One of her better habits, which she has kept up to this day. Around noon I would travel the 40 kilometres to Kötzting and begin strutting my stuff at the outdoor pool. I've no idea whether Oliver Kahn ever did somersaults in front of random girls – I did it every day. I trained in the afternoon, and then my working day was over. The brand new university of applied sciences in Deggendorf, where I wanted to study business, wasn't going to open for another year. I could live with a clear conscience.

But on the day the university finally opened its doors, it quickly became clear to me that I wasn't made for life at an institution of higher education. Forty of the university's first-ever students were buzzing around in the foyer – a lot of them were very nice, but there were a couple of 19-year-olds with side partings and crisp shirts who dreamed of a career at some big consultancy firm, yet still had mummy iron their socks for them. At the next table there were three students who had already left home. "Do I need to factor in more than eight marks per hour for a cleaning lady?" one asked the others casually. "Not for one from the Czech Republic," replied another full of arrogance. Maybe it was the atmosphere which made the supposed elite of tomorrow act as if they were today's crème de la crème. The university was housed in the Schauffler-Villa, a former private clinic.

During the introductory lecture I leaned back, bored; it felt a little bit like being on the subs' bench at a football match. No, far worse. At least on the bench you can jump up when something exciting happens. You can't jump up during a lecture, and it's not as if anything exciting happens anyway. With my arms folded, I slid further and further back in my chair, like an insulted national player banished to the bench who didn't think he should be there, while at the front a boring man in an ugly orange checked shirt talked about how far those present had already made it. "Each and every one of you, ladies and gentlemen," he pontificated in a voice that seemed far too high, "will decide on the future of this country." Amen.

Frustrated, I looked up at the ceiling. Neon lights. And then to the left: A pretty blonde student was making a note of every single word with her pencil. When I finally looked to the right, three chairs along I saw the only other person in the room who had slid as far down his chair as I had – his eyelids heavy, arms folded over his ragged T-shirt. He was well toned and nearly 10 years older than everyone else in the room. He looked somehow familiar, and I spent the next 10 minutes wondering where I knew him from. It turned out it was Hans Wurzer, who had been one of the biggest rising football stars from the Bavarian Forest before he tore his cruciate ligament. Nowadays that doesn't usually mean much more than six months off of training, but in the 1980s a torn cruciate ligament often meant the end of your career. It certainly spelt the end of Hans's professional ambitions – from then on he only played in the lower leagues.

"You're that Hans Wurzer," I said to him when the professor finally stopped talking and we had managed to claw ourselves up from our desks. "That's right," he replied, "and you're that Pfannenstiel, aren't you?" He had been recruited by the German border police and just returned from two years in Lebanon – but he hadn't lost track of the Bavarian football scene during his time abroad. "I heard you're on your way to the Bundesliga," he continued. "We'll see," I replied in true Beckenbauer style. It soon became glaringly obvious to us that we weren't destined to become your average business students. Little did I realise, though, that I wouldn't actually finish studying until 10 years later – in New Zealand.

Before long we were part of a group of 10 students who had more success with women than exams. At university we also acted rather like Lothar Matthäus was behaving at that time on the national squad – as if the world revolved around us. I can't say I demonstrated much self-restraint. Of course, it makes a difference if you're being cheered on at the weekend by 60,000 Bundesliga spectators or, like me, just 1,000 fans down in the fourth division – but you still feel like a star. A star who doesn't understand why he still has to go to his computer science lectures.

The day I walked into the hall for the first proper lecture, I knew straight away that I'd found my new favourite enemy. Professor Rummler was short, severely lacking in hair and a sense of humour, and frighteningly cross-eyed. It proved to be some time before I liked him. First of all I just noticed that he liked shouting, loudly: "Idiots, the lot of you. Why are you even here?" he would often cry, getting all worked up. "If this is the elite of tomorrow, then good night Germany!" I had arrived quarter of an hour late as usual. Rummler scrutinised me disparagingly, his gaze resting on my hair. Even in those days I used to tie my hair back in a ponytail and apply a generous portion of gel – not everyone's cup of tea, but it's become my trademark.

"You'd win the trial," he said in my general direction. I looked up as I sat down on the first seat I could find. "Which one?" I asked him. "Well, the one against your hairdresser," retorted the man, trying to wind me up. And I wasn't about to take that lying down. "You'd win yours too, mate," I replied, addressing my lecturer as if we were on first name terms, "the one against your optician." I doubt I'm remembered as Deggendorf's most submissive student, but that was how we communicated from then on, and after a couple of months we somehow even managed to develop a certain respect for one another. By the end we had something of a love-hate relationship.

I was a student and a fourth division goalkeeper, but in my mind I'd long since been playing in the Bundesliga. My performances were consistently strong, and after a few months a letter from Bundesliga team VfL Bochum came rattling through the ancient fax machine at 1. FC Bad Kötzting: "Having observed his performance this season, we would like to invite your player to a sample training session." In the early 1990s the club had lost its reputation of being immune to relegation, but it had just been promoted back into the top flight.

I sensed this was my big chance. The following day's computer science lecture took place without the male student and his ponytail in the back row.

As it turned out, I needn't have bothered spending that week in Bochum. Twice a day I slogged away with the two goalkeepers, Ralf Zumdick and Andreas Wessels, only to learn at the end that the club were just looking for a man for their amateur team. "No, that's out of the question for me," I said. Another club, 1. FC Nuremberg, had already tried attracting me with a deal offering similar prospects. "Either you make me a professional or I won't come," I continued. Coach Jürgen Gelsdorf stood up without a word, briefly shook my hand and walked out. Ralf Zumdick accompanied me to the door. "You'll find a way eventually," he said as we parted ways.

Outside, a man in a designer suit was leaning by the door. I had no idea who he was. "And?" he asked, as if we'd known each other for years, "did you sign?" I then remembered seeing him at the training session. He had been standing next to a couple of pensioners on the edge of the pitch. "No," I mumbled, "they only wanted me as an amateur." The slim man took a step closer to me. "If you really want to be a professional," he said as emphatically as a father advising his son on choosing the right career, "then go to Malaysia. I've seen you, you're good. Call me, and in two weeks you'll be living in your dream home by the sea with 5,000 dollars a month in your pocket." He thrust his card into my hand. "Football Management Agency," it read, followed simply by "Consultant". It was my first contact with a professional players' agent. "Thanks," I murmured and got into my BMW. On my way home I couldn't shake the thought: In two weeks I could be a professional …

A couple of days later I dialled the number. "I knew you'd call," began the agent confidently. "I've already got two clubs who want to see you."

"I need a little time," I replied and hung up. That night I couldn't sleep. Getting into paid football via a Bundesliga club's amateur team was the usual route which talented youngsters took.

Should I really stray off that direct path for the sake of an adventure? I spent several minutes staring at the ceiling. But surely even Ratko Svilar must have once upped sticks and left Serbia? And why shouldn't I?

The next afternoon, I had barely finished parking my car at Kötzting's ground when Michael Plötz, who was in charge of the club's administrative affairs, came rushing over to me from the offices. He was clutching another fax, this time from FC Bayern Munich. The country's most successful club had actually sent their scouts out into the provincial backwaters, and fortunately for me I must have been there that day. I was invited for week of training, a trial at Germany's biggest and most famous club. Malaysia would have to wait.

The patter of hundreds of football boot studs sounds different at Bayern than in other dressing rooms. It's somehow clearer, more echoing. Maybe it's because of the luxury tiles, or perhaps the fact that less talking goes on there than at other clubs. Each of the professional players, such as Matthäus, Klinsmann and Effenberg, was his very own medium-sized enterprise with a turnover worth millions of marks, and the atmosphere struck me as being correspondingly sober. I walked past the legendary laundry chute: The players would throw their boots into it after training – none of them had cleaned his own boots since signing with the club. The next morning their boots would be gleaming, back in their usual spot inside the dressing room, together with the freshly laundered training outfits. That chute contributed to a slightly pretentious overall image I had of the club; it was one tile in a larger mosaic. Still, when I saw it I couldn't help smiling to myself. To me it was the epitome of top-class professional football.

Players like Lothar Matthäus had their own fixed seats in the dressing room. It wasn't a good idea to leave even a towel anywhere near such top dogs. The papers like to speculate about team hierarchies, but they have no idea what goes on. In the dressing room – one of the last no-go zones, a forbidden area for journalists – they really come to the fore. At FC Cologne in the 1990s, Bodo Illgner had a brass plate with his name on it mounted beneath one of the showers. That shower was out of bounds for the muscular national keeper's teammates. It's advisable to exercise a certain amount of caution when you're in the dressing room of a new club.

My training gear had been hung up next to that of a grim-looking player who had just come to Munich from Karlsruher SC. Oliver Kahn shook my hand. "You're here for a trial, aren't you?" he asked. "Yes," I replied, "we'll see what happens." Kahn nodded and carried on lacing up his boots. I spent two hours training with him and goalie coach Sepp Maier; I fought as if I only had this one chance. And yet I struggled to keep up with Kahn's intensity. Until that day I considered myself pretty dogged. But if that word hadn't existed, then it would have needed to be invented for the guy doing his exercises next to me. Kahn concentrated on every ball as if the championship depended on it. When we stopped for lunch I ate my pasta with nothing on it, because I thought that was healthier. In the evening I went to bed at 9pm. I wanted to do everything right.

At the end of my trial, the head of Bayern's amateur department summoned me to a barren meeting room. A couple of chairs, a table and a nice view of the car park. I had brought my lawyer, Wolfram Zimmermann, with me, if only to seem more professional. His knowledge of football was so-so, but back then you didn't need to be an expert to work as a player agent – it was a fairly new profession. "You're not yet good enough to be a professional," the manager said to me. His words hit me like a punch in the face. "You'll play and train with the amateurs, and now and then you can train with the professionals." He spoke as if he'd already seen me sign the contract, and of course he was right: You don't turn down an offer from Bayern, not even for the amateurs. There's no better stepping stone into the world of professional football in Germany.

And yet, just one single message managed to penetrate the convolutions of my brain: You're not good enough for the professionals. "So you don't want me for the professionals?" I asked. The manager looked at me in amazement. "Listen lad, you're young. And we've got Sven Scheuer, who's a good substitute for Oliver Kahn. But your time will come, trust me." In my head all I could hear was the stranger from Bochum: "In two weeks you'll be a professional in Malaysia," his voice said, "... just two weeks ... house by the sea." Both the manager and my lawyer looked at me quizzically – I was so lost in my thoughts that I hadn't replied. "No, I'm sorry," I said eventually, registering out of the corner of my eye as my lawyer winced, "that's out of the question. Someone else has made me a professional offer." I got up and said goodbye. "No, no, Lutz, sit down," said my lawyer. He pleaded with me, his voice getting louder. But it was no use. "Can't you say something to him?" he asked my good friend Werner Neissendorfer, who had also accompanied us. "You know how he is," Werner replied. "If he doesn't want to, then he doesn't want to." My lawyer was still swearing as we got into the car.

Back in Zwiesel I called my old friend Hans. Over the past eight months he had often talked about going to Lebanon with me. He said the football was good there too, and he could work as my goalkeeping coach.

"Does your offer still stand?" I asked him.

"What offer?"

"Well, you wanted to go abroad with me," I said. "Would you consider coming to Malaysia?" Hans was silent at the other end of the line. After two years, the confines of the Bavarian Forest had long since become a huge burden for him. I briefly explained the situation before he interrupted me: "Well, let's go then." Over the next couple of weeks he was pretty much the only person in Bavaria who didn't think I was a total lunatic.

The few weeks before our departure seemed to fly by in seconds. If we weren't training or at one of our numerous farewell parties, Hans spoke almost non-stop with three Malaysian clubs on the phone; they seemed to trust the agent from Bochum blindly and agreed to cover the cost of our flights. Each of the clubs promised we would "definitely" come to an agreement; they wanted to pay around 5,000 dollars per month. Their contact in Germany had slightly oversold me as this great rising star from Bayern Munich.

While I was worrying about a visa for the first time in my life – a discipline I'm now a world-class expert in – the people in my hometown were busy bad-mouthing me. Why? Time and time again they would ask me: Why? I laughed at the doubters, although I did find it hard to say goodbye. "That Pfannenstiel's a lunatic," the people said. Once again – just like when I was eight years old – I didn't take it as a huge insult. Most of the people who were saying it had never been, and never would be, professional footballers. I on the other hand would have fulfilled my dream in less than a week. A professional. Just like Ratko.

CHAPTER 2
SWEPT OUT INTO THE BIG, WIDE WORLD

Kuala Lumpur welcomed us as if the city wanted to bite us in half and spit us out. The humid heat at Sultan Abdul Aziz Shah Airport slammed into us like a wall. It was overwhelming after the 12-hour trip, even though the sun had only just risen. The monsoon winds had driven hot moisture into the city, and we were plunged into the hectic hustle and bustle of the airport terminal. Sweat hung in the air, families with children rushed past us, and people selling water and sweets tried to drown out the groaning of the tannoy announcements and the seething crowds. In those days, 15 million passengers passed through the airport in Malaysia's capital each year, and I suspect no more than half would have been permitted under Western regulations. Utterly exhausted, Hans and I pushed past the queues of people. I hadn't slept a wink, as was to be the case on the hundreds of flights I took over the years.

The taxi driver threw my suitcase and kitbag, which contained no fewer than 10 pairs of goalkeeper gloves, into the battered boot and lined the car up in the solid stream of vehicles that rolled into Kuala Lumpur every morning. Shrill tones blared out of the radio. It sounded to me as if an army of recorder players were doing battle with hundreds of xylophonists. "Gamelan music. We play it at every family party," the driver called back to us. "Weddings, baptisms, divorces. Always, always." He giggled loudly and the recorders continued to whistle out of the tinny radio. The high-pitched sounds worked their way deeper and deeper into my brain. At least I was wide awake by the time we stopped outside our little hotel half an hour later.

We got out in front of an absolute hovel. "Congratulations Hans," I grumbled as we entered our room in the dilapidated hotel. Back then I wasn't at all confident speaking English. Hans, on the other hand, was a seasoned traveller who had lived in Lebanon, and he had taken care of planning our trip. I pushed the air-conditioning button in vain. Click. Click. Nothing happened. It probably hadn't worked in that room since 1970. Mosquitoes buzzed around above the two beds, and were probably the happiest insects in the world. Fresh meat! A dozen cockroaches had set up camp behind the bathroom door. "Relax," said Hans, "we'll just chill out for a couple of hours and then we can look for something better." Half an hour later we were back outside the front door – I couldn't have stood another minute there.

We headed to the nearest restaurant and ate our fill. I was moaning so loudly that eventually a couple at the next table noticed us and asked whether we needed any help. We nodded in amazement, unaccustomed as we were to this kind of friendliness. The couple turned out to be huge football fans and wanted to know everything about the Bundesliga. We – or rather Hans – chatted to them for the next two hours. I was too shy to talk in English. At one point the girl explained that her father was the manager of the Shangri-La Hotel and she could have a word with him. Soon afterwards we were safely inside the exclusive five-star establishment, the girl having arranged a dirt-cheap rate of 300 dollars per week for us. Half an hour later, we had settled into our little apartment – in the bathroom we found six different types of shampoo for guests to use in the whirlpool bath. I laughed when I saw a phone next to the toilet. The architects had obviously designed the place for extremely busy business people.

I changed into my training gear and spent a couple of hours in the weights room. My only thought was that I had to stay fit and sharp. When I returned to our room, Hans was sat on the edge of the bed and just ending a phone call. He looked down at the floor awkwardly. "They've cancelled," he said. We had travelled to Malaysia on the understanding that I'd been accepted for a try-out with Selangor FA, the biggest club in the country. "They don't want to use up any of their foreign player quota on a goalkeeper," Hans continued. Each club was only allowed four foreign professional players on its team, and most teams opted for forwards. I kicked the bed out of frustration and started to swear, but Hans picked up the phone again immediately and called our agent back in Germany. "Don't worry," he reassured us, "go to Malacca, it's a bit of a trip from Kuala Lumpur." He told us he had already spoken to the manager and that they would be in touch.

So we had to wait. But nothing happened. Hans and I lay on our hotel beds studying the pattern on the ceiling. Eventually the phone really did ring. It was the manager from Malacca: "I'll meet you tomorrow morning at 11 o'clock at the bus station near the red mosque."

Finally, at 6am the next morning, we boarded a bus along with a load of Spanish tourists and travelled to the wealthy coastal city. How idyllic that place is compared to the skyscrapers of Kuala Lumpur. We drove past tiny houses that wouldn't have looked out of place in Amsterdam – the Dutch colonial period had clearly left its mark there. Architectural preservation regulations still banned all buildings more than three storeys high. The bus headed lazily towards Christ Church, a Dutch church dating back to the 18th century. "I want to stay here," I told Hans.

The only place in town that seemed to be dirty was the bus station, and we had plenty of time to explore it. At 11am, the agreed time, there was no sign of the manager. We sat at the bus stop, in front of us our two kitbags and a scene like something out of some huge, crazy circus. The bustle of a market, broadly smiling traders peddling *roti prata* and *roti canai* – a fantastic type of flatbread, as we later discovered. Music blared from everywhere. Our nostrils were filled with the aroma of fantastic spices, and perhaps we might even have thought the place had a certain charm – if only the manager would hurry up. Dozens of buses stopped. Dozens of buses left again. Half of mankind seemed to hurry past us. But not a single football manager.

Shortly before midday, an old white Mercedes suddenly came to a halt at the bus terminal. A short man approached us. "You must be the Germans," he said. We greeted him warmly. He cut a professional figure in his black suit trousers and expensive-looking blue shirt. "We checked your CV," he said, "and we're glad you came." I smiled, but this was followed by words that made me want to punch his lights out: "We're sorry, but unfortunately this morning we decided not to use up any of our foreign player quota on a goalkeeper. We were unable to reach you by telephone."

I had never felt so cheated in all my life. The friendly manager left us a couple of minutes later. The next bus back to Kuala Lumpur wasn't for another two hours. More buses stopped. More buses left again. The other half of mankind walked past us. I've never boarded a bus feeling quite as aggressive as I did that afternoon. Hans and I spent half an hour staring out of the window in silence. The crowded coach left the station, and I came to life again on the bumpy rural road. The driver chatted incessantly with some of the passengers, who occasionally burst out laughing. There was an intolerable feeling of claustrophobia aboard that vehicle. "If this continues, then we're going to Iran or Lebanon, or Indonesia," I muttered almost inaudibly. "I'm not here to be screwed over." Hans's face was utterly expressionless. Stoically he watched as two children ran up and down the aisle. He thought it was just a couple of minor setbacks, nothing more. "Don't you worry, we'll find something," he said.

There haven't been many evenings in my life when I've got drunk, but that evening was one of them. Once we had arrived back at the hotel, I said to Hans: "We've been here for four days, I've spent four hours training every single day and we've taken buses all over the place on a wild goose chase. I think it's time we let our hair down." We dived into the glittering streets of the flashy metropolis and took in the lively night markets, moving from bar to bar as we drank, flirted with pretty girls and sang along to naff English hits.

We returned in a zombie-like state. Exhausted, I crashed out on my bed and fell asleep before I'd even managed to take my shoes off.

I woke in the pitch black, and in the distance a loud, persistent ringing. I glanced at the alarm clock, one eye only half open. It was 8am and I eventually realised that it was the telephone that had woken me after just a few minutes' sleep. I fumbled for the receiver without opening my eyes. An excited voice babbled into my ear. It was the agent from Bochum.

"Lutz, Lutz, get up. I've got a club for you. This time it's definite. Someone will be calling you soon." Some residual adrenaline shot through my body, but it only gave me enough strength to sit up slowly. Somehow word had got round that a halfway decent goalkeeper was in Malaysia. I've often seen how news can spread by word of mouth like this in football. But at that moment it was beyond me how anyone could get hold of the Bochum agent's phone number so quickly. The first division club Penang FA, whose stadium was on an island north-west of the Malaysian mainland, had succeeded. Apparently the club was dead set on signing me. "Honestly," the agent insisted. By now it was clear to him that his new clients harboured doubts whenever he made a promise.

A couple of minutes later the phone rang again. It was the Dato' Zain of Penang, one of the island's highest government officials. He was calling on behalf of the Chief Minister. The Dato spoke to Hans as if he were addressing a high-ranking state guest. The Chief Minister would be highly honoured, he explained, if we would accept his invitation. But we would need to hurry, if it wasn't too much of a problem. A friendly match was planned for 6pm between Penang and the top Hong Kong team, Happy Valley AA. He hoped this could be my debut match, and the flight tickets had already been paid for. "It would be a great honour for us too," Hans warbled down the phone as I lay exhausted in bed.

The flight was scheduled for 1pm. It was almost 100 kilometres from the hotel to the airport, so we needed to get going immediately.

Hans scooped our clothes out of the wardrobe and stuffed them into our bags. "I can't," I said, still lying there. I'd drunk alcohol for the first time in weeks, and what's more I'd barely slept – there was nothing I wanted less than to be standing on a football pitch that evening. "Come on!" Hans wouldn't take no for an answer. He ordered three Red Bulls from reception before shoving me into the taxi. All the drivers seemed to have the same cassette. This time the shrill of the recorders emanating from the speakers felt like some sophisticated form of torture.

The plane was supposed to land at 4pm, but we didn't touch down until just after 5pm. Two men in expensive-looking black suits were waiting at arrivals clutching a sign with our names on it. The Dato's staff hurried ahead of us, leading us to a gigantic Mercedes. We raced over the 13-kilometre bridge connecting the mainland with Penang at breakneck speed, the car drifting into the corners of the confusing road network. As if in a trance I sat on the back seat and saw the green of the island, with its lush vegetation, blur into a single green mass. My eyes kept shutting for a couple of seconds at a time, but then the driver would take some of the bends so tightly that I awoke with a start.

Bored-looking traders stood in their stands in front of the stadium, a few remaining lemonade cups and cigarettes strewn across their tables. At the foot of the stadium young boys on blankets were gathering together what was left of the almonds, oranges and bananas they'd been selling for the last couple of hours. We were too late. The 12,000 spectators had taken their seats ages ago and the match was supposed to start in a few minutes. An announcer screamed a few words of Malay into the noise of the crowd. Our driver grabbed me by the arm and translated: "They're already announcing you."

Bayern Munich's former keeper would be making his debut for Penang today, the announcer proclaimed. At least that's how the driver translated it. I wanted to protest and explain that I'd done nothing more than go there for a trial, but there was no time for that now. The noise of the crowd grew louder and louder as we hurried through the stadium's corridors: The first half had begun.

"They will substitute you in for the second half," the driver told me. He led me to the dressing room. It was deserted, but still showing the effects of the chaos that reigns before any football match. In one corner was a basket of fruit, and next to it a net full of balls. The floor was covered in chunks of turf that had become stuck to the players' studs while they warmed up. The coach had hurriedly scribbled players' names as well as arrows on a tactics board.

I sat alone in the corner of the dressing room. It was stuffy; the heat seemed to have sucked all the oxygen from the air. The shouts of the spectators sloshed against me like waves of sound. I had never played in front of more than 4,000 spectators, and out there 12,000 awaited me. I put on my shorts, socks, goalkeeper shirt, and finally the gloves – it was just like countless other times before. Only now I could hear the shrill voices of the Asian fans. My heart beat faster as the minutes passed. The adrenaline had allowed me to finally shake off my hangover.

As I was fastening the Velcro on my second glove, I began to hear the familiar pitter-patter of studs on concrete. It sounded like hail striking a skylight. The Penang players came in dressed in their yellow-and-blue shirts. They looked at me in surprise, some of them giving me a little nod before quickly sitting down on the benches. They had been told I would be arriving today, but it was evidently still a little odd for them to meet a stranger in their dressing room. A bald Malaysian man aged around 50 was last to enter. He was the coach. He approached me, his face beaming: "Mister Pfannenstiel, Mister Pfannenstiel, it is a great honour," he said in English, firmly shaking my hand. "We hoped you would still make it. It is fantastic that you're here to support us during this game."

He turned to the team and continued in Malay, frantically crossing out a couple of names on the board and replacing them with new ones as well as arrows pointing in every possible direction. All I could work out was that the team was losing 1-0, and that he had now written the slightly botched 'Panenstil' on the board in place of the original goalkeeper. "What the hell am I doing?"

I thought suddenly. "And doesn't the club need to see my player ID card before I can play?" Then all I could do was grin. None of that mattered now.

I was greeted by a hurricane of sound as I ran onto the field. They really thought I was a star from the Bundesliga. At that moment, the fact that I hadn't played a single match there didn't matter to me. In my head I was still one of the guys from 1. FC Bad Kötzting, swept out into the big, wide world and suddenly guided by the power of chance. Somewhat inexperienced, I gave the crowd a quick wave and ran over to the goal. More and more adrenaline was shooting through my veins. By now I was wide awake, and that was absolutely essential. It took less than three minutes for me to realise that Penang's defenders weren't a lot better than the amateurs who had defended my goal 10,000 kilometres west in the Bavarian Forest. The Hong Kong players were immediately allowed two easy shots on goal, and somehow I managed to deflect the ball for a corner both times.

We equalised. I longed for the game to end, my circulation threatening to succumb to Malaysia's sweltering heat. By the time the referee finally blew the whistle, we hadn't conceded another goal. 1-1. That was all that mattered to me.

I returned to the dressing room utterly exhausted. Chatting away, a couple of grinning players patted me on the back to show their respect. I laughed back, but even that was too much like hard work. My concentration waned. So it wasn't until I'd almost finished showering that I realised I was the only person to have undressed completely. My teammates, all of them dressed in swimming shorts, were trying not to look too embarrassed. Over the years, I often experienced such an awkward approach to nudity when playing with Asian teams.

The Dato picked me up from the dressing room. "The Chief Minister would like to invite you to dinner," he said politely before driving me and Hans 10 minutes across the island to a posh restaurant. In the warm semi-gloom I could make out imposing black leather chairs in front of small tables. Each seating area was separated from the others by huge aquariums and mirrored walls. Servants in brightly coloured traditional dress darted around the place. The Dato led me to the Chief Minister, a tall man who got up and welcomed me with a friendly smile: "What a great introduction, Lutz."

Everyone in the Asian football scene knew this man. He was continuing a tradition Malaysia had begun when it became independent from the United Kingdom in 1957. Back then, Tunku Abdul Rahman became the country's first prime minister exactly six years after becoming president of the Football Association of Malaysia. Rahman kept that job, and indeed, he proclaimed the country's independence at Merdeka Stadium. Malaysian politics began to flourish, and so did Malaysian football, which up until that point had lacked structure of any kind. The country's football team managed to qualify for the 1972 Olympic Games, a feat it owed in part to generous government support. After Rahman left office as prime minister in 1974, his political successor, Tun Abdul Razak, also took over his position as the highest official in Malaysian football. Having taken over as such an important figure in football, in the 1980s he ultimately transformed a purely amateur league into a professional one.

"We need people like you in the league," said the Chief Minister. Listening to his words, it felt as if I were dreaming. A beautiful servant had just brought my starter of shark fin soup, and I was having trouble processing all of this new information. A day earlier, had I not been totally pissed off and sitting at a bus station? And now I was negotiating my first contract over a glass of champagne. The next morning, I signed on the dotted line: 6,000 dollars a month plus bonuses for every win. The Chief Minister paid Hans almost half of that to be my goalkeeping trainer. Plus a car, an apartment in the best beachside hotel, and "of course," the Chief Minister emphasised, "jet skis." A professional contract. The high-life included.

One that did begin at 7am sharp, mind you. Due to the heat, the coach requested that we attend training – which took place on a pitch with perfect turf – early in the morning. And he certainly wasn't just being overly strict. Penang had more or less missed out on qualifying for the play-offs before I arrived, and the final four league matches were virtually irrelevant. It wasn't unusual for the coach to decide that 90 minutes of work sufficed for the day.

Those were the days of techno music. Nowadays few people dare to even utter the word, but when the 1990s were in full swing the whole of Europe was talking about Berlin's Love Parade. A number of German acts, such as Marusha and Culture Beat, had even made their way into Asia's clubs, and I had brought the latest CDs with me. It meant I was ahead of most Malaysian DJs, with many songs not becoming hits in Kuala Lumpur until months later. And so, helped by a few Marusha tracks I had in my luggage, I managed to secure three well-paid gigs at one of the city's trendiest venues. Once a week Hans and I flew over to Kuala Lumpur to help DJ at a nightclub called The Jump, before taking the first flight back to Penang the next morning and heading straight to training without having slept. I liked that double life. I was a shitty DJ but I'd jump around like a lunatic. But then the coach found out about my second career and threatened to end my first one as a professional footballer. "If I hear about this again, you're off the team." I was livid at the time. Now, though, I see the guy as something of a guardian of musical culture: He helped protect Kuala Lumpur from the screaming onslaught of Scooter, the permanently peroxide German techno legend whom the world has, unfortunately, still not quite forgotten.

Even without those nights in Kuala Lumpur, life in Malaysia was like a drug – easy, powerful and debilitating. I could have played in that country forever; the time would have slipped through my fingers unnoticed, just as easily as my salary, which I was investing entirely in the present. That's probably what would have happened were it not for the fact that, a couple of weeks later, a high-profile English team – although I can't for the life of me remember which – chose the island for a training camp. At short notice, the Dato arranged a friendly match in Kuala Lumpur. I felt like a handball goalkeeper. The ball flew at me practically every minute. We lost 2-1, but I had drawn plenty of attention to myself.

After the game a man stopped me as I was leaving the stadium. He was in Asia scouting for players on behalf of a few English teams.

"Impressive," he said, "but what are you doing out here?"

"Umm, playing football," I replied with a simplicity for which Arsenal player and German international Lukas Podolski would be known years later.

"Don't waste your time, you're still young," the scout continued. "I can get you into Wimbledon FC. They're desperate for a goalkeeper."

I couldn't believe my ears. Wimbledon played in the big-business Premier League. A few weeks earlier, their Dutch keeper Hans Segers had been accused of being involved in match fixing – he had allegedly arranged a result with two Liverpool players. The investigation had begun just before the start of pre-season, and if he were banned it would leave Wimbledon with a major goal-keeper problem.

Confused, I stood there with the scout's business card. This person was trying to tempt me away from a paradise into which fate had only just guided me. And yet, in my mind's eye I could already see myself playing for Wimbledon at an away match against Liverpool at Anfield. There are few nations who live and suffer for football quite like the English. Ratko Svilar, the idol of my youth, never played there. But I don't doubt that he spent his career hoping he might do one day. It's what every professional dreams of. For me the idea had so far been a utopian dream. No one has summed up the English nation's relationship with football better than Bill Shankly, who managed Liverpool back in the 1960s. He famously said: "Some people believe football is a matter of life and death. I am very disap-pointed with that attitude. I can assure you it is much, much more important than that." Those three sentences weren't a bad descrip-tion of my life so far. Playing in the Premier League was my real idea of paradise. It was just that I had almost forgotten it.

My journey to England started out just as chaotically as the one to Malaysia had. "Where's his bloody business card?" I shouted, rummaging through my bag. I had headed to London. The scout had congratulated me on my decision over the phone, and before hanging up told me to call him when I got to England so we could meet up at Selhurst Park, the stadium the club shared with Crystal Palace. But as I sat in the car, my bag emptied for the third time, it was clear that I'd lost his number. I couldn't even remember his name. Wolfram Zimmermann, my lawyer, had come with me just like he had done before when I had trained at Bayern Munich – and just like he had when I'd rejected Bayern's offer, he rolled his eyes.

We arrived in London one rainy November night and slept in a shared house where a guy I knew called Oliver lived. Oliver had been studying in England for the past couple of months. He lived in a house with small rooms laid with dark-brown fitted carpets and filled by the housemates with unwanted furniture from their parents' homes. We found the cosy atmosphere somewhat calming. Exhausted, I stretched out on the couch. "Tomorrow we'll just drive to the stadium," mumbled Zimmermann across from the bathroom, his toothbrush in his mouth. I noticed how much he could sense yet another disaster. "But they're playing tomorrow evening," I replied. My lawyer wouldn't accept my objection. So it was that we drove to the stadium the following evening and watched the match. Fog enveloped the pitch at Selhurst Park. It was a bad game, and with 15,000 spectators the stadium wasn't much more than half-full. Even so, I was spellbound by the atmosphere on the pitch – the uncompromisingly serious battle between those 22 players. Their football was reasoned and honest, and I wanted to play it too.

After the final whistle, Zimmermann managed to make his way into the heart of the stadium. He simply kept talking at the security staff until they moved the barrier half a metre to the side. I'm not sure whether they truly believed he was some sort of football official or were just annoyed. Zimmermann could talk anyone into the ground. For several minutes we wandered through the corridors. We finally found the scout, who had waited in vain for me to call the day before, in the VIP area. He wasn't too surprised by the slight setback. Back then, the league was rocked virtually every week by stars like Paul Gascoigne going on booze-fuelled benders, so minor unprofessional hiccups like mine hardly mattered. "It doesn't matter. The main thing is you're here. We'll get you signed up tomorrow, training with the reserve team starts at 10." They basically wanted to put me on what is called a non-contract and meant that I would be a paid professional footballer, but could be released at any time.

Ultimately I was in the same situation I would have probably been in at Bayern Munich. I was training with Wimbledon's reserves and would have to hope one of their professional keepers suffered an injury or a drop in form. But even so, in England the Premier League reserve teams still got to play each other in a league of their own; it was mainly to allow young players, or those who have been off injured for a long time, to gain valuable match practice. And so it was that my opponents included Liverpool and Chelsea, and a couple of weeks later I even competed against none other than David Beckham, who was recovering from a thigh strain – it certainly felt more like professional football than what would have awaited me at Bayern. At least that's what I told myself when I signed the contract. I was now part of the world of great professional football. My life, though, turned out to feel more like that of a student. And that was fine by me.

I moved into Oliver's shared house, where a tiny room with a single bed and an unvarnished wardrobe had just become available. Half of London seemed to be made out of such houses, and thousands of people lived in house shares like ours because of the exorbitant rents. Apart from Oliver I lived with a thin guy called Lee who had been studying literature for eight years and looked a bit like a modern-day Jesus, with his long hair, beard and baggy clothes. And with Lucy. Lucy the redhead, who was always very lively. The one with the spice allergy. Whose dress sense made me crack up. Sometimes she wore a pair of unflattering green trousers combined with a futuristic, iridescent silver shirt, and sometimes she'd just mix and match half a dozen different colours. Whenever I bumped into her in the kitchen in the morning, I was wide awake in an instant. Then there was the lovely Imogen, who enjoyed her lesbian relationship with a short-haired brunette for us all to hear.

Over the weeks I finally became aware that the world is bigger than the ultra-conservative Bavarian Forest. On what I was earning I could easily have afforded a decent flat in a better area. But even as we sat together on my first evening as a housemate, playing cards and discussing whether German or British politicians were the ugliest, it struck me that this house was the right place for me.

At 7am the next morning I was sat at the rickety wooden table in the kitchen, which smelled rather like a careful record of mealtimes past. Just like the dirty dishes piling up in the sink. "The rats have a whale of a time in here while we're all asleep," Oliver had said to me with a grin when he first showed me the kitchen, which is the problem area in any shared house. I hoped he was exaggerating. I quickly rinsed a plate, took two slices of bread from the wobbly shelves and covered them in butter and that bitter orange marmalade that probably only tastes good in England – it was a combination I ate almost every morning, always preferring it to a full English with sausage, egg and beans. Most British footballers at the time seemed to gorge themselves on a fry-up an hour before a match.

All of a sudden I was living in one of the most hectic cities in Europe. After breakfast I would take the crowded Tube beneath even more crowded streets and go to training, which was like travelling to some new world. Wimbledon maintained a similar style to that of FC St Pauli in Germany – slightly unorthodox and always with a bit of an 'us against the world' vibe. The training ground was public playing fields which consisted of two huts and five football pitches. There was an honest working-class atmosphere: Not much talking, but plenty of hard work on the rain-soaked grass. The showers and dressing rooms hadn't been cleaned for days – the club only took care of that once the tiles were more than half-covered in dirt. The grounds were fairly dilapidated. Football reporters and pensioners who wanted to talk shop would come and watch the 'Crazy Gang', as the club was known, as they trained; lifestyle editors and stupid, giggling groupies were not welcome. Wimbledon's players were known in the league for being pretty boisterous. And I soon found out that the reputation was deserved.

A couple of players gave me a nod when the manager introduced me in the dressing room. Others didn't even look up. I wasn't very good at making small talk in English, but that didn't matter to anyone there. The first and second teams systematically worked through their warm-up routines together with great focus, and among them was a keeper from Zwiesel. I didn't bother saying anything, instead concentrating on trying to get through the session without making any mistakes. The other players behaved as if I'd been part of the team for months. At least they did for a few minutes.

After a few exercises with the ball, the coach blew his whistle. Time for a half-hour cross-country run through Wimbledon Common, past all the playing children and pensioners. I hate running like that. Bored, I trotted along with the other troops. It must be three kilometres back to the club, I thought. And now it's raining. Suddenly one of the other players shouted: "Now." Before I knew what was happening, five players rushed me – and I became the victim of the welcome ritual that was tradition for all newbies at Wimbledon: Three grabbed hold of me while the others pulled my clothes off laughing. My T-shirt, shorts, underwear, even my socks and trainers. There I stood, stark bollock naked in the middle of the common. "Come on," called one, "no slacking!" They ran on. After a couple of minutes I ran after them, still naked. I did my best to seem unfazed. Back through Wimbledon Common, back past the playing children and the pensioners. Only now was I part of the team.

There was something a bit different about the players at Wimbledon. On that day I'd been the victim, but afterwards they left me in peace – unlike the apprentices. Talented young players aged 15 and 16, every now and then they were allowed to train with us, and in return they got to assume their position at the very bottom of the hierarchy. They carried balls, served us tea in the dressing room before and after training, and were utterly helpless if we decided to hide their boots again. But no one was safe, not even the established players. Take our striker Mick Harford, for example: We stuffed a dead fish under the wheel arch of his car. The ventilation was working beautifully, and weeks later his Audi still reeked savagely. Dean Holdsworth, another forward, had bought himself a new Range Rover in a special matte black finish. He would drive at walking pace over the muddy, sandy car park so as not to get his precious vehicle dirty. One day, while the proud car owner was in the shower, one of our midfielders took the keys from Dean's trouser pocket and raced his new motor three times around the car park. The £90,000 car looked like a Jeep after the Paris–Dakar Rally, its black paint utterly caked in mud. From then on, Holdsworth always parked outside the training ground.

One time I came into training with some nice shoes, but the dressing room was dirty so I put them on the bench. The boys didn't like this and when I got back in they'd nailed my shoes to the bench. I went home barefoot, and the shoes are probably still there now.

Gary Blissett and Mick Harford in particular became friends. They took me out drinking once and I nearly died. I didn't speak good English at this time and all they ever said was "f**king hell" and "stupid c**t". Once I went for a meal with them and two girls were looking over at me. Gary told me that English girls love polite foreigners. Go over and say, "Hello, I'm Lutz from Germany you little c**ts". I said: "What does it mean?" They told me it means 'darling'. So I went over and said it. The girls nearly choked on their cake. But they realised I'd been tricked and told Gary off.

Another time I went out on the beers with some of my teammates. As usual on these occasions I became very pissed very quickly, but at the end of the evening the lads kindly put me on a train. Unfortunately it was the last train to Newcastle, which is where I woke up the following morning (at least they had put a ticket in my pocket!). I had to get the first train back to London and go straight into training.

It was not long before I was a fully-fledged member of the Crazy Gang. One day we had a Nigerian player arrive for a trial. He was a little bit cold so he asked the kit man for some of those neoprene bicycle shorts which were in fashion at the time. The Wimbledon kit man was a bit stingy and didn't want to give him any, so I lent him some of mine ... but not before I'd slapped deep heat into the crotch. The poor guy slipped them on without any underpants and trotted off to get warmed-up. After five minutes he started running a bit strangely, after seven he had his hands inside his shorts and after 10 he suddenly sprinted off the pitch with tears in his eye and jumped into the showers. When we came into the changing rooms an hour later he was still jumping up and down in agony!

The players at Wimbledon might have been slightly crazier than at other clubs, but make no mistake: None of them were poor. The Premier League had just overtaken Italy's Serie A as the league with the world's highest-paid players. Professional footballers in England had already developed a fairly straightforward investment strategy – expensive cars and designer clothes were the order of the day, and as such there was an impressive fleet of vehicles parked up outside the huts at Wimbledon. In this respect I adapted to my new situation over the following weeks by buying myself an Audi A6 and jeans for 300 quid. But when I returned home after 3pm, it was as if I were coming back from uni just like my housemates. In the evenings we played football in the park against a group of Indians, doing our best to mark out a section of grass where there were as few dog turds as possible. I was no different from the others, only I spent vast amounts on clothes, didn't drink any alcohol when we watched videos in the evening and might bet £1,000 when we went to the casino – instead of no more than £50.

While my housemates sat in their lectures, I trained hard, sometimes too hard – not least because the back-pass rule introduced in 1992 was having a huge impact in England. FIFA had decided that goalkeepers would no longer be allowed to handle a ball that had been intentionally kicked back by their teammates – which meant I had to completely rethink my approach to the job. I suddenly became the eleventh outfield player, which was something English coaches already expected of their keepers. Traditionally in the English game, goalkeepers were used to becoming an extra defender outside the penalty area, acting like a kind of sweeper to clear up long balls. I spent hours after training stopping balls which were thrown at me by my goalkeeping coach, then would do hundreds of punts into London's autumn fog.

Fog. Nothing but fog. It lent the English reserve team games an air of mystic gloom, those silent games in front of maybe 300 spectators, or perhaps 500, in enormous, lonely arenas. The atmosphere was usually bleak, with a few shouts echoing across the wide space. We might have been competing against Manchester United and facing David Beckham and several other world-class players who were recovering from injury, needed match practice and against whom we didn't stand a chance. Or our opponents might mostly have been apprentices, little more than a reserve team. We usually played on Monday evenings. Who's thinking about football then? A couple of journalists were always there, and occasionally a local TV station would also turn up. I like honest, down-to-earth football, but after a while these reserve matches were a little bit too down to earth for me. I did everything I could to make it into the first team.

After a couple of months, though, it became clear that I wasn't going to get my big break at Wimbledon. The investigation into the match-fixing allegations against the regular keeper Hans Segers continued to drag on, but by no means did it impact negatively on his performance. He held strong. The second goalkeeper, Paul Heald, was also on good form and had the security of a long-term contract. What's more, their third keeper Neil Sullivan – who had been off injured for some time after breaking his leg – also began training with the team again.

There was no escaping the fact that I'd soon end up in the shunting yard of English professional football. The system was extreme in those days: Dozens of footballers served as stop-gaps, as modern, well-paid nomads who were always moving on to wherever their services were needed. Sieb Dijkstra, West Ham's huge Dutch third-choice goalkeeper, played on loan for eight clubs in just one season. Wherever a keeper was injured, he would be there. There were two guys ahead of him at West Ham, so the club sent him to teams at home and abroad to give him real practice and save on his salary. No one forces players to do it, but those who are reluctant to move will have problems when it comes to negotiating their next contract. Even though my contract was for a year, it could be terminated at any time – and mine was actually one of the slightly better contracts. Some of my teammates had weekly contracts that ran from Saturday until Friday and were extended automatically – provided the club didn't decide at the drop of a hat that they didn't need the player anymore. The non-bureaucratic American system of 'hiring and firing' was never as widespread in English football as it was in the 1990s. In the months that followed, I began to realise that I was one of the smallest cogs in the system.

CHAPTER 3
SURROUNDED
BY VUVUZELAS

The day before Christmas Eve in 1995, I heard the sentence that finally confirmed my role as a paid stop-gap in English football. Wimbledon manager Joe Kinnear called me into his cramped office, which consisted of a desk, two chairs and a 10-tonne mountain of paper. He got straight to the point. "It might be that we've got a new club for you," snarled Joe, who to be frank always sounded a bit grouchy when he had something to say. "But we'll sort that out when you're back in London." With a mixture of worry and renewed hope that I might yet get a regular place somewhere in England, I flew home to Germany for Christmas.

I had been looking forward to a couple of quiet days with my family, but the phone rang on Christmas Day. I was sitting on the pine corner bench in the dining room when my mother picked up the phone and frantically handed it to me. She always did that if she heard an English voice at the other end and didn't understand a word. "Hello Lutz, it's Joe Kinnear," began Wimbledon's manager. "Having a good Christmas?" he asked before immediately dispensing with the pleasantries: "Lutz, there is an opportunity for you to join Nottingham Forest, they've got an injured keeper and we want to send you there right away. Pack your things, you need to get going immediately. They'll be calling you any minute." It was great news for me, Kinnear added, explaining that the club would pay far more and offer me a much better chance to make the step up to the Premier League. I ate the rest of my roulade, called the travel agents to book myself onto an earlier flight back, and packed my things.

I already knew my new competition. Forest's regular goalkeeper Mark Crossley was a talented guy, but not a top keeper in my opinion. Their number two was called Tommy Wright; he had played in goal for Northern Ireland many times, but for years now he'd been suffering with chronic knee problems – and that was the reason they hired me, since he'd got injured again and no one could say how long for. They needed a back up for the back up. This is my chance to shine, I thought. The change was even easier for me after Forest's manager called me in person. As Kinnear had hinted, he was offering three times what I was currently earning. And it's not as if I had a choice – in English football, if you don't play along with the system it'll quickly spit you right back out again.

Two days later, it was a bright, bitterly cold day as I set off from London and headed along the M1 towards Nottingham, arguably the most creative and inventive city in the country. It was where, in the 18th century, a man named James Hargreaves invented the spinning jenny, a machine that was a true milestone of the Industrial Revolution. And then there was clergyman, William Lee – he was responsible for the world's first knitting machine in 1589. The list is endless: In the early 20th century a man from Nottingham presented the War Office with his plans for the first tanks, but his idea was rejected as "too cranky" – the machines didn't begin rolling off the assembly line until 1915.

So it's hardly surprising that the club, too, did all it could to revolutionise the game of football. Samuel Widdowson, an obviously faint-hearted player from the club's early years in the 19th century, one day decided he'd had enough of being kicked in the shins. He cut up some protective cricket gear so he could wear it while playing football – 100 years before FIFA made wearing shin pads compulsory for professional footballers. The man was a genius, a far too underappreciated pioneer – he also came up with the idea of the referee's whistle, goal nets and, a few years later, even wanted to introduce floodlights at Nottingham; that plan ultimately failed at the end of the 19th century due to safety concerns. Widdowson, people said, was a restless soul full of mad ideas. You might say he was something of an early Pfannenstiel, my brother in spirit.

In those days, Widdowson had a defining role at the club, and after all the inventions and his active career the members made him their chairman. Unfortunately, a good 100 years later the main man at Nottingham Forest was now called Frank Clark, a red-faced man with a slither of a moustache who usually wore boring suits, and he was certainly no kindred spirit of mine. Clark had been a legend ever since Forest won the European Cup twice in 1979 and 1980 with him at left-back. He continued to act the same way 15 years later, although now he was the club's fairly average manager. The position was his big chance; applying a mixture of discipline and tyranny, he wanted to win at all costs after spending his early years as a manager working down in the third and fourth tiers. By the time the club was promoted to the Premier League in 1994 he considered himself something of a 'chosen one'. When he welcomed me to my first training session, his face was expressionless and he didn't shake my hand. "You've got no chance," he said, "and you've got to make the most of it." Apparently that was his idea of motivation.

As casually as I could manage, I went out to the training area with my new teammates. In those days, Forest had considerably more money than Wimbledon. Originally built in 1898, the City Ground stadium had been renovated so often and at such expense that it was one of the most modern in the league. The offices and training ground were state of the art, and hundreds of fans would bustle about whenever we trained – quite a lot of them young girls hoping for a fling with one of the players.

During my first training sessions, I acted in the same way as I usually did after joining a new club – I went on the offensive. A new player's first few days decide whereabouts he will end up in the team's hierarchy, so if you hold back you can quickly become a doormat. I directed my defenders extra loudly from my goal during training matches, even if they were international players like Stuart Pearce. I responded to any criticism aggressively, and whenever a player crossed the ball in I dived into the tangle of defenders and forwards without any regard for my safety or theirs.

After training, our coach Clark nodded towards me almost imperceptibly – but approvingly. In England, being tough is one of a goalkeeper's most important qualities. The Premier League isn't just the best there is in terms of outfield play; it's particularly tough for goalkeepers too. In the vast majority of leagues, the six-yard box is a protected zone for the keeper, a place where he can't be harassed. In England, though, referees judge the keeper just like any other player and almost always let action unfold freely in the penalty area. Hardly any crosses went in without a striker committing a foul against the goalkeeper – even in the six-yard box.

But during just my second match for the reserves I had a truly disastrous day. We were playing against Barnsley, and nothing – absolutely nothing – was going right. My punts weren't landing as precisely as usual, I was coming across as nervous and jittery and I let in an own goal as well as a deflected shot. We lost 4-1. Clark had been watching the match. He didn't even deign to look at me. But the hairs of his moustache were vibrating, and they only did that when he was severely pissed off. In the weeks that followed I played for the reserve team or was left out altogether. I trained an extra two hours. Every day. Yet, I still couldn't get close to the first team, and I even began to struggle in the reserves. Shitty times.

I lay frustrated on the massage table, having pulled a hamstring punting a ball in training. My journey to become a member of the first team now looked even tougher. The physio massaged my leg while I stared up at the ceiling, as I always did when I had to think. "This is a case for Tunisia," he suddenly said casually, tearing me from my gloomy thoughts. "You'd best fly out with the others on Thursday." In the winter, English clubs sent their players south, where – and the players were quick to agree with the doctors on this – rehabilitation exercises paid off much more quickly than in the cold of the Midlands. And so it was two days later that I hobbled up a flight of aeroplane steps with four other injured players from various clubs, who didn't seem too dejected at all. Oddly enough my recuperation proved much more enjoyable at the luxury five-star hotel than it would have done in Nottingham, and what's more that was where I met Hetty, a slender Englishwoman of African descent, who was in Tunisia on holiday. She was from London too. We talked and talked, and by the end of the week I wasn't just feeling better, I was completely smitten.

Just like that, my life on the reserve team suddenly had meaning again. Hetty was fantastic. She worked as a TV journalist for travel channels and the music channel VH1. She took me along to awards ceremonies, and suddenly I found myself messing around with the Spice Girls or threatening to beat up Mark Owen from Take That because he had looked at Hetty a moment too long. I'd never have thought it possible, but I laughed more with that woman than I did with my beloved housemates. Before long Hetty and I moved into a flat in Edmonton, north London.

Edmonton is just as diverse as the rest of the city. Just two kilometres away from our flat crime rates were so high that few people dared walk the streets at night. On the other hand, two kilometres in the other direction rent was so high that even we would have had trouble affording a place despite our above-average incomes.

Our apartment was somewhere in-between, stylish but certainly no paradise, as we were soon to discover. We lived on the ground floor below Steve, a muscular guy in his early thirties. He was so well built that it looked like he didn't have a neck. We would meet Steve from time to time when we went to our local for a drink.

As Hetty and I left the flat at 7.30am one winter's morning, I stopped suddenly on the pavement: Someone had drawn a chalk outline of a person on the tarmac. "Look," I grinned and lay down in the outline, "we're at a murder scene." "Idiot," laughed Hetty as she got into her car.

When I returned from training that afternoon, Hetty was waiting for me at the door. "Come in, come in," she whispered, bolting the door shut behind me. She was clearly quite shaken as she led me to the upstairs hallway: The wall, the floor, everything was stained with blood. News of the events of the previous night had spread around the building like wildfire. Steve had met someone for a drink at the pub. At around 10.45pm John, the landlord, had rung the bell and called last orders like he did every night. In those days pubs still had to close by 11pm – a relic from the First World War when the government wanted to prevent munitions workers from drinking until the small hours so that they could concentrate on their dangerous work with weapons the next morning. Eighty years on, in peacetime, the law was still strictly enforced across England. Any landlord who still had any customers after 11pm risked a hefty fine. Regulars like Steve and his unknown companion had got used to the law by drinking extremely quickly.

We were able to read all the details about what happened after in the newspaper the next day: After the pub had closed, the two went to Steve's flat to have another couple of beers. Once there, the stranger suddenly pulled a knife on Steve. It wasn't unheard of for people to be robbed and murdered in the area, but Steve was able to fend off the attack with his forearm, taking the thief's knife and stabbing him three times. Wounded, the stranger dragged himself down the stairs before finally collapsing on the street. By the time the police arrived he was already dead.

Steve spent a week in custody. Once his innocence had finally been proved and he was allowed to return home, I was still absolutely terrified of him – my fear was a little bit put on, but there was definitely something there. Steve continued to accept post for us every now and then, as he had done before the crime. But now, whenever he rang our doorbell to give us the mail and I could see him through the spyhole, I ran out back into the bedroom. "It's Steve, it's Steve," I'd whisper as I rushed past Hetty. She was used to my little games, but had trouble answering the door because she was laughing so hard. Steve never saw me again.

Whenever he was outside our flat I either hid in the wardrobe or under the bed.

Despite the distance of nearly 200 kilometres between London and Nottingham, my relationship with Hetty held strong. I travelled the 90 minutes up the M1 almost every day, although it did prove expensive. Craig Armstrong from the first team had assured me that a fixed speed camera at a particular spot on a narrow stretch of the motorway had been broken for years. Without a care in the world I continued to drive past the camera without slowing down. I had no reason to doubt what my teammate had told me, and for months I didn't receive a single speeding ticket. My car was registered to a company that had hired it out to the club. It took weeks and weeks for the tickets to finally make their way to me. But then come they did, a whole box full of them. In one fell swoop I had to pay 49 speeding fines. I had to fork out £900 for the pleasure, and ultimately the ill-informed Armstrong shared some of the costs. He genuinely hadn't known that the speed camera was back in action.

Incidentally, my commuting also earned me the additional wrath of the club and of Clark, our irascible coach. He didn't appreciate his players spending their free time on the motorway instead of recovering. From his own experience as a former player, Clark knew all too well what some professional English footballers' idea of recovery was. I experienced an example of this once when, after a home match, one of our strikers invited the entire squad, plus a load of footballers from other clubs, back to his place for a huge party. It can't be often that 60 people manage to consume as much beer as we did. I was standing in the kitchen chatting to two other guests about who would be the favourites for Euro '96, which was about to take place in England, when suddenly one of my grinning teammates grabbed me by the arm and dragged me towards the bathroom. When he opened the door I could see about 15 men, a few of them my teammates. They were standing in a circle around a free-standing bathtub with their trousers down. I took a step closer and saw that a naked woman was lying in the bath and the men were masturbating above her. "What the fuck is going on here?" I asked my teammate. I went back to the kitchen in disgust. My love life was far more run-of-the-mill, but I was happy with Hetty – even though she was gradually coming to terms with the fact that she was in a relationship with possibly the most chaotic person in the country.

One cool day in autumn we played an evening match in London against Chelsea's reserve team. Afterwards I didn't have to go back to Nottingham with the team and was allowed to spend the night in London. I got to our flat at around 7pm. Hetty and I soon began arguing, over nothing really, probably because I hadn't paid attention to something she'd said again. It was often the same with such fights; at some point I would just leave. I'm still that way today. "I've had enough," I shouted, jumping up from the sofa and heading for the door. "I'm going to Johann's." He was a Dutch former professional I'd met through friends from my old shared house; by then he was working as a dealer in a casino. The door slammed shut, and I was far too proud to go back for my jacket, keys and wallet, all of which I'd left behind.

Johann was my saviour in such situations. He lived in a shared house that would occasionally take in stranded victims of relationships who had either been kicked out or decided to leave. Annoyed, I took the Tube – without a ticket, as usual. There were ticket machines at the main stations in London, but at Edmonton Station they hadn't bothered to install any and back then no one checked your tickets in London. I arrived at Johann's front door, but there was no answer. I went to Oliver's place, where I had lived until a few months earlier. No one home. I began to notice how cold it had become. The mercury had dipped below 0 degrees, and I cursed myself for having left in a rage without my jacket.

Freezing is more painful than wounded pride. I called Hetty, shivering. But she didn't answer – she never did after we'd been fighting. I was about to call some more friends when my mobile phone battery gave up the ghost. I took the Tube back to the flat. But this catastrophic evening wasn't over yet: Hetty wasn't home, and my key still lay neatly indoors on a cabinet beside the front door. Back I went to Johann's place – which was still deserted. I analysed my situation: By then it was almost 11pm, and I was standing on the dark pavement with £2 in change, no ID and a dead mobile. Frustrated and exhausted, I went for a walk in nearby Queen's Park; back then it was one of north-west London's somewhat more run-down recreational areas. The security guards patrolled at 11pm. On seeing their torches in the distance, I hid behind some bushes. When the men had left the park I stretched out on a bench and covered myself with newspaper I found in a bin. It's not something I'd like to do every day, but it keeps you warmer than you might think. Two minutes later I was fast asleep.

I would probably have been woken by the morning's first rays of sunlight, had I not felt a gentle pressure on my chest in the middle of the night. I struggled to open my eyes just a crack, and saw a dark shadow above me. I sat up with a jerk. The ancient tramp who had been touching me recoiled.

"Sorry, sorry, you haven't got any fags, have you?" he croaked.

"Fuck off, you tramp!" I screamed at him.

"And what does that make you?" he laughed.

I was speechless – that doesn't happen often. After the old man had slunk away, I got going and climbed over the park fence before running to Johann's flat. His Irish flatmate opened the door and offered me a sofa. Before settling down I used their landline to leave furious messages on Hetty's voicemail: "What kind of person are you, I mean who do you think you are?" I moaned, "I slept in Queen's Park because of you!"

Hetty still didn't get in touch on the Sunday morning. Utterly floored, I vegetated on the sofa and watched TV – unshaven and stinking like someone who'd spent the night in Queen's Park. Not until 11pm did the doorbell ring. Hetty entered the living room. She was dressed up and I could smell that she had put on her expensive perfume. "Okay, shall we go home?" she asked as if nothing had happened. She smiled warmly. I'd been expecting a continuation of last night's slanging match. We got into the car without saying a word, then she turned the radio on. We made our way through the heavy traffic, sitting in silence and I remember having to endure Peter Andre's *Mysterious Girl*. While we were waiting at a set of traffic lights Hetty suddenly burst out laughing. I looked at her, enraged, but she just laughed even louder. It was infectious, too infectious. We both laughed all the way home.

Professionally speaking I became something of a top stop-gap for the league – I was on consistently good form for the reserve team, but Crossley and Wright, who struggled with his knees but was usually fit enough for the first-team bench, were keeping me from getting anywhere near the Premier League squad. Clark called me to his office: "We don't have any need for you at the moment," he said in his usual unromantic way. "We want you to go to Watford for a couple of weeks. You start in two days." In the suburb of north London, the team's first-choice goalkeeper, Kevin Miller, was injured and they needed a replacement number two.

Players like me were like a mobile spare parts store for professional teams, and such sudden changes were utterly normal. In England, if you have a short-term contract your pay is calculated to the nearest week, so Watford, whose keeper had a swollen knee following a tackle, would be paying me as of Wednesday. He might have just sprained a ligament, in which case he'd be back after five days, or it could be a torn cruciate ligament, meaning six months off – no one could say. So my job depended on a 25-year-old Englishman's knee. I studied a map to find out how best to make the 25-kilometre trip from our flat in London to Watford, and began driving to Hertfordshire every day. For exactly two weeks. Miller recovered and I returned to Nottingham after having not played a single minute for the club.

I was an ever-ready temporary worker. I spent a couple of weeks in deepest, darkest Belgium with the first division team VV St Truiden. Just when I thought I might soon be booked as Father Christmas, I received a fantastic opportunity – a player agent was looking for a substitute keeper for Johannesburg's Orlando Pirates, the biggest club in South Africa. William Okbara, their Nigerian regular goalkeeper, had torn a ligament a few days before and would be out for a few weeks. Top-class South African agent Mike Makaab set up the deal, and I was soon on my way to Johannesburg.

Back in 1996, South Africa was one of the youngest democracies in the world – and football was recovering fast from its international exile. During the racial segregation of the apartheid regime, the country had been banned from almost every international sporting competition. So it came as quite a surprise when its football team sensationally won the 1996 Africa Cup of Nations.

The Pirates put me up in a hotel in Hillbrow, in the heart of downtown Johannesburg. In the 1970s it had been one of the city's fanciest neighbourhoods, with lots of companies' headquarters there. But its infrastructure had been unable to keep up with the population explosion of the past few years. The area had become one of the most dangerous in the world, dominated by crime, prostitution and illegal immigrants. High-rise buildings once home to international banks stood empty. The perfect place for new players to live, the club must have thought.

Johann came to South Africa with me. We'd had a pretty carefree time in England. Now we sat nervously on the back seat as the driver manoeuvred the limousine through an endless column of minibuses. Today such buses are still the most important form of transport in the nation which hosted the 2010 World Cup, keeping everything moving. Our hotel, the Holiday Inn, was one of the last ones belonging to a multi-national group that hadn't moved into the quieter part of the city to the north. Out of the corner of my eye I noticed the driver start to get nervous. At a set of traffic lights he turned to us: "Under no circumstances should you leave the hotel after sundown," he urged. The driver was silent for a moment. "And you shouldn't really before that, either." He slowly guided us through the built-up inner city. The road was full of both cars and people, everyone pushing forward simultaneously. It was incredibly claustrophobic. There was a palpable tension in the air. Johannesburg is now one of the cities that have invested the most in closed circuit video surveillance. Things have improved, even in Hillbrow. But when we stepped into the hotel back then it felt as if we were entering a golden prison.

The next morning a big Jeep came to take us to the club's offices. Today the Pirates' premises are in a fancy park area in Parktown, one of the city's most exclusive suburbs. They are the most popular club in Africa and merchandise sales alone generate huge revenues. But back then, before South African football became commercialised, you could sense the club's roots even at its main office. South Africa's oldest club was founded in the 1930s by workers from the gold mines, and many of its fans are from the city's poorer neighbourhoods. The offices were housed on the fourth floor of a dilapidated high-rise building just 10 minutes away from our hotel. Clapped-out cars, battered and falling apart, were parked outside.

Manager Lawrence Ngubane greeted me with a smile: "Welcome my friend. You will enjoy your time here. Just let me know if there is anything you need." Like most of the Pirates' players and staff, he was from South Africa's largest ethnic group, the Zulus. He told me about the club's history and the fans' almost religious devotion to the players. And about the part that football had played in bringing change to South Africa. Back in the 1970s there were several leagues. Blacks played against blacks, whites against whites, and people of mixed race against other people of mixed race. "We overcame those boundaries, more than any other sport did," Ngubane explained. "Wits University's white team accepted some black players. This spelt trouble for them, so they separated from the white league in the '70s and began playing with us." He explained that much of what was currently changing for the better in his country had been initiated by football. "Don't see the Pirates as just a club," he told me. "We're more than that."

Half an hour later a minibus picked us up for training. We squeezed onto the second row of seats right at the back; two players were already sitting next to the driver and three others on the row behind them. A Jesus on the cross hung from the rear-view mirror, and given our slightly chaotic ride I really did pray for divine intervention. For 10 minutes we zoomed past corrugated iron huts and improvised pitches packed with kids playing football, before finally arriving at the premises of a university – our training ground.

The club had just signed the Russian coach Viktor Bondarenko. He was the first ever coach in South Africa to hold his training sessions with the help of an interpreter, since he barely spoke a word of English. Bondarenko was a friendly man but he made us train so hard that even I found it difficult to keep up. The playing turf was perfect even though it hadn't rained for weeks. But there were no showers. Soaked with sweat after training, we forced our way back into the minibus, the windows wound down to make the stink less unbearable.

The Pirates had booked a twin room for me and Johann. After the first training session, we lay bored on the two beds and stared at the TV. Images of flooding in Cape Town, extracts of a parliamentary debate. The next six weeks, it suddenly occurred to me, were going to feel more like six years. I dozed for a while, ordered some sandwiches from room service, and carried on staring at the TV. By late afternoon I could stand it no longer. After training, one of the players had told me about the Golden Dragon, a huge casino. "What the hell, let's go," I said to Johann. "Where?" he responded, his gaze fixed on the TV screen. "Gambling," I said, already rummaging through my luggage to find a decent shirt. I was doing the top button up when Johann finally sat bolt upright. "Gimme five minutes, I'm coming too."

Were it not for professional football players, I imagine casinos the world over would be far less successful. I played for 24 clubs in 12 countries on six continents and there were none of them where players didn't love a good visit to a casino. Perhaps there's just one other occupational group who are of similar importance for the industry, and that's musicians. In New Zealand I once began teasing two young guys because of their shabby clothes and how unlucky they were at gambling. It wasn't until we'd been laughing away for five hours that a friend told me they were the world-famous singers Jack Johnson and Ben Harper.

I've seen players squander a year's salary before my very eyes, and others who won so much that they risked bankrupting the house. During my first visit to one casino in England I won £42,000; the operators found it so suspicious that they barred me. A couple of days later, they simply refused to let me back in. I blew a similar amount in another casino. Luckily though, over the years I've managed not to lose more money than I've won. That makes me something of an exception, since many former teammates of mine owe their bankruptcy to their gambling addictions. In Johannesburg there were dozens of casinos, many of them illegal, but I only ever took 100 dollars in with me.

We took a taxi and drove to the casino in Sandton, an upmarket business district. The entrance was guarded by a few beefy-looking characters in black suits. The casino was the best-protected building in the city, and it did exquisite food. I sat down at the gambling table where they were playing Caribbean Stud Poker with US dollars – a variation where you play against the bank with five cards, none of which you can swap. Two hours passed – my luck wasn't great, and my money was running out. But then, when I picked up my cards, I had my best-ever hand – a royal flush, an ace-high straight flush, all of them hearts. In any ordinary casino such a hand would bring you 100 times whatever you bet, so my 50 dollar stake would have meant 5,000 dollars – the chances of being dealt such a hand are like winning the lottery. As it happened, the dealer even rang a bell when I showed my hand. Dozens of players approached from the other tables. I beamed at them.

Unmoved, the dealer handed me a bottle of champagne before paying out a paltry 100 dollars for my 50 dollar bet. I stared at him incredulously. "Is this a joke?" The dealer politely explained that no, it was no joke. Since in that casino they happened to play without any form of bonus system, the best hand I was ever dealt ended up with a lousy profit of 50 dollars. I stormed out, furious, leaving Johann behind, and travelled back to the hotel.

But I still returned the next afternoon anyway. I preferred the frustration of the casino to the boredom of our hotel room.

That was how each week slowly passed during the Pirates' pre-season, match by match, sharing playing minutes with the other keepers in the squad. Despite the repetitiveness of our daily routine, every time I walked out onto the pitch the power of the fans penetrated every fibre of my body. For half an hour before kick-off, the stadium DJ would torture the speakers while the spectators danced to kwaito beats. Reggae rhythms combined with Zulu or Sotho vocals. Just before running out I saw the DJ standing on the sidelines dressed in his Pirates shirt and screaming into the microphone, clapping his hands above his head to the rhythm.

I loved those moments, that unbridled yet positive energy. The atmosphere was nowhere near as aggressive as in German stadiums, where spectators often concentrate their energy on insulting the other team's fans. That has no place in South Africa. Following the club is like a religion. If the Orlando Pirates were playing, nothing else mattered, not even the opposing team – unless the Pirates happened to be competing against their arch-rivals, the Kaizer Chiefs. Unfortunately I didn't have the honour of experiencing a derby between the two historic Johannesburg clubs.

We ran out onto the bone-dry turf. The fans leaned down to us from the front rows of the stands, stretching so far that they were almost falling, just to get that little bit closer to us. They shouted our names, laughed, danced – young and old, absolutely everyone. I've rarely experienced such a cult following. They were dressed wildly in homemade costumes that had been cut to size, and some wore headdresses made of plastic, some with oversized glasses and death masks – a reminder of the club's history. The club's emblem is a skull and crossbones. As soon as I came to Johannesburg, I kept noticing how people would imitate the sign by crossing their forearms over their chests – that gesture was how they greeted other fans, and it honoured Pirates fans who had already left this world. I liked it.

Trumpets everywhere, a dull sound as if 100 elephants were thundering in. Thousands of people had brought plastic trumpets, known as vuvuzelas, to the stadium. They are the soundtrack to football in South Africa, as was so often heard at the 2010 World Cup. FIFA had approved the horns for the World Cup – anything else would have been a huge mistake. No player or spectator could ever forget the noise of tens of thousands of trumpets. It reverberates through every fibre in your body. If the stadium was full of blaring trumpets, you couldn't even hear your own voice. I tried in vain to direct my teammates. All they saw were my lips as they moved, my words swallowed up by the sound of the vuvuzelas. Their energy was like a drug.

When we finally emerged from within the stadium more than an hour after the match had ended, almost 1,000 fans stood waiting outside. At the very front was one of the strangest figures I've ever seen. A one-legged fan on crutches, perhaps in his mid-thirties, dressed in the black shirt and scarf of the Orlando Pirates. His mouth was full of jagged teeth. I'd seen him a few times before near my hotel, a homeless man who always stood at the same crossing. He had greeted me warmly whenever I walked past him.

"Good job, Lutz," the man began, grinning. "I'm Freddy." He evidently had no trouble remembering my face, but then again the Pirates did only have one regular player other than me who was white. We talked for a while about the match and the club. Freddy seemed to be quite high up in the fans' hierarchy. After a few minutes he scribbled a number down on a scrap of paper. "The people in Hillbrow know who you are now. I promise you that, for as long as you play for the Orlando Pirates, nothing will happen to you if you go out during the day."

The entire neighbourhood was controlled by Orlando fans; in those urban canyons there was hardly a single criminal, big-time or small-time, who didn't worship the club and its players. Professional football players enjoyed what you might describe as immunity. A team supervisor later told me that professionals who played for the Pirates had a status similar to that once enjoyed by African clan leaders. In Zulu and Xhosa culture – the two largest ethnic groups in the country – it was completely taboo to touch an individual clan's leader or even say a bad word against him.

If I were to have any problems, Freddy continued, I just needed to call that number and he'd help me. Freddy handed me the paper solemnly. He had written down the number of the public telephone near where he spent most of his time each day. I thanked him wholeheartedly, carefully placed the paper in my wallet and got into the car. It was already dusk, and even with Freddy's number in my pocket I knew it was a bad idea to be out and about in Hillbrow after sunset. One evening a few days after arriving, I had met a young backpacker from England. The Holiday Inn was out of her price range and she couldn't be talked out of looking for some slightly cheaper accommodation a few streets away. The next morning she was found dead, having been raped and stabbed. The newspapers were full of gruesome details about the crime.

Nevertheless, my fear of Johannesburg, in particular Hillbrow, soon began to subside. Once, Johann and I even went to a nightclub. Johannesburg's nightlife was electrifying; its inhabitants had learned to live with danger but also to live life to the full. People invited me to sit at their table as if we were old friends, and families even invited me round to their homes. And they weren't just being polite. For them, community is priceless.

To this day I still don't know whether I was more in love with South Africa or afraid of it. I do know one thing, though: I was absolutely fascinated by the country and its energy, which resulted from dozens of different cultures living side by side – it has 11 different official languages, not to mention all the other languages spoken throughout the land. I met wonderfully friendly people, and at Kruger National Park I saw the 'Big Five' game animals, as the Africans call African elephants, rhinos, buffalo, lions and leopards. I encountered great people, the most fantastic of them in the stadiums. If there was one unifying element – at least among the black population – then it must have been the Orlando Pirates. During our away games, in Port Elizabeth on South Africa's beautiful coast and Bloemfontein in the heart of the country, the stadium ticket offices had to be guarded by armed soldiers; otherwise our fans might well have stormed them in the hope of securing the few remaining tickets. While league matches usually averaged 8,000 spectators, tickets for Pirates games were often completely sold out. We rarely played in front of fewer than 20,000 people. Our away matches felt like we were at home, since the cities were home to more Orlando supporters than fans of the local teams.

After four weeks, the Pirates' goalkeeper Okbara began training with the team again. The day I departed was the same day he was back in goal for the first time, playing in a championship match after his six-week injury lay-off. At the end of my contract in Johannesburg I briefly considered permanently working in Port Elizabeth. A professional team was currently being set up at the seaport, and they had shown an interest in me. But Hetty couldn't imagine living in South Africa. And I, too, was put off by the thought of an isolated life behind towering walls and electric fences.

I slowly packed my things in the hotel room. It struck me that I had never been to a country with so much positive energy. Fourteen years later I was angered by all the press reports about the 2010 World Cup, dominated as they often were by security concerns surrounding the tournament. Many people in South Africa, and the press in particular, were downright obsessed, addressing the subject in an almost paranoid way in spite of all the hard work put in by the host nation. Such people infect each other with their own fears. There was once a researcher who spent a number of months studying buffalo in the Serengeti from a small plane. Individual animals weren't bothered by the hum of the aircraft, but if he flew over an entire herd and just one hypersensitive buffalo bolted, then the whole herd would be gripped by panic.

Those six weeks in South Africa did me the world of good. I'd finally had some first-team minutes on the pitch again. I'd played in front of tens of thousands of spectators – a feeling your body can become accustomed to like a drug. And now I really was addicted. After returning to England, I often found myself leaning back on my sofa, closing my eyes and reliving those matches on the dusty pitches, with the drone of the vuvuzelas, once more. Then I remembered those desolate games with Nottingham Forest's reserve team, watched by a couple of fans and hidden in the fog. It was decision time: After almost two years of being a full-time stop-gap, I'd had enough of being ready to be sent wherever I was asked. I needed to play. As a regular player. No matter where in the world.

CHAPTER 4
ALL ABOARD THE FINNISH CHILL-OUT TRAIN

Back in England, I reluctantly slipped back into my life of meaninglessness. The days, it seemed to me, consisted of training, eating and sleeping, with the only variation coming at the weekend, when I would spend 90 minutes sat on some subs' bench or in the stands. Alternatively I might keep goal for Nottingham Forest's reserve team in front of a couple of hundred spectators. I became quiet, withdrawn, beginning to doubt myself. I couldn't stop remembering Ratko Svilar, my childhood hero, who spent almost his entire career playing in the small Belgian league – but at least he had played. I had now been in professional football for two years, but on the subs' bench I felt like a hyperactive little boy and found it painful to sit quietly while everyone else got stuck in just a few metres away. I wanted children – or even just one single child – to secretly switch on the TV at night to watch my saves. Just like I had once done with Svilar.

It was almost always the sound of a telephone ringing which heralded a change in my life. This time the call got me while I was in the dressing room after we'd just finished training. I took my mobile from the side pocket of my kitbag. It was an agent. I recognised him instantly thanks to his Belgian accent – Luc Vandenbon was a small fish in the business, and his working hours were based on when reserve teams were playing. After matches he would seek out dissatisfied players to shoot the breeze, inconspicuously obtaining telephone numbers and usually raving about the Asian leagues. He had excellent contacts in Asia. He would pocket a few thousand pounds whenever he organised a successful transfer. And he was good at what he did.

He knew I had had enough of my monotonous life as a reserve player in England. He explained that there was an interesting opportunity for me, asking whether I was interested in moving to Singapore. "Things are really taking off there now." He said there were several options, but Sembawang Rangers were desperately looking for a goalkeeper and their manager still remembered me well from my spell in Malaysia. Apparently the wealthiest club, Home United, and the ambitious Woodlands Wellington were also keen.

Over the past few months I had actually been following developments in the Asian football scene with interest. Singapore had been represented in Malaysia's professional league since the 1920s by sending over a representative team of its players. The Lions, as they were known locally, were one of the strongest teams there, although by and large the football played back in Singapore was only at amateur level. In 1995, though, officials from both countries had clashed. The league was rocked by a major corruption case, and two of the main perpetrators played for the Lions. The Australian, Abbas Saad, and the Czech, Michael Vana, were accused of match fixing. It was a spectacular scandal. Vana was released on bail for a million dollars, but the gambling mafia helped him flee to Indonesia by speedboat. The headlines about the affair and the Malaysian league's lax handling of the crime didn't exactly fit in with Singapore's squeaky-clean image.

Without further ado, the island's football association, the FAS, decided to establish its own professional league. Dubbed the S.League, it launched with eight teams in 1996 and was actually quite a success. Nevertheless it was a bold undertaking, since Singapore is only slightly bigger than Manchester and is home to just five million people.

I spoke to the manager of Sembawang on the phone that same afternoon. He could remember a match of mine with Penang from two years earlier where I had played well. He was adamant that I should come to Singapore for medical checks as quickly as possible. My contract with Forest was up in a few weeks, so with the club's permission I flew to Singapore a few days later. When I arrived in 1997 it was already the S.League's second year, but Sembawang Rangers were still very much in their infancy as a club. So far the clubs had been structured much like amateur teams, and for them the first season had been something of a low-budget trial run. Be that as it may, attendances at each match were around 7,000, and sponsors and television companies were now investing like mad in the league.

Invited from all over the world to try out for the Sembawang team, 15 players got stuck in at the freshly renovated training ground. It was a tough application process, with players from the Netherlands, Slovakia, Switzerland, Brazil, Argentina and a goalkeeper from Zwiesel. Two days later I flew back to London clutching a decent contract that was ready to be signed. I was going to play again. At that moment it didn't matter to me that it would mean switching from the most famous league in the world to one barely anyone had heard of.

Hetty forced a smile. We were sat at the kitchen table and she was passing her coffee mug nervously from one hand to the other. When we were together we would always discuss the important things in the kitchen. She was understanding: "I'm really pleased for you." But Hetty only managed to look me in the eye briefly before gazing back down at the table. She had been concerned over the last few months, having noticed how rarely I laughed, how few jokes I made. She had always known deep down that this day would come. "I'll just take you with me," I said a little too loudly. The laugh that followed was put on as well. Hetty smiled, her gaze still fixed on the table. Her career was well established, her income fantastic. She couldn't just drop everything and leave in order to sit in some flat in Singapore waiting for me to come home from training – that much was clear. I got up and returned with a piece of paper from the desk, on which I drew a line and beneath it wrote out the coming months: January 1997, February 1997, March 1997. "We can plan things so that we get to see each other at least every six weeks," I said. "I promise." For two hours we trawled the S.League season schedule for breaks and wrote down potential holiday periods for Hetty, little slots when we could spend time together. A week later I stood at the airport holding her tight until my flight was called. One final look back from the gate. Then I left. I didn't keep my promise. I never saw her again.

The Rangers coach, manager and two of their staff met me at Changi Airport in Singapore. I was immediately captivated by the present. The club had organised a huge apartment for me on the top floor of a stylish residential building. I looked out to sea from the terrace and took a deep breath. It was a good start, I felt alive again. I didn't have to worry about my position as the regular goalkeeper either, since the other two keepers were just 19 and 21 years old, plus they had some major technical weaknesses. That was also clear to the guys in charge after my first few training sessions. Five days later I signed my contract – it did only guarantee me 5,000 dollars each month, but on top of that there was the flat, a car and a virtual guarantee that I would finally be a regular keeper again. That feeling alone would have been worth signing any contract.

My path seemed clear for the coming season, but to be on the safe side my agent had also spread the word about me in several Asian leagues. In Singapore, too, there was a persistent rumour that I would actually end up starting the season playing for league rivals Woodlands Wellington, one of the country's top clubs. "Why did you sign?" snapped the agent that evening. Apparently I should have held off because better offers had been coming in for me every day since I'd arrived in Singapore to try out. He paused for a moment. "I want you to fly to China." I laughed out loud. But when the Belgian mentioned a few of the ballpark figures that had been discussed, I quickly shut up. A club in Guangzhou, a city in southern China with a population of three million, were apparently talking about a contract worth around 200,000 US dollars a year, several times what I could have earned in Singapore. "Okay," I said quietly, "I'll think of something."

The next day I was sitting on an aeroplane to China. I had explained to the baffled Rangers manager that I needed to return home immediately for personal reasons. I'd already contacted Apollo Guangzhou long before. I was lying, of course – but in the world of professional football lying is part of everyday life. In fact, that's the only constant in the whole business.

The agent had since informed me that, in China, a lot of businesses had bought clubs over the past few years that were previously administered by district governments. The same was true in Guangzhou. Suddenly vast sums of money were being pumped into the country's ailing football business, where people were fed up with settling for their teams' moderate performances in the Asian Club Championship. Meanwhile, the Chinese league had already become one of the best in Asia, their top players earning salaries worth the equivalent of 800,000 dollars a year.

The club summoned me to spend a day at its headquarters in Guangzhou. The manager wore a sophisticated black suit. With a friendly smile he really did talk of paying me 200,000 dollars a year – but that wouldn't be confirmed until after the training camp. The team had already been in Kunming for the last three weeks preparing for the new season. Kunming was a city in south-western China, they told me, where no fewer than 36 teams from China's top two leagues were currently staying because of the good climate. "I suggest you fly out there tomorrow," the Chinese man said in fluent English. I nodded. I didn't even bother unpacking at the hotel. It was only a few hours until my flight to hell was due to take off.

Guangzhou was a vast metropolis, an established industrial hub that had already witnessed the construction boom described so often in recent years. The small airport from which I now flew out to the mountains of Kunming, on the other hand, looked as if nothing had happened there since the 1950s. No one checked my hand luggage or even searched me before I boarded the tiny, ancient propeller plane that must have had its maiden flight back at the beginning of the Cold War. Not many business people took that route, since the plane landed quite far away from Kunming, nowhere near any other major cities. Ten cages with chickens in them were packed at the back of the plane behind a curtain. Their clucking accompanied us for the duration of the flight.

I was voyaging into a world far stranger to me than anything I'd ever seen before. My chauffeur guided the car along crumbling roads as we passed mountains and sprawling fields. Next to us, on the side of the road there were hundreds upon hundreds of Chinese people on rusty bicycles weighed down by huge sacks. After an hour we reached the training ground. It felt like I was entering a military camp. In fact that really was why it had been built originally, many years ago, far away from the city and with nothing but simple, unadorned prefab buildings and dozens of football pitches.

I checked my phone. No signal. Of course there was no signal out here in the arse end of nowhere. Without a word, my supervisor showed me to my room. A bare lightbulb shone, faintly illuminating my roommate; stretched out on one of the bunks, he looked up from the book he was reading. "Welcome. I'm Bjarne." I shook his hand. He looked tired. "This is the hardest thing I've ever done," he said. Bjarne was Danish and had previously played in Finland. Now he was in his mid-twenties and finally wanted to earn some money from playing football. Every day he ran 20 kilometres during the four training sessions; the intensity hadn't let up for the past three weeks. He explained that we were lucky, since most of the players had to sleep in eight-bed dorms. I was about to unpack my things and put them in the steel locker next to my bed when suddenly the light went out. "Ten o'clock," said Bjarne dryly in the darkness. "You can set your watch by it. The lights go off in the whole village, they control it centrally." I put my shoes on the floor, felt for my bed and got under the thin cover. Well this is going to be interesting, I thought to myself. The 200,000-dollar salary suddenly seemed like scant compensation for the pain and suffering I was about to endure. I fell into a restless sleep.

Rattling. Something was rattling loudly, again and again. I slowly opened my eyes and saw a Chinese man stood in the doorway. He was beating a metal sheet with a wooden spoon. He moved on once he saw that we were awake. All the lights were on. Outside, frantic voices echoed down the corridor. I gave Bjarne a confused look. He had dark circles under his eyes as if he'd been up drinking all night, but he still attempted a grin: "Six o'clock. You can set your watch by it." Similarly to Sembawang a few weeks earlier, the club had invited players from a dozen countries to try out, and they were required to report for the first exercises of the day at 6.30am. Kunming was known for its good climate, but at that hour the pitch was icy cold. The new day was only just dawning. Silently we performed hundreds of squats and press-ups. The gymnastics programme reminded me of black-and-white documentaries I'd seen on TV.

In the second session at 10am, the super-tough Chinese coach added sprints, barking his simple commands at us across the pitch. I hesitated. For almost a week I'd been suffering from a slight muscle strain in my thigh, which had already meant that I was only able to complete a reduced programme back in Singapore. Apollo Guangzhou had hired an English interpreter, but when I told him about my injury he simply didn't translate my request. "You seem fit," was all he said, smiling politely. After the morning session I was given an injection in my thigh.

That day went on to be one of the toughest in my life. Kunming lies at about 2,000 metres above sea level, and the Chinese training experts wanted the professionals to undergo six weeks of high-altitude training. Professional clubs around the world strictly differentiate between training outfield players and goalkeepers, since at the end of the day a keeper's performance depends on his strength and ability to respond fast rather than the ability to run for 90 minutes. It seemed that nobody in China had heard of that principle. Unaccustomed to the thin air, I took part in every run I could, and then there were the dozens of jumping exercises. It was as if the Chinese players, who had been doing this since childhood, had just been for a leisurely walk. But out of 800 people at the camp, 250 were foreigners. And they were all going through hell. Never before and never again was I subjected to four training sessions in one day – even in the run-up to the new season, German Bundesliga teams stop after no more than two.

That evening my body felt like it had been sliced up. I slowly crept to the camp's only phone booth, longing to hear Hetty's voice. Bjarne had warned me about the evening rush, but I was still shocked when I saw from afar that 80 or so players were waiting outside the booth. Some were leaning against the walls of the buildings, while others were sat on the pavement reading. The one inside the phone booth, however, kept looking frantically at the waiting players. He was aware of the impatient looks he was getting, and no one dared occupy the booth for more than a couple of minutes. Bored and tired, I sat down with the waiting crowd. I didn't have a book with me, so I studied the drained faces that surrounded me. Most of the players were from South America, but there were also a lot from Africa and a few from Europe. It was plain to see that none of them had ever trained under such conditions.

Suddenly I spotted a familiar face. Ten metres away a well-built guy with short hair and a flushed face was sitting against a wall. As I looked over at him, he saw me as well; Gary Blissett recognised me instantly. He had been a striker on the first team during my time at Wimbledon. Sometimes he would come on as a substitute, and sometimes he was in the starting line-up. But in recent years his performance levels had dropped. Some people made snide remarks about how he'd still been able to retain his regular spot at various pubs. Perhaps that was the reason the club was forever sending him off on loan to other teams. This time he'd ended up in China. "Lutz, the fucking German," he called. He was a really great guy and it was also fantastic to see a familiar face. I grinned from ear to ear. Blissett had a real nose for a goal and was fantastic at delivering powerful headers. He'd never exactly been a fitness fanatic, though – the daily half-marathons in China must have been a nightmare for him. We spent half an hour joking about old times in England, which couldn't have been more different from the days in Kunming. By the time it was finally my turn to use the phone and I ended my conversation with Gary, it was fairly clear to both of us that we weren't going to find fortune in the Chinese league. I chatted to Hetty for a moment while Gary waited. I spoke those same words that anyone who's been in a long-distance relationship knows: "I know, I miss you too." "We'll see each other in a couple of weeks." I'm not good at long-distance relationships.

After a week I informed Apollo Guangzhou that I had decided to accept the offer from Singapore. Gary looked at me enviously. He would have left China after the first day, if only he had an alternative. "If you hear anything, if any decent club is looking for a striker, let me know," he pleaded. I promised I would. My flight was that evening, and we spent the afternoon walking around the town – if that's how you could describe the area around the training camp, with its few scattered houses. Gary was limping. He had strained a calf during a sprinting exercise, and he was in so much pain that even the Chinese let him have the rest of the day off. We wanted to visit a market with a translator and Fabien, a black player. On our way there we passed an old lady out in a field, but as soon as she saw us she turned and ran away. The translator turned to Fabien: "She's probably never seen a black person before." Fabien laughed, shrugged his shoulders and retorted: "That must make me something of a pioneer."

After half an hour we reached the market square. This was where the camp kitchens stocked up on supplies, and in recent days I had discovered that we had been given not only fried chicks but also dog meat. I had assumed the latter was beef since that's what it tasted like. I didn't realise my mistake until a fellow player drew my attention to the fact. I didn't exactly lose any sleep over that meal. It taught me that the meat you can and can't eat depends entirely on your culture. I'm a big dog lover, but is it really more reprehensible to eat dog meat instead of beef? The answer is nothing more than a matter of socialisation. Throughout my career I ate pretty much everything – dog meat, snakes, squirrels, frogs, kangaroo, crocodile and beetles. None of it tasted truly awful. However, at the market, in an attempt to clear my conscience, I decided to spend 20 dollars on one live dog and one live cat and give them their freedom. Once we were a couple of hundred metres away from the stalls we set the dog and cat free. I hope they were lucky enough not to be caught again.

A few hours later I boarded the rickety plane to Guangzhou before travelling on to Singapore. Sembawang Rangers forgave me for having left the country for a fortnight even though I had signed a contract. In the small league they were used to foreign professional players, who often managed to land a better offer elsewhere, backing out at the last minute. And the club had, of course, worked out that I hadn't returned to Germany but had in fact been in China. Now though it was clear that I'd be sticking around in Singapore, and exactly the same thing happened that I had experienced in Malaysia, where they had introduced me as a former Bayern Munich player. Basically I was now the keeper who had come from the English Premier League, and the league instantly marketed this fact as an indicator of the S.League's sporting prowess. I never made a secret of the fact that I did nothing more than play for the reserve team at Nottingham Forest, but in Singapore no one seemed too bothered about the details. And when it then also turned out that Rangers were desperately trying to find a new centre-forward, I was able to point them in the direction of a certain rising star from the Premier League who happened to have already generated considerable interest over in China. It meant the Rangers manager, Yow Tian Bey, even forgave me for my little trip: Five days later, Gary signed a one-year contract.

I found it anything but difficult to adjust to life in Singapore, especially since I was on top form during my first league appearances. Sembawang was one of the league's poorer teams and our defence was pretty weak. Shots flew at me almost every minute, which made a wonderful change from the time I had spent on the sidelines in England. Every Monday morning I would painstakingly scan the sports pages of the newspapers. Even as a junior I used to keep statistics about all things football-related. After each game I would grade my performance as if I were at school and write it down. At the end of the season I calculated my average grade, which was far more important to me than what was written on some school report. The journalists in Singapore were similarly meticulous. They had stats for absolutely anything: The percentage of shots that were repelled, minutes per goal conceded, intercepted crosses and so on. After five matches Rangers were just sixth, but the statistics showed that I was the best goalkeeper in the league.

That was when the strange phone calls began. The first one came early one Tuesday evening when I was in my apartment. "It's Mike," said a young man. "Where did you get this number?" I asked. He laughed. "That's part of my job. Mr Pfannenstiel, I would like to meet up with you and introduce a few business models to you which I'd rather not discuss over the phone." Yow Tian Bey, our coach, had warned me about the Asian betting mafia; the league might be new, but it was already vulnerable to match fixing. Normally bookmakers would target young local players, many of whom earned just 700 dollars per month. But the goalkeeper's position is the most crucial to someone interested in manipulating the score of the football match. One blunder and the desired result can come about without much effort at all. "I'm not interested in doing business that can't be discussed over the phone," I said before hanging up.

A couple of days later we were playing away from home. Just like before any game, I went to bed at 10pm the night before – and shortly afterwards I was woken by the ringing of the telephone.

"How was your dinner?" asked the same voice as a couple of days earlier.

"What the fuck? Who is this?"

"It's Mike again. What will tomorrow's result be?"

"We're going to win, of course," I mumbled sleepily.

Mike continued, explaining that, if that could be changed, there'd be a decent bonus in it for me.

"Don't bother me with this shit, you prick," I said.

"Think about it. Down at reception there's an envelope containing 10,000 dollars, the porter will give it to you. If you lose, then afterwards there's another 40,000 dollars."

I won't deny that I thought about it for a moment. If you do that three times, then at the end you'll have 150,000 dollars in your pocket.

I never seriously considered it, because it would also have meant selling my dream of playing professional football. I would have bet my right hand that Ratko Svilar never cheated in his life. I wasn't going to do things any differently. Later I learned of players who had been unable to resist the temptation and then were blackmailed. The Asian betting mafia took photos of the money being handed over during such deals. If the player refused to play ball the next time they asked, then they would threaten to go to the press or do something to their children. Young players, in particular, often had to manipulate matches now and again whether they wanted to or not – these people were rarely content with a one-off deal involving just one match. "Fuck off," I said and hung up again.

I heard nothing more from the mysterious caller named Mike, and I quickly forgot the incident. In those days my life seemed almost perfect, like a dream come true. Unfortunately I never quite allowed myself to be satisfied; I always wanted all my wishes to come true at once. Every morning on the way to training I would pass Singapore's covered Chinese market. I had already driven past it dozens of times, but that afternoon I didn't have any plans, and curiosity has always been my most dominant trait. The stands, some of them selling fruit and drying fish and others piled high with mountains of fake designer T-shirts, were enveloped in a babble of voices and the smell of bananas, cloves, dates and saffron wafted through the air. I strolled aimlessly between the stalls, stopping to chat with a few Sembawang fans and savour the exotic atmosphere.

Next to two vegetable stands there was a shop with little cages containing mice, birds and reptiles. "How can I help you, sir?" asked the polite Chinese man behind the tables. I had always dreamed of owning little pet monkeys. "I don't need any mice," I teased. "But do tell me if you have any monkeys." The Chinese man was expressionless and didn't seem to get my joke. "I have two small slow loris monkeys," he said in all seriousness, waving me behind his stand. He pointed to two baskets. Two tiny monkeys no bigger than my hand were peering out of their cages at me, their enormous eyes wide open. "Lots of people have them here. You would have to take both of them, though. They need company." The man spoke so quickly and in such detail about the monkeys that it felt like he was trying to flog a second-hand car. He carefully neglected to inform me that it was illegal to own slow loris monkeys. However, I did learn that they were one of the most intelligent species on the planet and extremely adaptable to their surroundings.

"Can you keep them in an apartment?"

"Of course, where else?"

Fifty dollars and the two monkeys would be mine. I don't waste much time thinking in such situations. I gave the merchant the money and carried the cages to my car. At a set of traffic lights I turned to them both, their cages on the back seat. I waved my index finger at the smaller of the two: "You can be Glasnost." And then at the other: "And you can be Perestroika."

I was living with Gary in a spacious apartment which was well maintained thanks to a cleaning service. Even so, after half an hour Glasnost and Perestroika, which for those who don't remember the Cold War are the names of Soviet policies meaning 'openness' and 'restructuring' in Russian, had well and truly lived up to their new names. The expensive leather chairs were scratched, the spice jars in the kitchen knocked over and the curtains ripped. "Fantastic," I said to the two monkeys disapprovingly. They looked a bit scared and dismayed, but they always did that, no matter what they had done. They might have destroyed half the apartment, but there was something likeable about them and their propensity for chaos. I had always wanted to own exotic pets, and now I did.

Each day felt as if it consisted of no more than three hours, not 24. My last kiss with Hetty felt like it was months and months ago, but it had only been a few weeks. We had spoken a lot on the phone during the first few days, but I have never been the kind of person who likes talking about their feelings. After more than two years in England I was fluent in English, especially in trash talk – insulting and provoking my opponents. That was as much a part of the game in England as heading the ball. Only now was I beginning to realise that my vocabulary was considerably lacking when it came to relationship issues. While I was busy settling in in Singapore, I found myself ending more and more of our conversations early or not even answering when she called. My behaviour wasn't exactly gentlemanly.

To be honest, I enjoyed flirting with other women back then, and on Wednesdays and Saturdays I would go clubbing with my teammates – we didn't have to pay to get in anywhere. Every day the island's major TV stations broadcast several hours of current affairs shows and live coverage of S.League matches, and the club bouncers knew who we were.

I'd be lying if I said I wasn't dazzled by the island's shiny exterior. Everything in Singapore seemed new; there were the swanky clubs on Orchard Road, the modern stadiums and American-style shopping malls. Never before had I seen such a clean city. There was no graffiti, and the ground appeared so spotless that I would happily have lain down and been operated on outdoors. It wasn't until I asked for chewing gum at a supermarket that the penny dropped. "You won't find any chewing gum on the entire island," said the shop assistant. The government had outlawed the sale of the nasty pavement decoration in 1992 in order to keep public thoroughfares and subway seats clean. The man apologised, explaining that by selling chewing gum he would risk a two-year prison sentence. As a foreigner, he continued, I was still perfectly entitled to bring some with me from another country, but spitting it out on a pavement could end up costing me several thousand dollars. I shook my head and went to the checkout. Years later I smiled when I read an announcement in the paper. The sale of chewing gum was legalised in 2003 – a concession to the US. When negotiating a free trade agreement, the Americans had managed to overturn several such laws. In this case, the chewing gum giant Wrigley's had exerted considerable pressure. But their success was limited: The dangerously sticky stuff was only allowed to be sold in pharmacies if it was "chewing gum with a therapeutic value", and the pharmacies were also required to check that the customer had all the necessary paperwork – otherwise they still risked up to two years in prison. By the way, I also learned that chewing gum helps with blocked sinuses and stomach complaints. At least that was what a spokesperson for Wrigley's had hastened to add.

But when I was in Singapore, such revolutionary reforms were still years off. The then government acted like a schizo-phrenic legislator: Vandals who sprayed graffiti could expect to be beaten with a cane. Their wounds, as I saw myself years later, went all the way down to the bone. Absurdly enough, though, in Singapore the authorities' handling of prostitution was not at all consistent. Gary and I didn't know anyone from the industry personally, but if we went out on Saturday evening after a match we often got chatting to the club owners and everyone in Singapore knew that some of them based their business models on more than just nightclubs. After three weeks, Gary was better acquainted with Singapore's nightlife than most locals, and at home in England people would have expected nothing less from him. Today he leads a somewhat more sensible life coaching football in Philadelphia, having been co-manager of the German amateur team SV Elversberg. But back then he was a party animal, although he always managed to perform on the pitch. So when, in 1997, the England Under-20s travelled out to neighbouring Malaysia for the World Cup, one of the players called him to ask if he knew how to get in contact with someone who might be able to organise a girl for him, for the night after the team's final preparatory match in Singapore. They would leave for Malaysia the following morning.

Anyway, at 3am on the morning after the England match, Gary stormed into my room, his eyes wide open and with a face as red as if he'd just sprinted five miles. "We have to leave now," he shouted, "otherwise there'll be the scandal of the year." I asked what on earth was wrong. "There's no time for that now, I'll tell you in the car." Gary didn't have a driving licence, so he needed me to drive the Hyundai far too fast to the English team's hotel. The prostitute hadn't just had sex with the one player and left. At least that's what the woman claimed. She said that no fewer than 10 of the England players had had their way with her against her will. "She's sitting in the hotel room and wants to call the police," said Gary. He didn't need to tell me what that would mean for the young professionals, some of whom had already signed contracts with big clubs worth millions.

Once at the hotel we passed reception as if we were part of the team, nodded and climbed the stairs to room 312, which was from where Gary had received the desperate call. When we entered the room we saw a couple of sheepish-looking young guys leaning against the wall, dozens of beer cans on the floor and a beautiful Asian girl sat on the bed, her arms crossed.

"This whore wants to blackmail us," began one of them, but the girl interrupted him immediately: "It was rape, nothing else." Everyone began talking at once, but then Gary spoke up. "OK, guys, we need to find a solution. How much money do you all have on you?" The boys went to their rooms and each returned with 100 dollars. "Is this enough?" asked Gary. The prostitute gave a quick nod. In the end she went home with 1,200 dollars instead of the 100 originally agreed. And no, she didn't go to the police. I still wonder what happened in that room. Was the girl just trying to cash in or did those guys really force her?

It wasn't always easy, but despite the day-to-day chaos I was able to focus fully on my job. I trained for four hours a day. Secretly I hoped my good performance in Singapore would get people back in England talking about me again. Our defence still hadn't become much more stable, which meant I was a very busy man. "Pfan-tastic" punned *The Straits Times* newspaper after one match in which I made more than 30 saves. Suddenly I found myself so high up within the team's hierarchy that I was able to enjoy my penchant for practical jokes unchecked. One time I smeared a teammate's boots with butter; combined with the leather it produced a fantastically nauseating stench. Once when we had an away game I collected the room key of one of our forwards from reception and put shaving foam underneath his duvet. I held a hot teaspoon against the neck of one Muslim player, who had some explaining to do when his wife saw the mark – there's no better way to create a fake love bite. And one teammate wasn't at all pleased when he sat down on the toilet in our dressing room shortly after I'd covered it with superglue.

Bullying? No, you can't call it that; it's all part of a well-functioning team. Throughout my career, experience taught me that nothing, not even winning, is better at cementing the bonds between teammates – players from a dozen different countries – than shared laughter. In England, though, I had often held back from taking part in such tricks, since messing around like that only works if you're an undisputed regular on the team. Very often a team's social structure is governed by a strict hierarchy. It may sound stupid, but it's a golden rule in football teams: Not everyone has the right to play jokes.

One day after training, I returned from the showers and approached my locker, where my goalkeeper gloves were lying on the bench – mutilated. Someone had cut off the fingertips. "Who did it?" I asked my teammates, and soon found out. Razif Mahmud was 17 years old. He was talented but had only been a professional for a few weeks. The day before, I had cut off the toes of his socks – it's normal to mess with the younger players. Now though he was giving me a cheeky grin, the scissors still visible on top of his bag. He hadn't even bothered to hide them. I laughed, but in my mind I was already plotting my revenge.

A couple of days later we had a friendly game in Malaysia. The whole team was sat in the bus and we were ready to leave the hotel for the stadium – but Razif was running late. Eventually he turned up. Our coach, Yow Tian Bey, was passionate about discipline and eyed him severely. Razif lowered his gaze. "I can't find my boots," he said quietly, but not quietly enough. The entire bus burst into a roar of laughter. The coach glanced over at me and Gary. I shrugged my shoulders, but the old spoilsport had seen through our ruse. Our practical jokes had always been a thorn in his side, and he was in a particularly bad mood that day. Furious, he shouted at us: "Lutz, Gary, I'm going to your room. If I find those boots in there, you're out." Gary and I were two of the team's top performers, so we couldn't take him seriously. But as he got off the bus, returned to the hotel and asked for our keys, we did get a little worried. We headed up to our room with the coach, who proceeded to rummage through the wardrobes, check underneath the mattresses, and even look behind the toilet. In the end he gave up. "Why should I hide his boots?" I asked innocently. At the same time I was secretly thanking God for not drawing the coach's attention to our minibar. Or to outside the window. That was where Razif's second pair was hanging by the laces.

As expected, Rangers were weak that season. We came eighth out of 12 teams. Still, it was a good year for me: I had made the most saves and the sports journalists named me their goalkeeper of the year. Back in Europe, too, my name was on people's lips again. Clubs from Finland and Norway expressed an interest in me, and I wanted to give that option my best shot. At the end of the day, numerous professionals have made it into the English Premier League by coming over from Finland and Norway – back then they were the most important countries for players hopeful of breaking into the multi-million-pound league, the league I wanted to return to one day as a regular keeper. In the final few weeks of the season I intended to gear every fibre of my body towards playing my best football.

But then an old friend from London, Andrew, announced his arrival. Not Andrew. Please not Andrew, I thought desperately. In my first few weeks in London we had spent a lot of time together and often played football in the park. I actually liked him a lot, but I knew that he wouldn't exactly be planning to use his fortnight in Singapore as a relaxing spa break. Of course, I had to offer him my guest room; that was a matter of honour for me.

He had hardly changed. Grinning was still the only facial expression he had truly mastered. "Hi Lutz," he said as we met at the airport. "It's party time." That grin. Oh God. His belly had grown a little since we'd last seen each other a year ago. I didn't remember him having such a red face – I supposed he had utterly decimated the aeroplane's supply of spirits. At least that's what his breath told me. I hugged him but explained straight away that, if he was planning on exploring Singapore's nightlife, he would have to do so without me. Andrew was only half-listening. I thought for a moment about dropping him off at my apartment, but there was no time for that if I didn't want to be late for training. So we drove straight to training. Andrew sat in the empty stands, a broad grin on his face, while we ran our laps.

After 20 minutes it became obvious to me that the next two weeks were going to be hell. "Hey Lutz," Andrew bellowed, "how much longer will you be? Hurry up, let's go and nail a few Asian birds!" I tried to ignore the angry looks I was getting from my teammates. Rarely have I felt so ashamed. Five of our players were strict Muslims and really didn't appreciate that kind of humour at all.

On the way home I did my best to get it into Andrew's head that he would need to abandon his English lifestyle somewhat over the next two weeks in Singapore, and that the episode in the stadium had been extremely embarrassing for me. But he interpreted this in his own way: From then on Andrew did his level best to make me work off any sense of shame. He would come home at night completely plastered, usually not before 4am, and in the hallway he did a great job of letting not only me but also the neighbours know he was coming. Even Glasnost and Perestroika looked more confused than normal. They'd never seen anyone who could devastate an apartment faster than them. And I was pretty annoyed myself. A person needs to do a lot for me not to like them. Andrew succeeded. At least for those two weeks in Singapore.

I've never known anyone to talk as much as him. That lunatic could talk for hours about sex, he lectured me on the English Premier League and, even though he knew nothing about football, he felt the need to provide me with detailed analyses of the weaknesses in my goalkeeping technique. Andrew knew everything, and he knew it better than anyone else. What's more, he also managed to empty our fridge in record time. We would have only just finished refilling it and he'd be there helping himself. On a few occasions even Gary was inches away from beating the crap out of him.

Andrew brought out a mean streak in me I didn't know existed. Don't get me wrong, I know how to enjoy myself, but he really did hit on every single female he encountered. And he was so pushy about it that even I was embarrassed. The man needed to be cured, once and for all. One evening Gary and I joined Andrew when he went out on the lash – but not before giving Georgy a call. Georgy was special. Singapore is one of the main metropolises for Thai transvestites and they're a well-known part of the nightlife. There was a Thai player on our team whom they worshipped, and at every home game there would be a row of 'lady boys' in the stands. And one of them was Georgy. She – or he – was an institution in Singapore's nightlife; everyone knew the long-legged, lascivious diva. Apart from Andrew. We described Andrew to her in precise detail and she agreed to our plan.

After a couple of minutes in one nightclub, this beautiful woman came up to Andrew and spoke to him. He was downright terrified. He had clearly never attracted the interest of such a graceful creature. And interested in him she was, not even deigning to look at me or Gary. Andrew began to babble. He enjoyed being the centre of attention. Now and then he glanced over at us as if to say: Watch and learn, boys. We nodded approvingly, and after two beers Andrew and the lady boy were going at it, necking each other in one corner of the bar. I'm not too sure how he noticed that something wasn't quite right – it's quite possible he copped a feel of her crotch. But suddenly Andrew cursed loudly before storming up to the bar. He ordered four vodkas at once. The next morning my stomach was sore from laughing so hard. I gave Georgy a dozen free tickets to our next home match to say thanks.

Unfortunately, Andrew took our living together as a sign that he should continue to share every single detail with me. Things didn't get better. The fridge was still empty and he was still there. If I had something, then he had to have it too. Take tattoos – I had several. Nike offered me an obscene amount of money to have their logo tattooed on my right calf. I agreed. I admit it didn't look that good, and afterwards I felt like an advertising board. I suppose my brain must once again have been on standby when I made that decision. But no sooner had I returned home with my new body art than Andrew's interest was aroused. "I've always wanted to get a tattoo," he said that evening when he saw my leg. "You have to take me to the studio tomorrow. What do you think about the Chinese characters for power and strength?" I was about to object, because the next day I had to attend two training sessions and a TV interview. Plus there are better ideas than spontaneously deciding to get a tattoo – after all, body art like that is similar to marriage: You need to be sure of what you're entering into. But then I had an idea. "Sure, I can take you there," I said with a smile, "and the Chinese characters thing is a great idea."

I've rarely ever been as nasty as I was the next day. After training I went to the tattoo artist on my own. It cost me 300 dollars and a fair amount of persuasion, but eventually I got my revenge for the last two weeks of sleepless nights. As promised I drove Andrew to the tattoo artist, who had to listen to Andrew harping on while he worked for the next two hours. Oh, what a fantastic impact his tattoo was going to have on the ladies back in London! Looking at the characters on Andrew's upper arm, I had to summon all my strength to keep from laughing out loud. Happy with his tattoo, two days later Andrew flew back to London.

It was a good four years before I finally got the call I'd been expecting ever since that day. Andrew wasn't grinning like he usually did – that much I could tell from his voice. "Lutz, what did you do?" he roared down the phone. "You must have had a hand in this." I played innocent. Andrew continued. "I'm stood here in a Chinese takeaway and the owner's been pissing himself for the last quarter of an hour." He was the first person to notice that Andrew's upper arm had the word 'cocksucker' written on it. I started laughing, and evidently my denial didn't sound too credible. "You bastard, I'll kill you!" screamed Andrew, but I was laughing so hard I could barely hear him. This is the last I'll ever hear from Andrew, I thought. But somehow Andrew managed to see the funny side. He had the tattoo changed and has long since forgiven me.

I've never done anything that harsh to anyone else. But during those last few days, Andrew's forged tattoo gave me my inner peace. I continued to play well as the end of the season drew near, and by the final day I had received several offers from

Finland. The season there was due to begin a week after the last match in Singapore.

Hundreds of years ago, when people still crossed the world on foot or horseback, the journey itself helped prepare them for the changes in their lives, for their new surroundings. They spent months on the move, everything flowing gradually towards their destination as their environment, the climate and the temperature changed imperceptibly. Today, though, we're used to flying to the other side of the world as if we were just passing through a door. So it was that one morning the aeroplane tore me away from the concrete jungle of Singapore, spitting me out less than 24 hours later in the forests of Finland. Apart from professional football, there can't be many jobs that require you to play such an enormous game of hopscotch from one climate to another. I'm used to it by now, but I couldn't help but think such things throughout my career whenever I underwent such an extreme change to my environment at such short notice.

I spent a couple of months playing for Tampere PV before changing to FC Haka in western Finland. That was where I got to experience the harsh Nordic winter. The pitch felt as though it were made of concrete. The drumming of our studs on the frozen ground sounded like a herd of horses galloping across the prairie in an old Spaghetti Western. A grand total of eight spectators came to watch our friendly against Oulu in northern Finland. At kick-off it was minus 12 degrees; come half-time the temperature had plummeted to minus 17, and what's more we had to contend with the destructive force of the cold, stormy wind pounding our faces. I'd wrapped up warmer than I ever had done before to play in a football match and could barely move. Over my shirt from my new club, I wore a warm anorak, and beneath my tracksuit bottoms I was sporting thermal underwear as if I were some polar explorer. Before kick-off our manager, Keith Armstrong, had only briefly consulted the team doctor and the referee as to whether playing in such temperatures might pose too much of a health risk to the players. The result was a foregone conclusion: The saying "there's no such thing as bad weather, only inappropriate clothing" is something they still take literally in Finland.

In Germany they advise against performing any strenuous activity in temperatures below minus 10. Even in the bitterly cold regions of northern Finland, most matches take place inside in huge halls. In Oulu, though, the hall was undergoing maintenance, and since the training ground had no under-soil heating we were essentially playing on a hard court in the freezing cold, which tortured every single nerve cell in our bodies. The game felt agonisingly slow, as if we were all moving in slow motion and each half lasted 450 minutes. I've forgotten what the final score was, or it could be that I've just repressed it, but the hot shower after the match was the best I've ever had.

People who love a slow pace of life should go to Finland. The contrast to Singapore, with its glittering, superficial exterior, could hardly have been greater. Back then in 1997, the country was developing into a European centre of high-tech innovation. It was becoming a laboratory of the future, just a short time after being affected more than almost any other country by the consequences of the collapse of the Soviet Union. Now people across Europe were talking about Finland's technology sector and economic growth.

The Finns certainly knew how to hide this dynamism very well in everyday life – the 20,000 inhabitants of my new home, Valkeakoski, were particularly adept at it. People in Finland are friendly, but before any expression of emotion – or even uttering a single word – they carefully consider whether such extroversion is really necessary, as if they only have a limited amount before they die.

Finland is perhaps the best place for meditation on the planet. It's where I discovered one of my great loves: My love of long train journeys at night. Our team often travelled by train to play football in some of the country's remotest areas. Finland is almost as big as Germany, but home to just five million people – it's one of the most sparsely populated countries in Europe.

Rarely have I experienced a greater feeling of calm than in those moments when I was travelling towards the sunrise, millions of trees passing by, accompanied by the unchanging, earthy rattle of an old train. I admit I've never even looked at a medical textbook, but I'm pretty sure that a train journey to Rovaniemi or Oulu would be the best treatment for most mental illnesses of our age.

The train ride from Valkeakoski to our away match in Kemi, a tiny port in Lapland far away in the north of the country, took 11 hours. Millions of trees rushed past the window in a blur, interrupted now and then by a few scattered groups of houses. On journeys like this I learned how to focus my thoughts. I noticed how, after a few hours in the train compartment, I managed to concentrate more and more intensely on the upcoming game. How clearly I could picture the different situations that awaited me during the 90 minutes of play. So far I had been able to maintain the good form I had reached in Singapore. But now I began each match with even greater focus. Jürgen Klinsmann is an example of a manager who is synonymous with modern coaching methods, but if his playing career had ever led him to Finland then I'm pretty sure that his pre-season training would now consist of sending his players across Finland to meditate. On a train.

The game in Kemi seemed much the same as the five other away matches I had played in Finland so far. Four thousand fans came to watch us. That was a season record for Kemi. Be that as it may, the noise levels rather reminded me of what you might hear at a gentle tennis match. I was struck by how strongly the mentality of these people was reflected in their behaviour at football stadiums, more so than just about anywhere else.

Shortly after half time we were leading 2-0. Suddenly we heard a humming noise far away, it sounded as if all the men in the stands had brought their electric shavers with them and turned them on simultaneously. The pitch became dark. I looked upwards. Then the referee shouted: "Mosquitoes, everyone into the dressing room." We started running. Huge insects the size of dragonflies began flying across the pitch. While I was running, images from Alfred Hitchcock's *The Birds* sprang to mind. The mosquitoes didn't bite, but they weren't afraid of people running about in a panic either. Each May when the spring rains came to northern Finland, again and again huge swarms would descend on entire towns. Yelling and swearing, we reached the dressing room and slammed the door shut, the hum of the insects outside clearly audible. Two of them had made it inside the dressing room and were buzzing around the neon light in a nervous zigzag. Slowly the humming gradually became quieter. After half an hour the referee ventured to look outside the confines of the stadium. "The match can continue," he informed our captain. Uncertain, we went back onto the pitch. The insects were gone. Good. And so were the fans. Not so good. They had all fled and gone home. We played the second half without any spectators, which was certainly a career first.

Once again, on the journey home I spent hours staring out of the window brooding, as I had done so often in recent weeks. I still dreamed of returning to the Premier League. But my restlessness seemed to evaporate in the vast expanses of Finland's forests. Even the most restless spirit will find peace in a country where for part of the year the sun goes down at 2pm. I was now 25 years old and had spent the last six years travelling all over the world – for the first time ever I was suddenly struck by the serious thought of settling down. In Singapore I had begun a relationship with an Indonesian woman. Lilies was divorced and had accompanied me to Finland with her two children. She was also wondering more and more whether her family could withstand a life of constant change at the side of a truly global professional football player, who played a season here and a season there. She longed to live somewhere where her children could go to school permanently.

For a few weeks we'd been toying with an idea after I received a letter from a representative of the Indonesian Football Association. Back then the country's national team was weaker than it had been in a long time, and as such the association was seeking professionals from abroad who were married to Indonesian women and could be naturalised quickly and play for the national team. In addition to the former Yugoslav national player Midhat Gluhacevic, they had come across my name. I wasn't actually married to Lilies at the time, although we did tie the knot a few months later. But they could well imagine, they said, me playing for a professional club in Jakarta. The association and the club would share the cost of my salary. I'd never heard anything more ludicrous in my life. I couldn't help but laugh as I read the letter. I turned them down.

Over the past few years, SV Wacker Burghausen had also approached me on several occasions to ask whether I might consider returning to Germany. That was a more realistic option. In the mid-1990s, Burghausen played in Germany's third league, the 3. Liga. They were an excellent team with plenty of fully professional players, but they were still only in the 3. Liga – despite their lucrative offers, so far I had always politely declined. When they called me in the spring of 1998, though, I didn't hesitate for long. The club was now funded by its namesake, the chemicals business Wacker Chemie AG, which meant it now had the financial security it needed to stand a chance of being promoted to the second division of the Bundesliga, and what's more they were offering me a well-paid two-year contract. Lilies beamed at me when I told her about the offer. By that point I was fairly certain that my odyssey was destined to end at Burghausen – in a nice apartment, with a nice family life and a steady job keeping goal for a Bavarian third-tier team. Burghausen is only 100 kilometres away from Zwiesel. I would have come full circle.

Less than two months later we moved into a fantastic first-floor rented flat in a house in Neuötting, not far from Burghausen. Suddenly I was a normal Bavarian worker, dutifully carrying out my work on the football pitch, buying four pretzels at the bakery each morning and going hiking in the mountains on my days off. A normal worker who had, for a while at least, repressed his dream of a glittering career. One who was ready for the quiet life. One who came home one autumn day to find his Indonesian wife looking more shocked and troubled than he had ever seen her before.

She had checked the post and found a letter, with no sender specified. The piece of lined paper read: "YOU DON'T BELONG HERE! LEAVE! LEAVE IMMEDIATELY!" Lilies said nothing, but she was extremely upset. "It must be kids, it can't be more than a stupid joke," I said in an attempt to calm her down, doing my best to give her a reassuring smile. Nevertheless, I felt quite uneasy about the situation. I had grown up not far from Burghausen and had never heard anything about the place being hostile towards strangers.

The next afternoon Lilies was waiting for me at the door to our flat – she was in shock again, and this time she had been crying. She pointed silently at the kitchen table. On it was that day's post, which consisted of four blood-stained letters. Someone had put a bloody piece of beef in our letterbox along with another note written in capital letters: "YOU DON'T BELONG HERE. THIS IS A GERMAN TOWN." Lilies had placed the foul meat on top of a plastic bag next to the paper. "I'm scared for the children," she said. A man had called half an hour ago, she explained. "He said he doesn't want to see us around here for much longer, otherwise our big family won't be so big any more." My pulse rose like it usually only ever did when the opposition had a penalty. Nervously I dialled 110 on my mobile and told the police about what had happened. Half an hour later, Chief Inspector Klaus Straußberger from Burghausen police station was sitting at our kitchen table: "Under no circumstances should you open any more anonymous letters you receive, you must pass them on to us immediately," he said.

From then on I never let the children out of my sight. I took them to school every morning at 7am, and I picked them up after my first training session. Lilies stopped leaving the apartment; she became a prisoner in her own home. More xenophobic letters came, but this time they were addressed to the club. The criminal identification department at Bavaria's State Office of Criminal Investigation in Munich managed to create an offender profile based on the linguistic composition of the letters. The police installed a system at our apartment in order to trace malicious calls, and even searched several apartments across the district. But to no avail.

More post came. This time it was me who found a neatly wrapped little package in the letterbox – with no sender. I remembered the inspector's advice to pass on any such post immediately. I hesitated for a few seconds, but then I opened the package anyway. The moment I set eyes upon what was inside was when I knew it was time to leave Burghausen. In the box there was a dead sparrow. Two needles had been pushed through its head.

That night Lilies and I stayed up until 2am discussing our situation in the living room. "I want to go back home to Indonesia," said Lilies. I nodded. I had also been getting itchy feet again lately. And then I remembered the offer I had received a few months earlier from Lilies' home country. It didn't seem that crazy to me now. A Bavarian in goal for the Indonesian national team, who at 6'2" also happened to be a head taller than all the other players. I liked the idea.

My manager, Kurt Gaugler, and our fantastic coach, Kurt Niedermayer, both understood my decision. "We won't do anything to stop you," said Gaugler as I explained my decision to him. There hadn't been any more threats or gruesome letters for the past two months, but even so the light-heartedness with which we had lived up until autumn had disappeared entirely. The club had been deeply troubled by the events, and those in charge had done everything within their power to try to help find the mysterious sender – but unfortunately it was all in vain. Burghausen didn't insist that I stick to my contract, which still had over a year left before it expired. When Gaugler handed me my papers, he saw me off with a smile: "Indonesian national goalkeeper," he said, shaking his head, "one day you'll become Pope as well."

There weren't many things I was prepared to rule out during my career, but I promised him with a clear conscience that the next Pope would not be called Lutz I. Until then, mind you, I would have also considered the notion of playing for Indonesia's national side to be the result of some feverish delirium. One thing's for certain: As I write this, I am not the Pope. I kept my promise.

CHAPTER 5
DROPPING THE BALL

The scenario seemed almost unreal to me. One hot and humid April day in 1999 I found myself standing at a training ground on the outskirts of Jakarta, surrounded by three dozen Indonesians bustling around, all of them at least a head shorter than me.

The Indonesian Football Association had invited an extended group of players affiliated with the national team to a training camp, and that suddenly included me since I had married Lilies and there was now nothing to stop me becoming a naturalised Indonesian citizen. The national team coach stood at the edge of the pitch, forever nodding in almost exaggerated approval whenever I saved the ball. They acted as if I had been part of the team for years, and the football association had already sorted out the financial side of things: I was to play for the top league club, Persija Jakarta, with the association paying half of my salary. Even though I still found it absurd even to consider adopting Indonesian citizenship in order to play in goal for the national side, all the necessary steps had been taken. All I needed to do was say yes.

Throughout my life I've had many, in fact countless, sleepless nights. Back then though it was particularly bad. The Indonesians' football was far faster and more technically refined than I had expected. I had already kept goal during one of the national team's practice games against first division club Pelita Jaya, and the standard of the players had caught me by surprise. It's just madness, I thought as I grinned into the darkness of the bedroom. In my mind I could already see myself at the 2002 World Cup, which was to take place three years later in Japan and South Korea. As I slowly began to nod off, I pictured what it would be like to play in goal there. Not for Germany as I had always hoped, but against my home country. Attack after German attack surged towards my goal, but thanks to my saves we managed to keep it at 0-0. In a strong Bavarian dialect, the famous German commentator Gerd Rubenhauer was relaying the desperate scene to audiences back at home: "Ballack's complaining, Schneider's cursing and Klose is staring at the ground – can anyone beat this Pfannenstiel?" I'm sure I was smiling throughout that dream.

The fact that Indonesia wasn't even among the world's top 100 countries was something I only remembered during the hours of daylight. Then it hit home that I would have to renounce my German citizenship – had he known, my father would have had a heart attack on the spot. And then I started to get that feeling that was always so hard to shake: At 25 years old, was I ready to settle down to a leisurely family life in an Indonesian villa far away from the heart of major professional football? I spent a long time brooding over why the cracks had started to appear in my relationship with Lilies in recent weeks. There was still so much of the world I had yet to see.

The phone rang. I shouldn't have answered. I had just come out of the bathroom, my hair wet. In 10 minutes the taxi would be arriving to take me to Persija Jakarta's club headquarters to sign my contract. It was merely a formality, since the deal had been negotiated long before: a basic salary of 6,000 dollars per month plus bonuses for points won.

"Hello Lutz," said the person at the other end of the line. It was Alan Vest, the manager of Geylang United from Singapore. We had last spoken two weeks earlier. His club also wanted to sign me; I still had a good reputation there following my first season for Sembawang Rangers in 1997. I would have liked to return, but the fact of the matter was that Jakarta and the

Indonesian Football Association had made me the better offer. "Are you sure we can't change your mind?" Alan asked. "I've been able to squeeze out a bit more for you from the president."

I hesitated for a moment. I had agreed to Persija Jakarta's terms but still hadn't signed the contract – and at the end of the day that's crucial when you're talking about a professional footballer with no club. Plus it was becoming ever clearer to me that I really didn't want to give up my German passport – despite all my dreams of World Cup glory. We talked for less than two minutes. I accepted.

When I told Lilies about the whole situation, we got into a huge row. She screamed at me, totally unable to understand what I was doing. Perhaps I didn't even know myself. By the time we were done I was more or less single; leaving on such bad terms essentially meant we were separated. And so it was that, later that evening, a German goalkeeper was sitting on a flight to Singapore. One who had just made the biggest mistake of his life.

The next morning I arrived at Geylang United's headquarters half an hour earlier than arranged. In the office there was a pretty beefy guy who greeted me with a grim look. He looked over a few pieces of paper, signed, shook the manager's hand and then left without saying a word. "Who was that?" I asked Alan. The coach grinned. "Your predecessor." New Zealand's then national keeper, Jason Batty, had just signed his termination agreement.

Batty had only arrived in Singapore three months earlier, but he'd made a few crucial errors in his very first matches. Just like in any such situation, the usual mechanisms kicked in. He was whistled at by the fans, ridiculed by the press, and his manager was secretly on the lookout for a new goalkeeper. It was a situation I had experienced often enough myself, so it was hard to feel any sympathy for him. Like so many foreign keepers, Batty just didn't get along with Singapore's football culture. Matches are always played in the evening and thus always beneath the blinding floodlights, which is tough on goalkeepers. What's more, what the football lacks in technical excellence it certainly makes up for in unpredictability. Batty could have sat out the rest of his contract on the bench, but there's not much international demand for reserve goalkeepers from Singapore.

And so it was that Geylang changed goalkeepers within the space of 15 minutes. Just four days later I found myself standing in goal for them for the first time. I had no trouble saving the five or six shots on my goal, and we beat Gombak, who were sixth in the table, 3-0. The next morning *The Straits Times* ran the following headline in huge letters: "He's back."

There were just a few more matches to go before the end of the season, and life was going well for me. We ended up coming fourth, and out on the streets people greeted me enthusiastically. Even when my relationship with Lilies finally broke down for good in January 2000, it still wasn't enough to suppress my mood for long.

In the following months I thoroughly enjoyed single life, far more so than I ever had before. The rhythm never changed: During the day we usually had a training session, which wasn't too physically demanding, especially for me as the keeper. I didn't have any competition to fear either. The second goalkeeper, Shahril Jantan, was highly talented but he was also just 18 years old. The nights were what really tired me out: Three or four nights a week I would go out with my flatmate Mickey Jurilj. The Australian and I had been friends ever since playing at the same time during my first guest match in Singapore. And when I signed with Geylang, he joined my former club Sembawang Rangers. I called him and asked whether he fancied sharing an apartment with me and he agreed.

Mickey and I really knew how to make the most of any appearance in Singapore's nightlife, especially on Wednesdays when the most popular club in the country was reserved for its 'Airline Night'. Singapore's Changi Airport is one of the biggest in Asia, and stewardesses are among the biggest party animals there are. Those nights were legendary; they only let in cabin crew ... and professional footballers. Mickey and I had a ritual. On Wednesday morning we would drive to the airport, get lists of all the airlines' flights and work out which stewardesses would be coming to the club that night. Our motto was: The more exotic, the better. For example, we were curious as to what the ladies from Syrian Airways would look like. During the day we Googled everything we could on Syria, which we then passed off as our in-depth knowledge. There can't be many people who have flirted as systematically as we did.

Footballers are by far the most popular athletes in Singapore, and as such they enjoy a special status in the country's nightlife. At the time I also did a bit of commentating for the biggest sports channel in the region, ESPN, and every couple of months I made promotional appearances for the 'Armani Exchange' fashion line – in return I could take my pick of the range.

I wouldn't be surprised if Mickey and I came across as arrogant in those days. Dressed in designer clothes we would pull up in front of the nightclub in our sponsor's car, hand it over to a valet with the engine still running, and stroll past a queue of 150 waiting people. I soon got the impression that every single bouncer in the country must have been a football fan. "Can we bring two or three girls from the queue in with us?" we often asked. "No problem."

That life didn't end until, on one such evening, I got to know Anita a bit better – she was one of the most beautiful Eurasian women I had ever seen. She was willowy, with long dark hair and a stunning smile. We had seen each other a few times briefly back in 1997, because her mother worked as the head of administration at one of the local football clubs and Anita had come with her to a few events. I knew she sent most guys packing before they could finish their first sentence. Nevertheless I somehow managed to pluck up the courage to talk to her. I was unable to make it past a bit of small talk on this occasion, but I convinced her to meet me for coffee. It seemed like half an eternity before she finally came to trust me. Two months later, I kissed her for the first time. From then on I didn't waste any more thoughts on nightclubs.

Head over heels in love like a little boy, I started my second season at Geylang United. The club had been investing heavily in more new players, and we were favourites to win the championship.

Especially after our flawless start to the season, with six wins in a row. Although we had finished fourth the previous year, we did still manage to get through to the qualification round of the Asian Club Championship, but to be frank we always lost those games quite heavily. Still, it did mean losing matches while playing against the vast stadium backdrops I had dreamed of as a child.

We played against the Iranian team Esteghlal Tehran in their huge Azadi Stadium. When it was built for the 1974 Asian Games it held an incredible 140,000 spectators. By now the capacity had been reduced to 100,000, but playing in front of that many noisy fans was still an unforgettable experience – far more so than the match itself. Such games always aroused my curiosity. I wanted to know everything about all the countries I played in, even if it was just one match. Before these games I would read up on the place or quiz teammates from the country in question. Iranian football, which had been viewed critically by the ayatollahs, was experiencing something of a golden age after the country had sensationally beat its nemesis, the USA, 2-1 at the 1998 World Cup.

We arrived in Tehran in the middle of a heatwave, with the temperature struggling to drop below 35 degrees even in the early evening. I had never played before such a wall of noise. The whistling from the crowd was so loud that you could insult the referee without fear of punishment – he simply couldn't hear you. Esteghlal also played technically sound football. We didn't stand a chance from the beginning, and lost 3-0.

"Why weren't there any women in the stadium?" I asked one of my teammates, who had spent a season playing in Iran, during our flight back to Singapore. "They are allowed in the stadium," he replied. "But it's extremely complicated and they have to apply for a permit." I hadn't seen a single one. To all intents and purposes football stadiums were taboo for them.

His former teammates, he continued, had told him that football had galvanised the whole country. All the country's political leaders – the Supreme Leader, the President and the Speaker of

Parliament – had praised football's influence at the time. Following the success of the national team, people's enthusiasm was simply too great, and so even the critics – who up until a few weeks earlier had branded the country's 'football fever' a delusion produced by the imperialist sports world – fell silent. It was a time when the country celebrated football on the streets, like Germany did during the 2006 World Cup – and even women were included. Since then, I've heard, it has become easier for them to attend matches.

We had already been prepared for our defeat and Asian Club Championship exit, so it was no great disappointment. But then we lost a home league game and became more and more inconsistent, and by the end of the first half of the season we were four points off the top. A nervous atmosphere gripped the club. It was as if the disaster that was to unfold in the coming months already hung in the air.

There are coincidences in life that can change everything. A friend of mine once forgot to buy tomatoes when he went shopping, so he went back to the supermarket and met the woman he later married. Some people suddenly believe in miracles because the plane they only just missed then crashed. In my case, the coincidence worked the other way around: I missed my plane, as it were, and boarded another one that was destined to crash soon afterwards.

Our final match before a break of a few weeks ended in sensation: We lost a home game at our own Bedok Stadium 1-0 to the middle-of-the-road team Jurong. Feeling frustrated, after the usual interviews I got into my Honda. When I started the engine, the fuel gauge lit up: I only had enough petrol for another 40 kilometres or so. There was a petrol station very close to the stadium. "Shall I stop there or not?" I wondered, before deciding to queue up behind the other waiting cars. As I was filling the tank, a huge Indian man with a vast belly came up to me. "You're that Geylang goalkeeper," began the sweaty man. I nodded casually; I had a dozen similar encounters every day. "It's a shame you didn't win," continued the stranger, "I often watch you guys.

Maybe we'll meet again." "Yeah, perhaps," I replied wearily before making my excuses and getting back into the car.

Twenty minutes later I had reached the Orchid Park Condominium in Yishun, where Mickey and I, as well as a whole host of other professionals, had our apartments. The grounds are fenced off – anyone wanting to enter has to wait briefly in front of a small driveway. Lost in thought, I was rummaging through my kitbag on the passenger seat looking for the chip card for the gate, when suddenly a car flashed its lights behind me. It was the Indian man, who proceeded to get out and come up to my window. "Ah, so this is where you live," he said. "My apartment isn't far from here. I'm a golf coach, by the way. If you like, maybe we could play a round some time. No charge, of course." I was surprised that he was there after leaving him at the petrol station, and had no desire to get into a long discussion. "Yes, yes," I said, probably just to get rid of him, "why not." I drove through the gate, slightly annoyed by how pushy he had been. It wasn't until later that I would discover the Indian man actually lived miles away and had deliberately followed me.

Four weeks later, I was sitting in a restaurant with Mickey. Suddenly someone tapped me on the shoulder. I turned around and saw the Indian man again. "Hey, how about that round of golf?" he asked, "I could get you into the Orchid Country Club." That was the swankiest course in Singapore, and nobody got in without an invitation. Mickey and I looked at each other and nodded. Keen to make the most of such an opportunity, we were happy to give him our landline number.

The stranger called the next day. He asked whether we had time now. We arranged to meet for a coffee at the golf club. Oh, and his name was Sivakumar, he told us. Despite working as a golf coach he seemed to be interested in nothing but football. We talked about the English Premier League, about football in Malaysia and the German national side, which had just been through two poor years under the rather embarrassing manager Erich Ribbeck. At some point we got talking about our next match against Home United, who were third in the league. "Can you beat them?" asked Sivakumar. "Of course," I replied, "we are in good form." In the not-too-distant future, uttering that sentence would see me thrown in jail.

Weeks later, Mickey and I were at a shopping centre. Someone tapped me on the shoulder again. Before I had time to turn around, I could already hear the Indian man's offended voice: "The match against Home United only ended in a 2-2 draw." I had to think for a second. The match hadn't gone well for us and I'd really had my work cut out keeping us in the game. I had been named man of the match after the final whistle. "I did my best," I replied to Sivakumar, "but they just played well." The Indian man calmed down. "Next week you two are playing against each other," he said, his gaze alternating between me and Mickey. He was right; our clubs Geylang United and Sembawang Rangers were due to meet. We had been trying to outdo each other with witty one-liners for days. "What will the result be?" We had won our first meeting that season 3-1, and Rangers were down in 11th place. So I replied that we would obviously win, and was surprised to hear Mickey being unusually realistic.

"If we're lucky we might pinch a draw."

"Who knows," said the Indian to Mickey, "perhaps I'll risk a bet on that."

In the end we won 2-1. A completely normal result. But Sivakumar, as I learned later, claimed that he had bet a large amount of money on Geylang pulling off a big win.

Three weeks later there was a repeat of the strange little game. Sivakumar called to ask whether he could stop by for coffee. I didn't have anything on, so I said yes. Once again we talked entirely about football and not once about golf.

"Next week you're playing against Woodlands," he said. "What do you think?"

"We'll win that one."

"Yes, of course," he answered fiercely, "that's what you always say."

We joked about my predictions, just like how anyone talks about football. I explained to him that Woodlands were lousy in terms of tactics and it wasn't by chance that they were second from bottom. Never did it occur to me that he was planning on betting a large sum of money based on what I had said.

But that is exactly what he did, only this time he didn't leave anything to chance. On the Friday evening before the match, Woodlands' two best players were attacked by two strangers. The Englishman Max Nicholson was able to escape, but the Croatian player Ivica Raguz, the team's most dangerous striker, didn't stand a chance: They slammed a hockey stick into his right knee. The two assailants fled without taking anything. The motive was clear: Someone wanted to stop Raguz and Nicholson from playing against us. Suspicion fell on the Asian betting mafia. And even though Nicholson had been able to flee from his attackers, the betting mafia's plan worked; Raguz couldn't play and we easily won the match 2-0.

In recent months the headlines in Singapore had once again been dominated by rumours of match fixing. The league had originally been founded with the intention of being cleaner in this respect than every other league in Asia. Now though it was considered one of the most vulnerable on the planet, combining all the necessary factors bookmakers needed with the energy of the criminal underworld. On average just 5,000 spectators attended the matches, and local players rarely earned more than 3,000 dollars per month. It was easy for them to double their income in just 90 minutes by accepting bonuses from book-makers. What's more, the betting mafia already had a firm grip on football in Asia back in the 1990s. While German referee Robert Hoyzer, who was responsible for a huge match-fixing scandal in 2005, was still at school, people in Singapore were already placing bets with bookmakers worth up to one or two million dollars per game.

There had been a number of surprising results in recent months. Mediocre clubs like Tampines and Balestier had won against top teams, only to be utterly thrashed by someone at the bottom of the table the following week. The hockey stick attack escalated the whispers into a genuine public scandal. Pressure on the government mounted – after all, even back then Singapore was more worried about its squeaky-clean image than most other states. A corrupt league didn't really fit the picture.

While the matches carried on as normal, behind the scenes investigators pulled out all the stops to find the two attackers. Singapore's notorious CPIB, the Corrupt Practices Investigations Bureau, got involved. It was a special agency established in the 1950s by the British colonial government. Its officials were widely regarded as the most brutal in the whole of Asia. No sooner was it involved than it planned to make players take lie detector tests after any unusual results.

In Singapore, the attack was on everybody's lips for a fortnight, until the day when, before our match at Marine Castle, we received an anonymous fax at our offices. It had also been sent to our opponents and the Singapore Football Association. "Geylang will win the match 1-0," it read. "Geylang's captain, Billy Bone, and striker Brian Bothwell have given someone a considerable amount of money to place on a win." Although Bone and Bothwell had nothing to do with the fax, the anticipated result turned out to be right; we won 1-0 in the pouring rain. For a few days, the fax managed to push the hockey stick attack out of the headlines.

Before long the CPIB discovered who had sent the fax. The document had been sent from an internet café, and the owner was able to identify the sender from surveillance footage as Sivakumar, the fat Indian man. Officials searched his apartment, with lists of phone numbers leading them to further suspects. The hockey stick used in the attack was found at one of their homes. By sending the fax, Sivakumar had hoped to divert the attention of those investigating the attack away from him. A few hours later he was in custody. He faced several years in prison.

But the successful operation was of little use to the CPIB. It was evidently difficult to persuade the public that convicting an overweight golf coach constituted a breakthrough in the fight against match fixing. Sivakumar offered the investigators a deal. He told them he had been receiving information from a number of players over the past few months. He said he would cooperate fully in return for impunity, and the investigators agreed. He gave the investigators seven or eight names – including mine and Mickey's.

The following Sunday afternoon Anita, Mickey and I were sat at home watching the rather stupid American comedy *Deuce Bigalow: Male Gigolo*. Not exactly a classic, but still we cracked up at every little joke. Halfway through the film there was a knock at the door. Mickey went to see who it was and peered through the spyhole: There were five Asians, dressed casually in polo shirts and jeans, standing outside our apartment. "I don't know them," he called into the living room. "Maybe they're Jehovah's Witnesses," I joked from on the sofa. "Tell them we don't need anything." Mickey opened the door. He had barely opened it a fraction when a fist came flying at his face. He lay sprawled on the floor as the men stormed past him.

"CPIB!" they shouted. "CPIB!"

Confused, Anita and I stood up in front of the sofa while the plain-clothes policemen spent the next five minutes taking apart the entire apartment. "Would you mind telling us what you're looking for?" I asked when one of them peered inside our coffee jar.

"Evidence."

"What kind of evidence?" I asked with a combination of anger and sarcasm. "Perhaps we can help you. Why don't you try looking inside the lamps?"

Anita, on the other hand, was petrified and didn't say a word. Anyone who grew up in Singapore knows you don't joke with the CPIB.

In the end Mickey, Anita and I had to go with them to the CPIB headquarters. Wearing T-shirts, shorts and sandals we got into a Honda that belonged to one of the investigators. "In half an hour we'll go and have dinner, then move on to a club," I said. The situation was far too surreal to be taken seriously. It was to do with betting on S.League matches, the officials had told us, but us being involved in betting was about as likely as the Pope going clubbing with us on 'Airline Night'. I was certain that we would be leaving the building a few minutes later. I was wrong.

The policemen led us down a long corridor before separating us and depositing us in three cramped rooms. I was left alone. A desk, two chairs, no pictures, no windows, the walls completely white. After five minutes, a short man came in and began to shout: "You will not leave the country in the next five years." I was so surprised that I couldn't help laughing. He left the room again once he had finished shouting himself hoarse.

Nothing happened for the next hour, maybe two hours. I was alone. The walls, I could literally feel it, were coated in the sweat of the hundreds of interrogated suspects that had taken place in the sweltering room. Another investigator entered the room. He was friendlier and spoke to me patiently, although his message was the same and so just as ridiculous. I laughed at him. His expression didn't change in the slightest. "Okay, then let's see if the lie detector agrees with you."

The investigator led me out of the room. We walked along the corridor, which seemed never-ending. In one of the final rooms there sat a young Chinese woman. The equipment that surrounded her made the place look like a recording studio. The investigator stood behind me menacingly. Without saying a word, the woman lifted my T-shirt up and wrapped a strap around my chest. She attached small sensors to my fingers.

"Are you currently in Asia?" It was the first thing she said. Her voice was stern, like that of an embittered old Latin teacher.

"Yes."

"Are you currently in Europe?"

I replied no, surprised by the ridiculous questions. A printer was sketching a diagram on a roll of paper, and there were barely any variations. But then she got to the point.

"Did you manipulate a match at the beginning of March?"

I knew how important this question was. I answered no. Even though I had done nothing wrong the diagram showed the tiniest of variations.

"We've got you," said the woman. She pulled the paper from the roll and hit me on the head with it. I got aggressive.

"Like hell you have, I didn't do anything!"

She had in fact been bluffing. I discovered much later that the swings on the chart were much too small to be considered a lie. I had passed the test, but this wasn't even mentioned in the investigation file.

The policemen took me back to the white room, where I spent two more hours sat on the chair alone. I wanted to speak to my lawyer. Instead, an investigator came in. He was called Wong. Wong was in his late thirties and about 5'5". He wasn't exactly likeable. He slammed the door shut and shoved the table in front of me aside. "Just confess!" he screamed. "Just confess!" I wanted to speak to my lawyer, but in Singapore a suspect can be questioned without their lawyer for 48 hours. I was getting angrier. I looked at the man and asked him if he was suffering from 'short man syndrome', which only made him lose it completely. He hit me.

"If you hit me again," I said, "then those colleagues of yours who are watching us on camera will have to scrape you off the wall."

That was the last self-confident thing I said that day. The investigators turned the air conditioning down to 10 degrees and stripped me naked. They tried to trap my fingers in a drawer, shouted in my ears and slapped me in the face. The investigators took turns, some going and others coming. It was like a bad Hollywood movie. Eventually, after being interrogated for 28 hours, I had no strength left in me. Wong produced a document which contained Sivakumar's statement.

In it, the strands of his story had been carefully woven together. He said he had deliberately befriended Mickey and I in order to make money from betting. He claimed he had asked my opinion on three matches, and that I had said we would win each time and I could guarantee it. He alleged that he had promised me a share of the winnings. After the first two games didn't turn out the way he had hoped, he said, I had manipulated the third match in order to pay off my debts. Two pages of nothing but lies. Even so, that was the moment – another 12 hours into my interrogation – when I began to feel a real sense of unease.

I then made my own official statement. Yes, Sivakumar did tell me that he liked to bet on the odd match now and then, I dictated, but he never mentioned his intention to bet money on our fixtures. By the end, three A4 pages explained what had really happened. I was thus signing the exact opposite of Sivakumar's version of events. After 48 hours, my interrogation came to an end. I left the building – without my passport. The CPIB held onto that.

When I stepped out of the door I was blinded by the midday sun – it had been 48 hours since I'd seen the light of day. I called Anita on her mobile; she had been released after just a couple of hours of questioning. It went through to voicemail. Eventually I managed to get hold of her brother: "She doesn't want to talk to you," he said curtly before hanging up. Back at home I met Mickey, who had been let out some time before me. "In the end I just signed," he said blankly, "I just wanted to get out of there." And then came the sentence which made me momentarily doubt his sanity: "I really needed to shave," he said. He was being serious. I had no time to ask about the details. I had to go to training, even though I hadn't slept.

Nobody demanded an explanation about why I hadn't turned up a day earlier; they all knew why. The news of my questioning had been all over the TV and the newspapers. I was closely watched by 10 policemen, while more than 50 media representatives crowded around the ground. My teammates looked at me coolly as I ran onto the pitch. During the two hours of training that followed, none of them said a word to me. The newspapers were packed with all the details of my arrest. In a statement, the football association had announced its intention to use lie detector tests next season in cases of suspicious matches – they neglected to mention the fact that my test had been negative. Later on I called Anita again, trembling. She still wouldn't answer. "If your fear of the CPIB is more important to you than I am, then let's just forget it," I muttered to her in a voicemail.

I'm not quite sure how, but in the next few matches I was able to block out what was going on as soon as I walked out onto the pitch. Under such extreme pressure my body seemed to emit substances that put me in a whole new league. I had six clean sheets in seven games. After a few days I met up with Anita. She apologised for the way she had behaved and we lived together as a couple again. Some semblance of peace returned, and even the newspapers began to write more about football again than about betting. I quietly hoped that my statement had put an end to the case for the CPIB.

But just before the end of the season I found a post-it note left by my manager on my locker in the dressing room: "Please contact the CPIB immediately. Important!" They must want to return my passport, I thought as I set off for their headquarters. Ever the optimist. That morning Mickey had already had an appointment with the CPIB to renew his bail. I called him. Voicemail. I called one of Mickey's friends, who told me that Mickey was still in there after two hours. My optimism vanished. Reluctantly I entered the police building. Before I knew it, an official was barring my way: "Mr Pfannenstiel, you are hereby officially charged by the state of Singapore." I stood rooted to the spot, having just received the worst shock in all my 27 years. All I could say was: "Can I make a couple of phone calls?" Once I had calmed down, I called Anita as well as my lawyer. The court hearing was already scheduled for the following day. Anita signed for my bail. In the event of me doing a runner she would have had to cough up 100,000 dollars. Journalists and photographers were waiting outside the building; within minutes they knew the scandal was getting bigger and bigger.

That night we lay in bed staring at the ceiling in silence. Mickey and his girlfriend were in the next room. They barely slept a wink that night either, since he had been charged at almost exactly the same time as me. In his statement he had described some things he had kept from me until then, which put pressure on me as well. The CPIB had lured him into a trap. Mickey was friends with Ivica Raguz, one of the victims of the hockey stick attack. After interrogating him for 20 hours, the investigator had told him they needed his testimony in order to lock that tosser Sivakumar up: "That will be the end of it for you and Lutz," they had said. In the end though, Mickey actually signed a document stating that, when promised by the Indian that we would receive some of the profits, he had said: "Okay." That was nothing less than a confession. There had been no mention of my name. But since I must have been at the encounter in question, as far as the CPIB was concerned I had known about the situation and was therefore an accessory to the crime.

The next morning the courtroom was packed with 100 people. The hearing lasted just two minutes.

"How do you plead: Guilty or not guilty?" asked the judge.

"Not guilty."

"Then the case will go to trial," he said before ordering that we be detained in the courtroom's holding cells.

Mine was no more than 10 square metres and had no windows – I counted 18 cockroaches crawling across the concrete in the sweltering heat. Bail had been set for each of us at 100,000 dollars. A guarantee was no longer sufficient, meaning the money would actually have to be deposited. It was a fortune – even for a professional footballer. At least for one who had mostly played for clubs in lower leagues. It would take a few days before my parents and Anita were able to raise the full amount.

That evening after the hearing, we were taken by bus to the remand prison along with 20 other detainees. Having seen a prison cell in Singapore, I now have a good idea of what hell must be like. The uneven floor was covered in straw mats just a few milli-metres thick for us to sleep on, while in the corner there was a hole to pee and shit in – no toilet paper, of course – and next to it a bucket of dirty water for rinsing and drinking. It was 40 degrees, and an acrid stench hung in the hot air. By 3am I couldn't keep calm any longer. I started to cry. It soon became clear to me that this place might break me.

Anita tried everything to raise the bail money, even pawning necklaces, rings, and all her jewellery. After five days my parents managed to transfer the rest of the money to Singapore. While I was waiting I couldn't stop thinking that, if I actually were to lose the case, I should just go to the top of a skyscraper and jump.

By the time the bail had been deposited and I was allowed to leave the prison – without my passport – seven days later, I had developed a nasty skin allergy: I was red from head to toe. A paparazzo promptly jumped out from behind a corner and took a photo. "If you take any more pictures of me, I'll shove that camera down your throat," I snapped at him. Even so, the next morning the front pages of the two biggest daily newspapers showed a man with dark rings around his eyes and a thousand red pustules.

We drove to Anita's place; she took Mickey in as well as me. Our clubs had already suspended us, given our cars to other players and cancelled the contract on our apartment. Even my bank account had been frozen. I spent two hours in the shower. That evening I started preparing for the trial, since it's not like I was able to sleep – I didn't sleep for five nights. The itching, the mental images I had from the prison, I just couldn't. Every day I spent two to three hours at my lawyer's office. We collected statements from more than 100 witnesses confirming that my conduct had been flawless in all three matches. My teammates confirmed that I hadn't incited any of them to match fixing. Just one witness would be testifying against me: Sivakumar.

All the facts spoke in my favour. Still, I did wonder whether I should flee: In private conversations, staff from the German Embassy had recommended I consider taking such a step and illegally leave the country via Thailand or Malaysia. They knew what everyone in Singapore knows: Anyone accused by the CPIB was bound to lose. But by doing that I would have brought serious financial difficulties upon Anita. Defiantly I said: "Then I'll just be the first one to win."

I called everyone I thought might possibly have contacts in the country's betting mafia. I needed to prove my innocence. After a couple of days I got a call from Sivakumar. "Hey, sorry about everything, I had no choice," he stammered down the phone. "We really need to meet up. I can help you leave the country." I shouted and swore at him, making it absolutely clear what I thought of his offer. He did give me the address of an internet café in town, though, where he said I would find someone who knew Pal. Pal was the most important illegal bookmaker in the city and just so happened to be Sivakumar's boss. He had a dubious reputation in Singapore. He had already spent a year in prison because of his involvement in illegal betting, but he was in there for eight months before a mobile phone was found on him. A guard had slipped it to him. No one before or after him ever managed to manipulate games from inside a prison cell.

The café owner was a football fan. He immediately recognised me, led me to a table with three men and introduced me as "one of Pal's business partners." The man I was looking for was in his mid-thirties; he greeted me like a courteous bank clerk might greet a customer seeking investment advice. "You will lose, the CPIB has only lost one case in the last three years," he said after a while in a friendly tone, taking a sip of his mineral water. The two other men said nothing. "We can get you out of the country. Every Friday there's a car that drives across the border into Malaysia. The border guards know the car and let it through. Believe me, you don't have any other options." I had to bite my tongue so as not to tell the man what I thought of him. "Thank you," I said as I got up, "but I will find another solution." Fleeing would more than likely have resulted in my international player's permit being revoked and the end of my career. I was innocent, and I wanted that confirmed in black and white by a court of law. My Bavarian stubbornness had accompanied me to Asia. I walked out of the café. Later I learned that one of the two silent men had been Pal. Apparently he rarely revealed his identity to a stranger on meeting them for the first time.

The trial proved a total farce from day one. The prosecutor, Tan Boon Gin, knew absolutely nothing about football. Mickey and I had played against each other in one of the matches in question, and the prosecutor asked whether we had been in direct contact with each other immediately before the game, since "the dressing rooms are right next to each other, aren't they?"

"Yes they are, but do you think I dug a tunnel between them?" I replied, earning laughter from the onlookers.

But we must have seen each other somewhere inside the stadium as we made our way out onto the pitch, the man continued. "It's relatively unlikely for two opposing players to meet outside the dressing rooms, hug, agree what the result will be and then give each other a peck on both cheeks," I pointed out. I suppose I was never destined for a career as a high-ranking diplomat, but I just couldn't do it any differently. That day I laughed so much that I had to loosen my tie.

The trial had been adjourned for a break when I bumped into the prosecutor in the toilets. "You must think you're pretty clever," he said. "And maybe you are. But in a couple of days you and your friend will be back in the bunker." I was furious. "Then you'll be able to look in the mirror and proudly say to yourself that you've locked up yet another innocent person," I replied. The prosecutor was silent for a moment. "Don't get me wrong," he said a shade less callously, "I'm just doing my job." He knew as well as I did that they just wanted to make an example of me.

The verdict was due on 27 December 2000, but the judge called in sick. I think she at least wanted to spare me having to spend New Year's Eve behind bars. And so it was that 4 January 2001 became my darkest day: "The defendant may rise," said the judge. I still hung onto the feint hope that I would be flying home a day later. Ever the optimist, like I said. The judge continued: "On count one you are found guilty. Count two: Guilty. Count three: Guilty." Her justification was that she had no reason not to believe Sivakumar's statement.

I was to be sentenced four days later. The newspapers claimed I faced up to five years. Mickey had been sentenced to five months shortly before me and was already in prison, so I knew that I could expect a similar sentence. For the last few months, apart from my research, I had been doing high-intensity strength training and eating plenty; if I did end up being convicted, I wanted to be strong enough to make it through prison. The day before I was sentenced, I went to a hairdresser and had my ponytail cut off – I wasn't about to let the hairstyle that had been my trademark for more than 10 years be destroyed by a pair of prison scissors. What's more, inmates with long hair were more likely to fall victim to attempted rape, and I certainly didn't want that to happen. In the afternoon we visited one of Anita's friends whose daughter was celebrating her birthday with a fancy dress party – I had to distract myself somehow. My final meal as a free man was a pizza in a fancy Italian restaurant. I hardly ate a bite.

When the judge announced the sentence of five months, Anita burst into tears. I stood up, bereft of emotion. I gave one last furious glance at the club and league officials, who had already made their judgement months ago. I then got changed in the adjacent room. Anita came in. We held each other for a minute. Then I was taken to prison by bus along a route I already knew.

CHAPTER 6
WELCOME TO HELL

Guards in Singapore use a new arrival's first night to instill respect into them. They locked me in a cell with a mentally unstable double murderer. He was on strong tablets that kept him in a state of semi-sleep, but as soon as the dose began to wear off he swore at me loudly. He tried to hit me, but the medicine slowed his movements down so much that it was easy for me to shove him into the corner of the cell. He stayed there, but I didn't sleep a wink.

At least after a couple of days I did end up sharing a cell with Mickey. As well as 10 drug smugglers, murderers and rapists.

I instantly found the tangible stickiness of the humid air and the stench of rotting leftover meat on the food trays unbearable. At night I could hear the whir of dozens of mosquitoes. I hate those creatures, and throughout my life I must have spent thousands of nights hunting the vicious little things. I've never understood why, despite the deaths of billions of their kind before them, the insects continue to enter people's bedrooms and, driven by a combination of suicidal and sadistic desires, spend many hours on their final, fatal flight. In our cell they flew undisturbed. Most of the inmates couldn't sleep anyway.

The staff from the German and Australian Embassies had advised us to stay well out of any fights – if we behaved well, they said they might be able to apply enough pressure to secure our early release from prison after three months. But none of them had seen Queenstown Remand Prison from the inside. Different rules applied there, especially when it came to people awaiting execution who had nothing left to lose. Our food was served to us on trays inside the cell. There was always rice, and often we got manky vegetables with plenty of curry and chilli. There was barely ever any meat. In the first few days, without saying anything, whenever we got food some of my cellmates took two of the three little bowls from my tray. I didn't react.

One day we were exercising in the prison yard when Mickey and I were approached by a muscular man. Joga was a former boxer serving time for manslaughter. We'd often seen him, usually on his own leaning against a wall. With his expressive facial features and large, alert eyes that always kept track of what was going on around him, there was something of an unapproachable aura about him. The smaller criminals didn't dare speak to him, and the beefier guys sensed it was best to leave him alone. Joga was the prisoner who never spoke, but now he was talking to us in a deep voice: "Guys, watch your backs. You have to defend yourselves, otherwise you'll soon have real problems."

Word had got around that we were allowing people to take our food.

"Outside there were laws and lawyers," he said, "and perhaps now and then the Embassy will help you. But there's none of that in here."

Regardless of whether you were serving time for unpaid parking tickets or mass murder, if you didn't earn people's respect then you were putting yourself in mortal danger. "They're like animals," Joga continued. "They test to see who is the weakest and then move in." He didn't need to tell me that inmates also got raped from time to time. Everyone knew about it. One frail old prisoner needed medical treatment after one such night because his bowel was hanging out of his backside.

I had thrown myself into the fray in the penalty area thousands of times, and suffered a broken nose or arm on several occasions as a result, but life hadn't prepared me for this new situation in the slightest. Joga assumed that job. If we did run into trouble, he said, apart from hitting the person we should also kick their knees, because "they're one of the most sensitive parts of the body".

The next time a Chinese prisoner, who had been convicted of drug smuggling, reached for my tray, I punched him twice in the nose and kicked his knee hard. By the end both he and the tray were on the floor. I earned myself a broken nose five or six times, but it was nothing compared to what I did to the other prisoners' faces. A couple of days later I survived an attempted rape by several Chinese men in the showers. They left me alone as soon as they noticed how ready I was to hit back, no holds barred. I didn't get any more hassle after that.

As time went by I began to make friends with Joga, as far as that was possible. He didn't tell me much about his life, but did at least reveal why he was in prison. In a pub brawl he had killed a knife-wielding man in self-defence, and that had earned him a 12-year prison sentence and 24 lashes.

Mickey and I had the pleasure of witnessing such punishment a few times. The prisoner's bare buttocks are beaten with a wooden cane. Three gashes, each deeper than the last. The screams echoed around the prison grounds every Friday – you could hear them in every cell – and sometimes I can still hear them at night if I can't sleep. With each lash the wood dug its way about a centimetre into the prisoner's flesh. Most lost consciousness after no more than six or seven lashes. Then the official would stop, the wounds would take a couple of months to heal, and the punishment could be resumed.

When it came to dishing out Joga's lashes, he refused to have them divided up into smaller amounts. "I want all my lashes at once," he said. He endured his 24 lashes without so much as a sound. His wounds went right down to the bone, yet Joga suffered it just like he had suffered so much else in his life: in silence. He insisted on walking back to his cell unaided. For three weeks he was only able to lie on his stomach. We heard nothing of his pain. Joga was already one of the most highly respected inmates, and now his aura of being untouchable was there to stay.

After a few weeks, Mickey and I got a job in the prison laundry. That meant between four and six hours of work a day, a tin of biscuits at the end of the week and, most importantly, immense luck. The laundry was a task normally reserved for long-term inmates; it at least freed you from the confines of your cell for a couple of hours, and sometimes you even got to go out into the yard and get some fresh air. The German and Australian Embassies had spoken up for us, and I thanked the heavens once more that I had not chosen to swap my German passport for an Indonesian one.

In that respect we were no ordinary prisoners. Many Singaporean citizens had already believed in my innocence in the months leading up to my trial. It's true that there were always some who would shout "Kelong" – "cheaters" – at us, but the majority recognised the inconsistencies in our case. Behind bars, too, the guards also treated us well, especially one Indian man. He was a fan of Geylang United and asked me a thousand things about football. If I received a visit from my lawyer, sometimes he would even let me sit in the visiting room for three hours instead of the normal 60 minutes – that was a blessing as it was the only air-conditioned room in the sweltering heat. The other guards didn't give me much grief either. Inmates who wanted to speak to them were required to crouch down. I never did that: "If I talk to you, then I'll do so as your equal," I said from day one. None of them had any objections. Apart from one.

A month of eating so much chilli had left me with intestinal inflammation. There was so much blood in my stool that I suspected I might not survive another week. It must have redefined my cellmates' idea of what was disgusting – after all, the toilet was an open hole in the floor and I had to do my business in front of them. Admittedly, though, even a person's perception of disgust does change somewhat in a place where cockroaches lay their eggs inside prisoners' ears. No one complained.

The prison doctor said I should eat plenty of bread with kaya, a coconut paste, along with unseasoned vegetables. When I explained this to the kitchen, that afternoon the guard responsible for distributing our food walked up to my cell. He hit the bars repeatedly with a truncheon. "Listen, you dog," he roared, enjoying the power he had. "You're not in a six-star hotel. Do anything like this again and you'll find yourself in solitary confinement."

That dark hole, where a prisoner might sit alone for days on end, would be a step up from the hell we were already experiencing every day. Things like disciplinary complaints didn't exist in our prison, so it would have been advisable to beware of this man. Even so, that was the last straw. I went right up to the bars so that barely five centimetres separated his face from mine. "Alright then, open the door," I screamed at him. Other inmates came up to the bars, their voices a raucous cacophony. It felt like I was about to spark a huge riot. "Put me in their right now. Right now. But let's hope it doesn't affect your secret dealings." I was well aware that he did the odd favour for the dreaded Triad members – they were prisoners, often tattooed from head to toe, who belonged to the Chinese mafia. Many of them were awaiting execution. The bawling of the other prisoners got louder and the guard began to look less sure of himself. From the next day on I was given the food the doctor had recommended and made a quick recovery.

Each day seemed to last a fortnight. "Don't think too much," people say in prison. I never managed not to. A couple of cells down from us, they once carried a prisoner out in a bin bag. A narrow stream of blood dripped from the bag and made a trail along the floor. The night before, I was told, he had repeatedly run head first into the wall until he was dead. If Mickey hadn't been around, I'm sure I would have lost my mind in there as well. It's true that his false statement was what had got us convicted in the first place, but I had long since forgiven him. Such difficult experiences form strong bonds between people. If he should ever need anything from me, whether it's tomorrow or when he's 80, I would do anything I could to help him.

The monotony began to hammer away at my head. Every morning we had to get up at 6am, woken by a shrill noise that echoed through the whole prison wing. Then we had to hurry and go straight to the bars of our cells, where we waited until the guards had counted us. That beeping must have been composed by the devil. I can still hear it to this day.

Our time in prison just dragged and dragged – especially on weekends, when the laundry was closed. Then I had time to think. Would I be banned from FIFA? For a year? Forever? And even if I wasn't, would I be able to find a new club? I realised that, apart from my secondary school qualification and a couple of terms at uni, I had nothing that could help me secure a future without football, and what's more I had spent a fortune on legal fees. At the beginning there was fear. But the emptiness slowly began to spread inside me, suffocating everything. In that darkness Mickey and I would sometimes talk without really listening to each other, both of us drifting off into our own worlds. In such a situation, the final step towards death doesn't seem that far anymore. I don't know whether I would have made it through that time were it not for Anita, my family and Mickey. They kept me alive during what was quite simply a disaster, an apathetic existence where I did nothing but vegetate. I had been brought up a Catholic, but until that point I had never really read the Bible. In prison I read it three times without skipping a single verse. It took such an extreme situation for me to understand just how important religion is and how much support it can provide.

The worst part was when prisoners from Bangladesh were transferred to our cell. They didn't understand a word of English, so we spent days on end not exchanging a single word. Even the slightest change in our daily routine was a godsend. At the end of February Singapore celebrated *Chunjie* – Chinese New

Year was a major event on the island. Outside the prison people partied all night, while inside we were like little children excited at the prospect of slightly better food – there was a bit more meat and even a cake for dessert. For us it meant just a few seconds of variation in our otherwise dreary daily routine. Then the empty plates were cleared away again.

I had little else to do each day other than my 60 minutes of press-ups and abdominal exercises. That training defined my daily rhythm. I managed to keep it up for most of my time in jail, but by the end I was too weak because I had lost so much weight. I tried to keep up my programme for as long as possible. Darwin's theory of evolution is more pronounced in prison than anywhere else in the world: Only the strong make it. We simply couldn't allow ourselves to become weak. Above all, mentally. Those exercises became a daily ritual for me.

Apart from Mickey, Anita was my second great source of comfort during this time. I spent 101 days in prison and I received exactly 101 letters from her, each of them handwritten and spanning between two and four A4 pages. The colour of the envelope would always vary; they might be red, or perhaps blue, and sometimes she drew little hearts on the outside. Those letters were like a drug to me, an elixir that provided all the strength I needed. If the guards didn't deliver any post for four days, which happened frequently, it would almost drive me insane. I was plagued by the fear that she would give in to the pressure from her father, who pleaded with her every single day to end our relationship.

Anita was allowed to visit me every four weeks. We got to spend 15 minutes in a small room, with 10 centimetres of bulletproof glass between us and next to us five other inmates chatting away at full speed with their loved ones. We had to shout to make ourselves heard. Anita laughed a lot during those few minutes, trying to appear happy and cheer me up despite the dark rings around her eyes. She later told me that she only managed to hold the tears back until she was back outside. The sight of me was always a shock for her: When she met me

I had long hair and wore expensive suits, and now she saw me emaciated and wearing a prison uniform. She couldn't get used to the sight. Each time she visited I spent the next two days at rock bottom, since the next time we would see each other felt like it was an eternity away and one look at her was enough for me to see her pain. Apart from my lawyer and a priest, she was the only friendly face I was allowed to see – I wasn't allowed to transfer visitation rights to my father or mother, so our only option was to communicate via letter.

After three months in the worst place on the planet, both Mickey and I heard that our sentences would be reduced for good behavior. Mickey was released seven days before me. "If I could stay in here with you, I would endure the seven days," he told me as we said our goodbyes. "Are you mad?" I replied. "Go home and see your family." But then a day later, when Joga – the only other person I was close to – was suddenly transferred to another prison, I spent the remaining few days in a total panic. You can never rest easy in prison if you don't have any allies.

Nothing happened to me, although the prison guards did try a bit of psychological terror. The closer my release drew, the worse it got. Sivakumar had been incarcerated for a few days. His statements had of course helped him avoid a lengthy prison sentence, so it must have been the pressure exerted by the German Embassy that saw him eventually end up in prison. The guards led Sivakumar past my cell. I'm positive that it was no coincidence.

A day before my release, a guard then led me to the visiting room. I was waiting for my lawyer when suddenly they led Sivakumar in. He saw me and panicked. I felt my blood pressure rise and broke into a sweat. At that moment, if nobody had been watching us I would have let loose and seen to it that he left in an ambulance. But there were guards in the corner and I was just about to be released. So I just stared at him in silence. He probably still dreams about the look I gave him. Saying that, I don't really blame him because the

CPIB put pressure on him and he just tried to do the best for himself.

That afternoon I was taken to the room again. This time two people in dark suits were waiting for me. They reminded me of the CPIB officials who had interrogated me. "We wish to advise you not to bring our country into disrepute by making untoward remarks," said the older of the two. I was shocked, but it didn't really come as a surprise. "What would happen if I did?" I enquired. "It's a recommendation, nothing more," replied the official. I didn't exactly follow their recommendation.

On 13 April 2001, the day of my release, I was handcuffed and had my feet chained together before being taken to the Naturalisation Authority. There I received a one-day passport and only then did a guard release me from my bonds. No less than 16 kilos lighter, I walked out of the building and threw my arms around Anita. I couldn't cry. My relief was overwhelming. But there were no tears, not any more. I haven't shed a single tear since my imprisonment in Singapore. The tears just dried up like an old well.

I had to leave Singapore by the evening. But before that, my first walk as a free man took me to a place that would have left any Bundesliga player's nutritionist in a state of shock, and which really didn't tally with my principles of healthy eating: Kentucky Fried Chicken. I wolfed down eight chicken burgers and three enormous colas.

My stomach was full for the first time in three-and-a-half months, but I still felt like I was on the run. I drove to a hairdresser, where a young woman did her best to make my military haircut look a bit less like a military haircut. While she trimmed my hair I was already arranging my departure over the phone. We went to the apartment and hurriedly packed my things.

At the airport, my one-day visa meant that I had to go to a special check-in desk. The passport officer looked me up and down long before I reached the desk. "Ah, I've been expecting you," he said. My heart sank. Was there now going to be a problem with me leaving the country? For days the only thing I had wanted was to get the hell out of there. But the official smiled. "My daughter is a big Geylang fan," he said. "Would you mind giving me your autograph?"

I gave him one. And then I laughed.

CHAPTER 7
BACK TO SQUARE ONE

ired, I waited with Anita for our cases at the baggage claim at Munich Airport. And it felt fantastic. I had endured that wait hundreds of times before over the years, but never had I been so happy to be able to do something so ordinary from my old life. I stared at the bags and cases like a little boy as they slowly passed us, watching as some were pulled away frantically while others disappeared behind the curtain again because their owners hadn't reacted quickly enough.

We were almost the last passengers to get all of our bags, but I didn't care. I could feel every muscle in my body relaxing. The plane had made a stop in Malaysia, and up until that point I had sat absolutely rigid in my seat. It was only when we had lifted off for Munich that the tension dissipated. "I'm free!" I had said. Apparently somewhat louder than I had meant to, because a number of confused passengers turned round and stared at me.

Anita and I gradually made our way from the baggage claim towards the arrivals area. I was excited at the thought of being able to give my father a hug in just a few seconds' time. We hadn't seen each other for more than a year. It felt more like 10. I was pushing six bags: two of Anita's and four of mine – it was everything I owned.

At the exit, the automatic doors opened and there was no sign of the peace I so longed for. I was greeted by a crowd of screaming voices, and my first glimpse of my home country was into a dozen camera lenses. The baggage hall had acted as a protective cocoon, and now I had the feeling that hundreds of people were about to pounce on me. Journalists surrounded me while the other people waiting at arrivals looked quizzically, probably wondering who this gaunt bloke was – back then I could actually count my ribs. Maybe they assumed I was some drug-addict rock star, not a professional football player.

Despite my 'welcome' I was overjoyed to see my father and wrapped my arms around him. My mother had stayed in Zwiesel, which was a good thing since the hubbub of the airport would have been too much for her. The reporters were literally all over me. It was ridiculous really. I had given football everything I had for my whole life, but now all the people were interested in was something I hadn't even done: match fixing. "Can you imagine anything worse than being in prison in Singapore?" asked one. No, at that moment in time I really couldn't, I answered into his microphone, still doing my best to get to grips with this sudden sensory overload. There had already been a good deal of media attention in Germany during my trial, and 100 journalists had been present in the courtroom when I was convicted. But the chaos that awaited me in Munich was worse than I had feared.

It later occurred to me that stories about people imprisoned in Singapore seemed to have an excellent impact on newspaper sales. Shortly after I was released, a young German teacher called Julia Bohl, who was living and working out there, was given a death sentence because around 700 grams of marijuana had been found in her flat. The story was all over the front pages for weeks and it really got to me at the time, because I had briefly met her during my first visit to Singapore – back then I held weekly football courses at her school. In the end her defence team managed to have her sentence commuted to a lengthy prison sentence at the last minute. It shouldn't have been possible: In Singapore, anyone caught in possession of more than 500 grams of marijuana automatically faced death by hanging, so on paper Julia didn't stand a chance. However, the drugs found were of such low quality that the defence successfully argued that she only actually had 250 grams of pure marijuana since it had been cut with something else. This stroke of genius on the part of her lawyers saved her life.

My situation wasn't as dramatic – although it wouldn't have surprised me if they had tried seeking the death penalty during my trial. The reporters were just as interested in me as they would later be in Julia's case. I spent half an hour answering questions I had recently asked myself many times. "Why were you convicted?" "What traces will three months in Singapore's most notorious prison leave on you?" And the worst question of all: "What will you do now?" I shrugged. I simply couldn't say.

My father drove the car along the motorway towards Zwiesel and I looked out of the window as the forests of Bavaria raced past. I had my arm around Anita and we were listening to the radio station Bayern 3. Sat behind the wheel, my father was uncharacteristically talkative, almost prattling on. Whatever I listened to, I was surrounded by a strong Bavarian dialect – I felt better by the minute.

Anita, on the other hand, couldn't understand a word. It was her first time in Germany. It meant completely new surroundings for her, and just like me she had been through a tough few weeks. Even so, she seemed happy. She had stood by me against all the odds, even in the face of her father and his daily phone calls. He and his parents had moved from Sri Lanka to Singapore in the 1950s. After studying medicine there, he had set up a number of highly lucrative cosmetic surgery clinics. That had made him a multi-millionaire, but also something of a megalomaniac. Anita told me how he had once walked through his villa staring at his hands and cried: "These hands are a gift from God." Again and again. "These hands are a gift from God." He was strange. It had been 15 years since his wife had divorced him and moved to England.

Our relationship had been a thorn in his side before my conviction. But when I was charged he did everything he possibly could to drive Anita and I apart. "Leave that corrupt failure," he yelled into the phone while Anita wrote her daily letters to me. Another time he said in a low voice: "You're no daughter of mine. Consider yourself disinherited." Then he simply hung up.

As my release drew closer and he realised that Anita intended to come to Germany with me, he had tried a different tactic. Anita ran a small Montessori school in Singapore. It was a type of school that paid particularly close attention to each child's individual strengths and weaknesses, and Anita was a great advocate of the methodology. A day before I was due to be released her father called, apologised for the things he had said and offered her a huge amount of money to set up a far bigger Montessori school. He didn't say it in so many words, but of course his offer was tied to the condition that she broke up with me, since as soon as I was released I would have to leave Singapore – not that I would have wanted to stay. After my release I had to assume that I would never be granted another visa. I had never met the man, but when Anita later told me about the phone call, without further ado I called him and yelled: "Even if all the allegations against me were true, trying to buy your own daughter is a hundred times more corrupt." Anita didn't know I made that call, but she didn't let him buy her anyway.

All the anger, all the tears now seemed so far away. After driving for a good hour we pulled up on the little drive outside the Pfannenstiel family home in Zwiesel. The morning sun bathed the blue wood panelling of our house in a warm light. In the last few years I had usually only ever seen the place covered in snow when I was back for Christmas. Now I got to see it on a wonderful day in April. It had never seemed so beautiful to me.

My mother threw the front door open as soon as she heard the familiar sound of the engine on the drive. I had barely got out of the car when she threw her arms around me. My sister was also waiting in the doorway, and I was surprised at just how happy I was to see her. My father set the phone to silent – it hadn't stopped ringing for a month. Exhausted, I sat down on the pine bench in the corner. It felt like I had travelled back in time: The crucifix and the four pictures from the Old Testament still hung on the wall. That familiar, hearty smell of goulash with pasta was wafting out of the kitchen, and slowly my thoughts of Singapore evaporated. My return to life had begun.

The next morning I walked to the sports ground, the symbol of my carefree childhood. I dragged myself around the turf for 15 laps. I had never found it so difficult to exercise – I felt almost paralysed, my muscles no longer used to the stress. But I was determined to return to professional football as soon as possible. In the afternoon, Gerd Bielmeier finished his shift. The 'Indian', who had launched balls at my goal every day when I was a youngster, still had long hair and still ran his laps there every day. We only talked for a few seconds; he seemed to sense that I didn't want to talk about my time in prison. Then he got started with the ball and I caught the leather again and again. It felt just like the old days. He said nothing, and neither did I. Two lunatics on the grass, neither of us wanting it any differently. All you could hear was the dull thud when he kicked the ball followed by the even duller sound of me stopping it with my gloves. It was good to feel the smack of the leather once more. No psychiatrist would have been able to achieve such a positive effect. We never did talk much, but it hit me hard when, at the beginning of 2009, I heard that he had passed away.

But I couldn't quite settle in Zwiesel. A week after my return the phone continued to ring, with reporters constantly wanting to hear my story. On a couple of occasions we even had journalists waiting outside the front door. It was just absurd. Normally I would have found it funny, but I was in no mood for laughing. Anita, too, desperately needed a bit of peace and quiet after those awful months in Singapore. So we decided to visit her mother in England for a few days. She had returned to her hometown of Bradford 15 years earlier after divorcing her husband.

Anita's mother was a slim, resolute woman in her late fifties who lived in a new house. She welcomed us both with a friendly hug. Her good nature meant she was the exact opposite of her ex-husband. "Come in, come in." We spent a while drinking tea out of fine bone china cups. "What's in the past is in the past," she said to me, placing her arm around my shoulder. "We'll get you back on your feet. This time next month you'll have forgotten all this crap." Anita and I unpacked our things up in the attic, where the bed had been made up in readiness for our arrival.

After a couple of days we went for a walk through Bradford and took in the city's wonderful old buildings, very few of which had been destroyed during the Second World War. It had once been the centre of Britain's wool industry, a good honest working-class city. Anita's mother led us to Bradford Park Avenue's Horsfall Stadium, one of those tiny arenas of English football built in the 1930s with ancient seating for perhaps 3,000 spectators. A couple of years earlier they had painted the little stands green and white, and also given the interior a bit of a makeover, but here and there the grass of the football pitch was still invading the surface of the synthetic track that surrounded it. The stadium exuded the dilapidated charm that I so love about lower division English football.

Bradford Park Avenue's players had just begun their training. The seventh-tier team's players were powerful guys who had travelled straight to the stadium after finishing their shifts in the nearby factories. A tall, older man with reddish hair stood on the sidelines. Without hesitating, Anita's mother entered the stadium and greeted the manager. Anita's mother always spoke incredibly fast, and so it was that she explained my situation to him in a matter of seconds. The manager introduced himself to me as Trevor Storton, a former professional who had played for Liverpool. "You'll be coming tomorrow," he said. "Of course you can train with us. If there's anything else I can do to help you, just let me know." He had a firm handshake. We didn't know each other, but right away I sensed that he really meant what he said.

The next day, I returned to my life as a footballer. I spent every morning in the gym before training with Bradford Park Avenue in the afternoon, and each night I went to bed at no later than 10pm so as to be fit the next day. When it came to technique and tactics, the level of the English non-league players didn't pose too much of a problem for me, but physically my form had declined so much that I found myself nursing bruises almost every evening. Once I even broke my little finger. But that happened to me a dozen times over the years – by now my hands look like crooked pitchforks.

Alas, it had been a long time since my future had depended on those crooked hands alone. After my conviction, the football association back in Singapore had announced my lifelong ban from professional football, at the same time launching something of a crusade against me. Following a request by the country's officials, the Asian Football Association extended my ban to the whole continent and requested that FIFA impose an international ban on me.

I had a few sleepless nights in the run-up to the meeting of the international body's Disciplinary Committee, but my worries came to an end when the fax finally arrived: FIFA was of the opinion that I hadn't been given enough of an opportunity to defend myself in Singapore to make my position clear. The application for me to be banned internationally was thrown out, with FIFA rejecting the judgement from Asia. It's true the Asians refused to apply this decision on their continent and insisted on banning me in Asia, but I could live with that. I never wanted to set foot in Singapore again, and the thought of not spending any more time as a professional footballer in Malaysia or Indonesia didn't bother me either.

But I hadn't reckoned with Sepp Blatter, the powerful boss of FIFA. He was bidding to be re-elected as president in 2002, although his chances hung by a thread in the wake of speculation about financial mismanagement. Back then people thought that the Swedish candidate, Lennart Johansson, also had a good chance of being elected. Blatter fought for every vote, and without the backing of the small Asian associations he would have barely stood a chance. He changed sides after a storm of indignation broke out in Asia following FIFA's rejection of my ban.

One late evening in June, I received a phone call from an English journalist I was friends with. He worked for a newspaper and was reporting on the Confederations Cup in Tokyo, the mini tournament that took place a year before the 2002 World Cup in South Korea and Japan. "Lutz, you'll never believe what Blatter just said into my voice recorder." The journalist knew my case well, and had asked FIFA's President about the lifting of my ban. Blatter had objected, saying that lifting the ban was out of the question. "FIFA will uphold the Asian association's objection," the journalist went on breathlessly. Apparently I was going to be banned for two years. Laughing, I said to him: "April Fools' Day is over. Even you can't really believe that." I was familiar with the structures that underpinned FIFA and knew that Blatter didn't have the right to overrule the Disciplinary Committee's decision. But instead of responding himself, the journalist played some of the things Blatter had said about Mickey and I. "They will be banned immediately ..." I couldn't believe my ears. Blatter wanted to enforce an international ban for both of us.

The next morning, my English agent Mark Steele contacted me. "Turn the fax machine on. It's true, they want to ban you." He sent the official FIFA letter to Bradford Park Avenue, which revealed my case was going to be debated again. I was devastated.

I called my lawyer back in Germany. "Get ready to sue for damages. We need to get the ball rolling first thing tomorrow." Then I spoke to Mark for an hour on the phone, who promised to sort out another lawyer. But even that wasn't enough for me, and I worked late into the night. My insomnia was back. While Anita slept in the next room, I called every agent I had ever had anything to do with until I finally found someone who could give me Blatter's telephone extension at his office in Zurich. The next morning, I called the number every five minutes until his secretary finally answered.

"I don't know who Lutz Pfannenstiel is," the woman said. "And how did you get this number?" It took all my diplomatic skills, but she listened to my story from beginning to end. It took more than an hour. The line sounded strange. I'm certain that she played the call over the speaker and that Blatter must have been listening.

Afterwards she said goodbye and promised that she had made some notes and would explain the case to Mr Blatter from my point of view. I don't know whether she really did do that. But the following day, contrary to what Blatter had said, FIFA spokesman Andreas Herren suddenly announced that FIFA would no longer be concerned with the issue of Lutz Pfannenstiel. I was banned for six months by FIFA, but the punishment was backdated to the day the Singapore FA banned me. In other words, I was free to play whenever I wanted.

I had never been so relieved, not even after my release. I had just spent a few months in prison, but a ban would have taken away what I loved for the rest of my life.

Bradford Park Avenue would have been happy to keep me, but the club couldn't pay me enough for me to be able to earn a living playing football alone. After a couple of weeks, Storton found me a job with Second Division (now League One) Huddersfield Town, whose players were all professionals. Back in the 1970s and 1980s, Huddersfield's assistant manager, Joe Jordan, had been widely regarded as one of the most fearsome players around. While he was playing for Leeds United, he lost four front teeth following a scrap during a match. Doctors gave him false teeth, but for safety reasons he took them out while playing – a good many of his opponents later reported having been intimidated by his toothless grimace.

Jordan became something of a father figure, and so did manager Lou Macari. I trained with Huddersfield in the mornings and with Bradford Park Avenue in the evenings to regain my fitness. By that point I had regained some 10 kilos of muscle mass and was beginning to return to my old form, so we quickly came to an agreement. Just like years earlier during my first stint in England, I was given a 'non-contract' by Huddersfield which could be cancelled each month but was still enough for me to cover my basic expenses. But that wasn't what swayed me. Storton and Macari inspired me and helped me get back on my feet – but not by pushing me or trying to get me to go over what I had experienced in Singapore. Storton in particular always had time for me and liked talking to me. He knew my unusual story, but he treated me like he would any other player. That kind of normality worked wonders.

At some point, word soon got round the Bradford Park Avenue team that the new goalkeeper had done time. Once in training when I let in a ball that I should really have been able to save, two of my teammates ran behind the goal and shook the net as if it were prison bars. I couldn't help but smile and was surprised at myself for being able to laugh about it. It seemed that I was slowly beginning to process what I'd been through.

Even so, after impressing for the reserves, Huddersfield wanted to enter into negotiations with me for a professional contract that would have covered the rest of the season, but I turned them down. It had only been three months since my release and I still didn't feel ready – neither physically nor mentally. A lot of football fans knew me in England, and after all the headlines that had been published even there during my trial in Singapore I knew that any away match would have been like running the gauntlet. Once when I was playing a match for Huddersfield reserves against a neighbouring town's club, the spectators threw coins into my penalty area. The message was clear: In return, would I mind letting a couple of goals in? I collected them after the match, all 23 of them: "More for the family budget," I said to Anita that evening, attempting a smile. But I didn't find it funny. I wondered what might come next – what about bigger matches? I thought that the opposing fans would mock me with their songs for a full 90 minutes.

In the end it was a friend I had met years earlier at a training camp in Brazil who brought the next unexpected twist in my life. Bruce MacDonald was good friends with the manager of New Zealand top division team Dunedin Technical. He knew that despite my hardships in Singapore I'd easily be one of the best goalkeepers in the league there. After Dunedin's manager had seen a few videos of me making saves, he agreed too.

Football is something of a minority sport in New Zealand, but to me the country's seclusion and tranquillity seemed to offer ideal conditions for my comeback. I also wanted to finish my studies in New Zealand. A few years before, I had started studying sports and tourism in Düsseldorf via a distance learning programme. It had become clear to me that I wasn't going to be able to build my entire future on the beautiful game alone. Now I wanted to spend the next six months getting through the remaining exams.

I flew to New Zealand just a week later in the autumn of 2002. It was my first long-haul flight since 9/11, and the first of dozens of similar flights where I could really feel the effects that those terrible attacks were to have on air travel. Until that point, in many countries I had boarded planes without anyone so much as looking inside my hand luggage. Now, though, I had to endure interminable checks and take my shoes off. The endless security checks at Manchester, London, Los Angeles and Auckland meant that my journey to Dunedin took more than 48 hours, so I arrived in New Zealand absolutely shattered. An inconceivably large man in an oversized red Hawaiian shirt was waiting at the airport, in his hand a cardboard sign with the not-exactly-correct "Lutz Pfanestil" written on it. When I greeted him, his entire face became one big smile: "Hey, I'm Jonny Warren. It's great to have you here, man. You'll be staying with me and my family." I was a little shocked, but it turned out that ending up in that house was a stroke of luck.

After my strenuous flight, their president Marc Chidley had told me not to join them for training until the following day. Out of the question. So I appeared for the afternoon session on the day of my arrival despite having had about two hours sleep in two days. In training I was determined to show what I could do, especially since we hadn't agreed my salary yet. So for an hour they fired balls at me and I played like my life depended on it. I was so intense and full of adrenaline that the other players thought I was crazy. I was on fire, I stopped everything. At the end of shooting practice I was exhausted. I thought I was going to collapse in a heap on the side of the pitch. But the chairman was open-mouthed and I said to him: "You decide what to pay me".

I slept for 24 hours and the next day they made me the best-paid player in the club's history and one of the best in the league.

It was a big decision to fly 19,000 kilometres to try my luck in New Zealand, but as soon as I'd trained with them once I realised that Dunedin Technical were something truly special in the world of professional football – things were just so informal. When I turned up for that first training session I had greeted every single player, shaking hands with each one, and it wasn't long before we were all laughing away. My decision to go to there was one of the best I've ever made, even though I was still only earning 4,000 dollars each month which was less than at most stages of my career.

Anita had not come with me as I needed time to clear my head, so I moved permanently into Jonny's house, a fairly old building close to town. Like many New Zealanders, he was blessed with a tremendously hospitable side. Jonny was more of a teddy bear than a human. He was one of the finest people I've ever known. He could have had a starring role in any anti-ambition TV advert; he oozed a certain lethargy that was magnificently soothing. He was simply happy with what he had, and perhaps that's why I liked him so much. Because to this day, unfortunately, I still don't possess the ability to be satisfied. Jonny's children had long since flown the nest, and I was living in his daughter's old bedroom. A couple of posters of pop stars still hung on the walls. He was happy to have me move in, because he had more or less been Dunedin Technical's number one fan ever since leaving England and moving to New Zealand 26 years earlier. He hadn't missed a single home match for years, and experienced fans wouldn't sit behind him in the stands because otherwise his enormous frame would prevent them from being able to see half the pitch. Jonny had worked as a chef in his own hotel for years. He cooked up sensational dishes, and I'm convinced he was the best chef in all of Oceania. An angel in a fat person's clothing.

But everyone at Dunedin Technical was fantastic. Presumably they had all heard about my time in prison – after all Google was nothing new by then and a person only had to type my name in to get an idea of what had happened. But that didn't count there. Almost all of the players were friends with each other, and most had been playing together for years. Some were professionals, some were at university, and others had a day job on the side – the team functioned well despite all these different lifestyles. The boys wanted to win the title, and they knew that I was an excellent goalkeeper by New Zealand standards. I slept for 17 hours after the first training session, but I was integrated right from the beginning.

I immediately fell in love with the city too. With its many hills, small houses and surrounding forests, it reminded me of Zwiesel. It had been built on the solidified lava of a volcano that cooled down millions of years ago, and even though the region was fantastically green with its many forests, here and there you could still see the different types of stone that had developed throughout the ages. The people of Dunedin had created one of the most beautiful cities in the country and weren't even put off by the occasional geographic oddity. One of my teammates lived on Baldwin Street: With a gradient of 35 per cent, the *Guinness Book of Records* recognises it as the steepest residential street in the world, making it about as steep as a ski jump. The houses looked like they might slide down the hill at any moment. It's legendary in Dunedin: Every year in February, hundreds of mad people race down the street on roller blades before hurrying back up – if they still can. Whoever manages it in the fastest time is the winner and treated like something of a superstar in Dunedin for the next few days. The street attracts all sorts of idiots: Shortly before I arrived, the Bavarian Thomas Hugenschmidt set a speed record by racing down it on his bike at almost 120 kilometres per hour. Even I'm not that stupid.

Within a matter of days I felt as if I had been part of the team for years. We trained hard, and of course the pressure to perform well was no lower than anywhere else. At the same time, however, the club had the kind of atmosphere probably not seen in German professional football since the 1970s, back in the days when a reporter might swing by during training every couple of weeks and the players took things with a pinch of salt, not automatically believing themselves to be some sort of inter-galactic superstar just because they had scored a goal in the Bundesliga. At Dunedin it didn't matter whether you were a professional, a nurse or a student. After a match we would have a beer with the fans in the clubhouse, and on days when we didn't have training the players and their families would go on outings together or meet up for coffee. Quite simply, people in that city laughed more and swore less than elsewhere. And the same applied to the team.

It was also just a few days before I managed to rediscover the sense of humour I thought I had lost forever in Singapore. In the mornings I would work out in the gym room, then study at university for my final exams before going to train with the team in the afternoon – but my day couldn't just consist of deadly serious activities like those. Phil Kelly was one of our strikers. He was already 32 years old but still mastered fantastic headers and powerful long-range shots. For his day job he lectured at Dunedin's prestigious university, where almost half of the city's residents studied. We were running one morning. "Sorry, Lutz," he said after just half an hour, "I have to dash. My lecture starts in an hour." As he was getting into his Jeep I remembered the seminars I'd attended a decade earlier in Deggendorf. In those days I had found the subject matter incredibly boring, but I always absolutely loved annoying the professors. I decided to refresh my memory.

After showering I drove to the university's medical school and parked right outside the building. I watched through the window as Phil explained graphs in a video presentation – he was giving a nursing course and almost all of the students in the lecture theatre were female. When I opened the door all the colour drained from Phil's face. "Sorry I'm late, professor," I said and sat down in the back row. Phil was silent for a few seconds before continuing: "Left-sided heart failure involves a weakness in the left ventricle. If there is a volume overload, then the left side of the heart is unable to pump enough of the blood arriving from the pulmonary veins into the systemic circulatory system ..." I shouted something out. No reaction. Phil did his best to ignore me, but I began clicking my fingers loudly. Before long a number of students had turned around and he was no longer able to simply carry on. Annoyed, he asked me what I wanted. "Professor," I began with a grin, "you haven't scored in your last three games. The fans' hearts would suggest that there is a shortage of goals scored by you at Dunedin Technical." The aspiring nurses, who obviously knew about Phil's football career, laughed out loud. Even the striker couldn't suppress a grin. "Next weekend, next weekend," he said. In fact, Phil did score a goal at our next home game. From then on I considered my visits to his lectures to be a good luck ritual. But whenever I sat down with his students, beads of sweat formed on his forehead instantly.

I quickly recovered from the difficult year that now lay behind me and began to focus on my future. I was obsessed with finishing my degree and pushed myself mentally and physically to the limit, as I wanted to prove to the world that I was not a failure after being in prison. I got up at 7am every day and started studying for my final exams. Then came two training sessions, and if I wasn't busy annoying Phil or Jonny I would study late into the night. Even so, my past kept catching up with me. In my first few weeks I was extremely aggressive on the pitch, and if my team-mates hadn't stopped me it's likely I would have received one red card after another. I would often lie awake at night, unable to shake from my mind the image of the old man they had carried out of his cell in a plastic bag. Or I could hear the screams of the inmates as they endured their corporal punishment.

Just like back in England, nobody on the team poked around my old wounds. They just acted as if I had never been in prison. Apart from once, when there was no ignoring it. Every Monday, the day after we had played, we drove to a public swimming pool for a spot of recovery training. It was always the same routine: A bit of swimming, aqua jogging, and finally the whirlpool. The whole team would lie there, their eyes closed, while behind them the artificial waves raged. Suddenly a loud siren went off, which was the signal to bathers that the wave

GERMANY

I was always a bit of a show-off too!

From as young as I can remember, all I wanted to do was play football.

Carrying a bag of balls during my trial with Bayern Munich, not long before I turned them down.

CHINA

Looking miserable at the Chinese training camp where I found out they were serving us dog meat.

1

Ex-S-League keeper jailed for match-fixing

Former Geylang goalkeeper gets five months' jail. He is the second player found guilty of match-fixing in a month

By ELENA CHONG

I knew I had made it when I appeared on a football trading card while I was with Geylang United.

I spent 101 horrendous days in the worst place in the world, Queenstown Prison in Singapore.

It took me a long time to recover from the prison experience and I still have nightmares.

NEW ZEALAND

Playing football in New Zealand was great, but I would have been back behind bars if I'd been caught with the endangered penguin I kept in my bath.

CANADA

ENGLAND

Here I am with an opposition mascot in Canada in 2004… everyone else is watching the ice hockey.

I died three times on the pitch at Bradford Park Avenue on Boxing Day 2002.

ALBANIA

Lining up for Vllaznia Shkodër in Albania in 2006, where the fans would try to kill you if you lost.

Right, where is nice at this time of year?

In training at the Vancouver Whitecaps, where I settled down – for a few weeks.

In action for the Whitecaps – not long after I played against David Beckham.

My proudest day: In Brazil in 2008 after achieving the record of playing as a pro in all six FIFA confederations.

In 2008 I became goalkeeping coach for the Cuban national team, but I still had time for a bit of modelling.

NORWAY

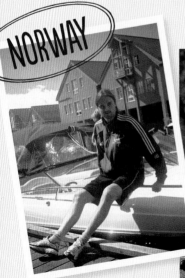

Part of my deal with Flekkerøy in Norway was that the club gave me a boat.

A nasty moment at Manglerud Star, I'd just broken this guy's leg.

NAMIBIA

After many years hunting, I finally captured my prey… oh yes, and there is a cheetah in the picture too!

Rambling round the six-yard box in Namibia.

Being goalkeeping coach for Namibia was one of my greatest challenges as the keeper, Athiel Mbaha, could not hear a thing.

Lining up for the anthems before we drew 1-1 with South Africa before the 2010 World Cup. On the right is Belgian manager Tom Saintfiet.

Proudly walking out for the pre-World Cup charity match for Global United FC, the climate change charity I started. The player on the right is Stig Tøfting.

Addressing Vladimir Putin at a German/ Russian political and economic forum.

Helping out with some food aid in Pakistan. The guy next to me is US footballer Tony Sanneh.

Me and former German international Fredi Bobic play with some African kids before one of our Global United FC matches.

7

ENGLAND

My wife Amalia and I hanging out on the beach!

I went back to the old Wimbledon FC training ground, but someone else had moved in. My shoe was still nailed to the bench!

You can now see me on TV all over the planet thanks to my work for BBC World and ZDF.

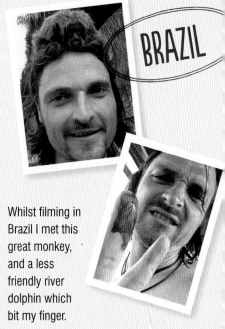

BRAZIL

Preparing for the 2014 World Cup with my friends Dante (top) and Zico (above).

Whilst filming in Brazil I met this great monkey, and a less friendly river dolphin which bit my finger.

machine was about to come on. My teammates were used to that horrible noise, but it tore me from my dreamlike state and I sat bolt upright – it was exactly the same siren they had used in Singapore to wake the prisoners each morning at 6am, giving us just a few seconds to get up and stand next to the bars at the front of the cell. In an instant I jumped up in a panic so quickly that I splashed the players around me. It wasn't until a few seconds later that I realised I was at a swimming pool in Dunedin and not in prison in Singapore. My teammates were laughing about the little incident for days – and eventually I managed to laugh about it too.

With three wins and three defeats, we had a fairly mediocre start to the season, but I was fast approaching the form I had reached before my arrest. I found myself back in the normal routine of a professional player – which had, in my case, always included a good portion of superstition. For years I had only ever played wearing white socks over my shin pads, and any other colour would have been out of the question. But even my socks hadn't been able to prevent my bitter experience in Singapore, so from then on I insisted on black socks – with white ankle braces.

What's more, ever since I was a lad I had always responded to a defeat or an error I made as the keeper by changing my goalkeeper shirt for the next game. But that was getting more and more complicated because my rule was that the shirt could not be the same style, and it needed to be a different colour. It was a quirk of mine which was so firmly rooted that I would insist that I needed to be able to choose from a variety of shirts when negotiating a new contract with a club.

Most of the time it didn't bother anyone too much, especially considering the fact that footballers are known for being the most superstitious people there are. In the mid-1970s, Eintracht Frankfurt's manager Gyula Lóránt insisted that his players drank coffee and ate a piece of marble cake before kick-off: The team were undefeated for 21 games in a row. And in 1987, legendary manager Udo Lattek refused to take off his knitted blue pullover – even in the middle of summer – until FC Cologne finally lost a match after winning 14 games in a row. Some people even put France's success in the 1998 World Cup down to the fact that defender Laurent Blanc kissed the bald head of goalkeeper Fabien Barthez whenever they won.

I had been careful to bring one red, one yellow, one green, one black, one white and one blue goalkeeper shirt with me to Dunedin, and the club put their main sponsor's logo on them before the season began. But when we had a few bad matches in the middle of the season and I had to change from one shirt to the next, that supply soon ran out: I made an exception, and instead of worrying about my shirt I changed my tactic. Instead of black shorts, I wore grey ones. This change served its purpose and our performance began to stabilise. At the end of the season I was chosen for the league's all-star team and named goalkeeper of the season. I really was back on my feet. And I definitely owed some of my success to wearing the right colours.

Away from football, Anita had been out to visit but she was becoming more and more reluctant to accept such an unsteady life by my side. Be that as it may, I did settle down in Dunedin, as far as it's even possible to settle down as a professional footballer. The season lasted from November until April, meaning it only provided an income for me for half the year. As a result I ended up keeping goal during the summer months at clubs in Canada, the USA, Norway and England – returning to Dunedin in the winter months.

My supply of goalkeeper shirts was utterly decimated right at the start of my second season in New Zealand. Unfortunately Jonny had fallen seriously ill, so I had moved into a larger house with my teammate Craig Smith and a female student. Craig and I returned home after training, and on entering my bedroom I saw that my clothes were strewn all over the floor. I don't doubt there are tidier people than me in this world, but did it really look like that when I left that morning? Then I heard Craig shouting in the room next to mine: "What the fuck? Where's my PlayStation?" At that point I noticed that a few things were missing from my room as well. The DVD player was gone, as were two pairs of sunglasses, some cash, and I soon discovered that my goalkeeper shirts were no longer folded up in the wardrobe. Burglars had pried open the little window in the bathroom. They had climbed into our house in broad daylight.

We called the club's president as well as the police, and half an hour later the house was full of people. The bored-looking policeman recorded the details: "We've had a lot of similar break-ins in this area over the past few weeks," he said. "I wouldn't hold out too much hope that you'll see your things again." I had heard that burglary rates were above average in New Zealand, but I didn't want to accept what he was saying. "Is this all you can do?" The policeman looked up. "We will of course do everything we can," he said in his bored voice, "and you could try going to the pawnshop tomorrow. It could be that the thief tries selling your things there." I turned to the president immediately: "What time do they open?"

"Nine o'clock."

"Right, I'll come to yours at eight and we can drive over there."

That night I wrote a list of all the things that were missing and estimated their value: 5,000 dollars in total.

At 9.01am the next day a goalkeeper with a pulse of 180 was sat in the pawnbroker's entering the list of his stolen belongings into a form. The table was in the corner of the office. Out of the corner of my eye I could see the counter, where an elderly lady was serving the day's first customers. A huge Maori 6' 5" tall and easily weighing 110 kilos joined the queue. He was wearing a red-and-white Tommy Hilfiger ice hockey shirt. That shirt's cool, I thought before returning to my form. But then it was the man's turn to be served. "I'd like to deposit this DVD player. How much will you give me for it?" I looked up incredulously and saw my DVD player lying there on the counter. And then I recognised the ice hockey shirt as well – I had bought it just a couple of months earlier in Bradford. That was one of those moments where I lost control completely. "You wanna know how much you'll get for it? You'll get a smack in the face,"

I shouted. The Maori turned around, and after punching him in the face I kicked him as hard as I could in the knee. I remembered the advice I had been given in prison.

It suddenly occurred to me that the police had been looking for this idiot for months. As far as I was concerned he was an outlaw. I rushed the giant of a man, who was so surprised that all he did was raise his hands to protect his face, he didn't even defend himself. The president rushed up and pulled me off him. A couple of minutes later, the pawnshop worker came in with two policemen she had found. They still had to hold me back from the Maori, who then finally spoke: "I'm not the thief," he stammered. "The one who gave me the stuff is called Bryan Clark. He's owed me money for months. I knew I would never see it again so I agreed to let him give me this stuff instead." I burst out laughing. "What a loud of bullshit. I've never heard such rubbish." But the police believed him. Bryan Clark was a drug addict with a criminal record longer than the Bible, and they had been looking for him for months. I slowly began to believe the Maori, but continued to shout at him. "If you see him, tell him I'm gonna bite his ears off. I'll make him pay for every dollar he's stolen. And if I see you on the street again, then I'll carry on from where I just left off." His eyes wide with panic, the Maori turned to the two policemen: "He's mad, he's threatening me." With more than a trace of boredom in his voice, one of the officials explained to me that it was a crime to make such threats, but then they headed to the door. For them, the case was settled. The Maori hurried away too. A couple of months later I bumped into him in a pub. We laughed about our little brawl. "It's fine," he said. "I've never seen anyone so crazy. It was like an unstoppable avalanche. You were well and truly out of control."

I laughed, because by that point the whole affair had gone on to become so bizarre that it surprised even me. The evening after my encounter with the Maori in the pawnshop, the president gave a highly imaginative retelling of the incident back at the clubhouse. Not much went on in Dunedin, and so the story was soon on everybody's lips at the club – and it still was three days later, when we were at the pub after a home game and I had to describe the fight yet again. "Well," I said as I came to the end of my story, "I got almost everything back, apart from my goalkeeper shirts." I was also missing 1,500 dollars, but I managed to see the funny side. "If you happen to see anyone who doesn't look at all like me but has the number one and the name Pfannenstiel written on their back, do give me a call!" I joked.

Amazingly, the following Tuesday, my phone really did ring. I looked at the screen somewhat annoyed, since Craig and I were enjoying our post-training muesli in the kitchen and I don't like to be disturbed when I'm eating. "Westpac Trust" was written on the display. It was my bank, so I answered. "Hey, it's Moose," said the bank's director, who played on the Dunedin seniors' team. There was excitement in his voice. "Listen. This is not a joke. There's a man standing with his bike in front of the bank and he's wearing a black goalkeeper shirt. Guess what it says on the back." My heart rate doubled in the space of a second. "Make sure he doesn't leave. I'll be right there."

It was two kilometres from our place to the bank. That day I discovered that a car can cover the distance in 60 seconds. Moose was stood outside the bank, and of course he hadn't been able to stop the cyclist. But I could still see the thief. He was a picture of calm as he wheeled off with his bike. I hurriedly strode after him, recognising one item after another. My goalkeeper shirt was far too big for him and flapped around like a black nightgown. The thief's red hair shone bright beneath my baseball cap – which I hadn't even noticed was missing. I also recognised the sunglasses he was wearing, which belonged to my housemate Craig. I tapped the man on the shoulder from behind.

"Bryan Clark?" He turned around with a smile.

"Yes man, what can I do for you?"

"There's a lot you can do for me," I hissed before ramming my forehead into his nose.

Clark recoiled in fright, and I realised that he was high as a kite. But I lost control of myself too, just like I had a few days earlier during the scrap with the Maori. Moments like those can unleash an immense rage within me. I pushed the thief again and again, and he staggered backwards before stumbling in front of me. "Nice hat, where did you get it? Give it to me." I yanked it off him and smacked him on the head with the palm of my hand. "Your sunglasses? I don't even need to ask, they're not yours." Clark stumbled into an alleyway as I relieved him of one stolen item after another. "The shirt? Seems very, very familiar to me. Take it off." A couple of minutes later he was standing there with his skinny torso exposed. "Your shorts? You know whose they are, don't you? Take them off."

So far Clark had acted as if he were in a state of shock. Now the thief began to resist. "I'm not taking them off." I whacked his temple with my fist. Dazed, he loosened his belt. And there he stood: Trainers, socks and a pair of ugly grey underpants. Out of the corner of my eye I noticed that a number of passers-by had stopped to watch us from the entrance to the alleyway. One was obviously phoning the police – they must have thought I was the criminal and Clark the victim, but at that moment I didn't care. It's not like anyone dared to intervene.

I found 1,000 dollars in Clark's wallet, 500 less than had been stolen from me. "Where's the rest?" I yelled. "I don't have it anymore," Clark stammered. He explained he had spent it on the bike and drugs. That provoked me to take another swing with my right fist. I was sorely tempted to force him to take his underwear off and then chase him down the street.

But by this time the passers-by had edged a little closer. Then a police car also stopped at the entrance to the alleyway. Three officers hurried up to us. They recognised Clark instantly. To the surprise of the onlookers they didn't arrest me but the victim of my beating. I reluctantly let go of the burglar, but my adrenaline was still through the roof and sometimes my mouth is, quite frankly, far too big. "Inspectors of Dunedin," I boasted, "I was burgled on Friday. Finding him cost me four days. Do you spend all day smoking marijuana?" One of the policemen knew me since he was a big fan of Dunedin Technical. He couldn't suppress a grin. But then he got serious. "Why is Clark bleeding so heavily?"

The thief was quick to chime in: "Because he wouldn't stop hitting me." The policeman wanted to know whether that was true. "No, he kept falling over," I replied. "Constantly. I've no idea why." The policeman hesitated for a moment before nodding: "Yes, that sounds about right. He kept falling over. Come to the station in a couple of hours and you can give a statement, then you can forget about this whole affair."

They were wrong, of course. The newspapers and TV channels had a field day with the story. The *New Zealand Herald* ran the headline "New Zealand's dumbest burglar" and I received calls from dozens of German journalists for the first time since the Singapore story had died down. I even heard from Tommy Hilfiger representatives, who sent me a couple of shirts because I had kept saying in interviews that I had recognised the Hilfiger shirt the Maori was wearing. I found that pretty funny, since I hadn't had any intention of advertising for anyone. On the other hand, when interviewed I wasted no time mocking the New Zealand police and their failure to find Clark. The police officers certainly got wind of that, but they didn't really hold it against me. When I was leaving a supermarket a few days after the incident, a police car was driving past. The officers turned on the loudspeaker on the roof. "Hey Sherlock Pfannenstiel," echoed a voice over the street, "searching for criminals again?"

In Singapore, my experience with the police had been awful. But, well before the burglary, during one of my first nights in New Zealand, local policemen had already put paid to my previously unshakeable belief that anyone wearing a uniform was automatically a humourless sadist. After a match I had borrowed Jonny Warren's old Ford and driven to a teammate's house 15 kilometres away from Dunedin. I picked up another teammate on the way. Neither of us noticed that the fuel gauge was at zero – until, at 2am, the engine died on the way home. In the middle of a lonely country road. The nearest petrol station was three kilometres away. I swore like a sailor, got out and looked for the jerry can. There wasn't one. I tried to call Jonny but there was no reception. In the end we just started walking, and instead of a petrol can we carried an empty two-litre cola bottle to the petrol station. We arrived half an hour later. I gave the bottle to the attendant. "Two litres of LPG, please." The New Zealander looked at me incredulously and started to laugh.

"Is this some kind of a joke?"

"No, why? I'm out of petrol, and the owner said I need to fill the car with LPG."

The pump attendant just laughed even louder. "LPG is gas, you idiot. You need to bring a gas cylinder."

I began to rant, moaning about Jonny, my teammate and the sardonic attendant. But to be honest I was mostly annoyed with myself.

We would have needed to somehow transport the car to the petrol station. But by then it was 3am, so we decided it could wait. There was a telephone at the petrol station, but neither Jonny nor the local taxi company answered. So we walked. Five kilometres to Dunedin. A nightmare. We walked along the dimly lit country road in silence. Every couple of minutes a car would drive past, but none of them stopped. But then one did. It was the police. "You're that German goalkeeper, aren't you?" asked the driver. He had a season ticket at Dunedin and hadn't missed a home match for years. "Get in, we'll drive you home." We gratefully accepted his offer, and it reminded me of when I had to get into police cars back in Singapore – albeit under completely different circumstances. I was happy to chat away with the Dunedin fan about our last few games. Then he suddenly told me about Wolfgang, a German policeman who had emigrated a few years ago. He was on duty that night at the station. The policeman picked up the radio. "Hey, can you do me a favour? We'll radio in, and you insult him in German, just say whatever." The man was clearly bored. I took the microphone. "Okay. But let's make a deal. Afterwards, I get to drive the car through town with the lights and siren on." This had been my dream ever since I was a child, along with appearing on TV one day just like Ratko Svilar. I was only too happy to radio in to the station.

Wolfgang answered. "This is Markus Neumann, German Ambassador to New Zealand," I began in German, letting my imagination run wild. "We now know everything, so there's no use denying the allegations." Wolfgang suddenly became very confused. "What allegations?" he stammered. "I haven't done anything." Hearing the doubt in their German colleague's voice, the policemen reacted like two excited little children. "You know full well what I'm referring to. You do realise that having sex with sheep is illegal in New Zealand?" I barked into the microphone. "Present yourself to the German Embassy tomorrow morning. The paperwork has already been taken care of." The two policemen in the car lost it and burst out laughing. Wolfgang laughed as well once he realised it was all a joke. He signed off and promised to come and watch our next home match. "Okay, now let me have a go behind the wheel," I said to his two colleagues. And they really did let me drive the remaining three kilometres to my house – they said nothing when I turned on the lights and raced through town in the long, white police car at 70 kilometres per hour. I yelled into the empty streets over the loudspeaker, my voice echoing far and wide. The policemen didn't stop me. A couple of months earlier I wouldn't have dreamed it was possible, but all of the police officers I met in New Zealand were great guys.

The football club at Dunedin became something of a second family to me. On the pitch I did my job, and off it the New Zealanders forgave my follies – small and big. Just after my second season at Dunedin had begun, some of the players and I travelled to visit one of the largest reserves for little blue penguins, the smallest species of penguin in the world, which wasn't far from the town. We went on a guided tour and I grinned when I saw them – the creatures reminded me of ugly doves, but I liked their gullible look and the awkward way they moved around.

The biologist gave a little presentation about how intelligent the penguins are when it comes to adapting to the different climatic conditions they experience. I remembered Glasnost and Perestroika, the two monkeys that caused me to redecorate my apartment in Singapore – but they also used to make me laugh so much.

A pet penguin. Why not? I couldn't stop thinking about it. At night I lay awake in bed, annoyed by the tick-tock of my alarm clock. I turned the TV on, but still couldn't get the penguin out of my head. I reached for a football magazine – and put it back down again. After an hour I got up and did what I normally did when I had a mad idea: I put it into practice. Quietly I put on a black hoodie and black jeans and grabbed my rucksack and a pair of goalkeeper gloves before setting off in my car. It was raining when I parked near the beach where the penguin colony nested. I walked the last kilometre so as not to attract the attention of the keepers, who were on duty in a beach house.

I pulled my hood down over my head and stood next to the fence, my shoes half-sinking in the boggy ground of the car park as I pulled on my goalkeeper gloves. I got going, my torch lighting up the way. I couldn't see any of the creatures, since they slept in holes in the ground. I reached blindly into one of the holes. It was empty. Another hole was empty too. In the third hole I felt something soft. I reached in, hauled the penguin out of its hole and put it inside my rucksack. It was barely moving, probably because of the huge shock. But then it started to respond to the situation and pecked at me with its beak. Fortunately I still had my gloves on, otherwise it might well have managed to escape. I ran back to the car, placed the rucksack with the penguin inside on the back seat, and drove off.

It was a stupid idea and, in case anyone reading this is an animal rights activist, yes, it was a mistake. The penguin wasn't exactly thrilled, but I told myself that it was bound to make friends with me eventually. It scratched away at the fabric of the rucksack as it lay on the back seat. I turned and looked at it. "You'll be happy with me," I promised. Only then did I begin to wonder how I would be able to provide a decent home for the penguin. I stopped at a 24-hour petrol station and bought 10 kilos of ice.

I quietly carried the rucksack into our bathroom and lifted the penguin into the bathtub, which I had filled with ice. It looked up confused, giving me a few aggressive pecks with its beak and squealing like a rabid duck. I slowly became aware of the fact that this was going to be a lot more complicated than I had imagined. The sun was rising, and Craig wanted to use the shower. He stood rooted to the spot as soon as he saw the penguin. He didn't say anything, busy as he was trying to process what he had just seen. A penguin in the bathroom of a shared house in New Zealand, at 7am on a Monday morning. "You can't shower right now," I said. Craig knew me by then. He gave a wave of his hand and went without a shower that morning. The bath seemed like a practical place for the penguin to spend a few days, especially considering that our toilet was in a separate room.

I quickly drove to the pet shop, where I bought the penguin a few fish in a plastic bag full of water. Pleased with myself, I presented my new pet with its breakfast. I tipped it into the bath. It really did eat the fish, but even that wasn't enough to improve our friendship. It just sat there looking angry, if penguins *can* look angry. "Just relax for now," I said. "I have to go to training, then we'll take it from there."

That afternoon our president Marc Chidley came back to my place. We often ate together. "Don't mind the penguin if you go into the bathroom," I said casually when we got in. "I've got a new pet." Chidley laughed as he hung up his jacket: "Was there ever a day in your life when you took things even slightly seriously?" He didn't believe me until he opened the bathroom door and was greeted by a hideous stench and a little penguin staring up out of the bath. The president's good mood disappeared in an instant. His face turned slightly red, like it always did if anger was on the horizon. "Lutz, what the fuck?" I couldn't get a word in edgeways for the next five minutes. He lectured me in detail about how important penguins and environmental protection were in New Zealand. "If this gets out you'll face a 10,000-dollar fine and before you know it you'll find yourself in prison or on a flight back to Germany." The bit about prison certainly got my attention.

I waited until nightfall, put the penguin back inside the rucksack and took it to the beach. It had long since become clear to me that it had been a totally stupid idea. The penguin didn't look back, waddling towards the water as fast as it could. We hadn't become friends.

The next day, Chidley came round to eat again. I had bought chicken. When I served the meat he cocked his head and gave me a puzzled look. "What? It's chicken," I said. To this day I still don't know whether he really believed me.

CHAPTER 8
NIGHT
AND DAY

ollowing the end of my first season in New Zealand I had gone back to Bradford Park Avenue in England to keep myself fit until the start of the new season down under. And there was another reason for returning to the land of fog and fish and chips: Anita was now seven months' pregnant, and we wanted the baby to be born in England, where we would have the support of her mother. However, I very nearly didn't live long enough to witness the birth.

The day I died three times began just like every other in England. It was drizzling as I drew back the curtains at 8am. I did 225 sit-ups to work on my stomach and then 100 push-ups. A quick shower, muesli for breakfast, a look at the paper: The sports section was twice as thick as usual. Eight pages of special previews and features for Boxing Day, one of the highlights of the British sporting calendar.

I hadn't spent Christmas in Zwiesel this year, but in Bradford. We had a small tree, and Anita's mother had cooked a turkey. It would have been too draining to travel to Germany, because any professional footballer who doesn't prepare properly for 26 December may as well forget playing in England. Even though in Germany there's no way you could get the Bundesliga to come out of hibernation the day after Christmas, this is one of the most important match days of the English season. They say that if you win on Boxing Day then you'll be blessed with good luck for the rest of the season.

I sat down at the kitchen table and opened the newspaper. Just like every year, columnists were debating the origin of such a brutal-sounding name – Boxing Day – for what is in fact a Christian holiday, St Stephen's Day. I must have heard a dozen different theories over the years. The version I find most plausible is that the term dates back to the days of serfdom. On Christmas Day, noblemen's workers were required to keep working, but they had the following day off and were given the leftovers from the Christmas banquet as well as one or two presents – all of which was packed up in a little box. Thanks to these little boxes, the day has still kept its name centuries later.

Less traditionally, many people in England go hunting for bargains in the post-Christmas sales on Boxing Day, but many also go and watch the football – often in the mood to get rather boozed up. For me, Boxing Day in England means one thing in particular: hard work. Traditionally, plenty of goals are scored on this match day – one somewhat tongue-in-cheek theory claims this is because the defenders spend the Christmas period filling up on a little bit too much Dutch courage, and any striker who's taken it a bit easier should have no trouble getting plenty of chances to score. It's probably a myth, although Boxing Day in 1963 saw a record-breaking 66 goals scored in 10 top-flight games, so maybe that's the root of the legend.

I hastily scanned the local paper's preview of the day's league game against Harrogate Town. The author declared us the clear favourites. Anita was still asleep. Back then, because of her pregnancy I didn't want her to have to lift a finger. "Of course I'll come to the stadium later, mum's coming too," she said drowsily as she woke up. "It is *Boxing Day*!" I wanted to protest, but knew it would be no use. As soon as Anita had made up her mind, there was no dissuading her. I gave her a kiss, and then from outside I heard my manager Trevor Storton, who had come to pick me up, beeping his horn. Ever since he had let me train with the team following my prison sentence in Singapore, a deep friendship had developed between us. Around that time his daughter, who was just 19 years old, had been in a serious accident. She spent months fighting for her life; I'd often accompanied him when he'd visited her in hospital, until – thankfully – she finally recovered. Our two destinies had forced us together.

In the changing room, I put on my purple-and-black goalkeeper's shirt. I'd chosen the shirt deliberately, because for years it had been one of the ones in which I'd lost the least matches. A lucky charm I urgently needed. Our recent performances had been pretty poor, and I'd even been the subject of some odd headlines. A couple of weeks earlier, I'd dragged myself to a match despite having a high fever, but not before consuming just about every flu remedy I could find. As a result, I could see three balls instead of one. After going for the wrong ball three times, we were 3-0 down! Back in the changing room I collapsed, and a defender had to go in goal for the second half. The British newspapers had a field day with the story.

But no player wants to miss the Boxing Day match. I ran onto the pitch, my pulse racing faster with every step. I was already completely soaked after warming up, and the biting wind worked its way through my clothes. I've always liked rain. It refreshes the soul and reminds every fibre in your body that it's alive. It frees football matches from tactical constraints, rendering the ground so unpredictable that both teams have no other choice but to accept that their fight alone is the truly decisive factor. Few smells are more satisfying than that of a pitch which has been battered by rain and ripped apart by the studs of football boots for 90 minutes.

The game, a local derby, got off to a rough start. It was one of those matches with no midfield. Taking a huge risk, we sought to go from our defence straight to attack. Big, long balls, with everyone chasing after them. The other team did the same. Kick and rush. Nowadays it would be wrong to sum up English football using such simple terms – after all, in the Premier League they play some of the most technically sophisticated football in the world. Nevertheless, this style of play is still widespread in the lower leagues.

If our defence made a mistake after one of these long balls, it almost always resulted in a major opportunity for Harrogate Town. Every minute the ball would come flying at me, and in the first few minutes of play alone I was elbowed in the face twice. It was one of those games I loved.

We were the superior team. We were leading 1-0 after just one minute thanks to ageing former professional Simon Collins, and a few minutes later Robbie Painter put us 2-0 up. But then came the 29th minute. From the midfield, Harrogate passed the ball forward, where nobody seemed too bothered about Clayton Donaldson. Of Caribbean origin, the dreadlocked striker had begun one of his sprints, the kind which would one day see him play league football for the likes of Hull City, Brentford and Crewe. After a through ball from midfield, he was suddenly clean through in front of me. The ball was directly between us, we were both 10 metres away from it. I didn't know for sure whether I would reach it in time before he would. If I didn't, I'd look past it. But it was my only chance to prevent him scoring an easy goal. My feet all but sank into the squidgy ground. Water splashed everywhere. The spectators got up from their seats, yelling like mad as if they were witnessing the climax of the men's 100 metres. My gaze kept switching between Donaldson and the ball. He was slightly closer than I was, but I was determined to get there first. I had to get there first. Just two more metres. At the edge of the penalty area, I slid towards the ball but Donaldson was already there. He kicked the ball at me at full speed, then as he fell he hit me in the chest with his right knee. It felt as if I'd been struck by dozens of lightning bolts at once. I couldn't breathe.

I stood up and wanted to shout at the referee – after all, Donaldson had gone in pretty roughly for the tackle. And then everything went black. I fell over. Collapsed. As if struck by lightning, I landed on the soggy grass. It was as if from one moment to the next my body had been turned to jelly.

I don't remember what happened in the next few seconds, but my fellow players told me later. The referee let the match continue, and the ball rebounded for Paul Sykes to tuck it into my empty goal to pull one back for Harrogate. The noise from the stands adopted that angry tone which always surfaces when the home team concedes a goal. The referee pointed towards the centre circle – now it was only 2-1.

Then suddenly the spectators began to notice that I was still lying motionless at the edge of the penalty area. A person can sense when another is in serious danger, and the feeling coming from the stands now was one of absolute horror. Most of the fans quietened down in an instant, and an eerie silence fell over the stadium. One of my teammates later told me that it became as quiet as a secluded meadow. Over in the stands, Anita clawed at her mother Margaret's anorak as the shock set in. The 10 seconds that it took for help to arrive where I lay must have felt like an eternity for them. One of those truly scary moments when time seems to stand still.

Our physio Ray Killick was the first to get a hold of the situation. He ran over with his medical box, at one point stumbling and almost falling over. The players were yelling like mad at each other and waving frantically at the subs' bench, from where the Harrogate team doctor then also came running. Slowly, worried murmuring began to be heard from the stands. When Ray reached me, I lay motionless, a whitish-yellow fluid pouring out of my mouth. Ray, a bony fellow with grey hair which he usually hid underneath a green baseball cap, had been there for the team for more than 20 years. His methods were a little out-dated, but nobody could have imagined the club without him and his dry sense of humour.

Ray felt my pulse and started swearing. "Nothing." I'd stopped breathing. "He's fucking dead," he cried, panic gripping him. "He's fucking dead!" Ray held first-aid qualifications from the Football Association. But he'd never found himself in a situation where he actually needed to administer mouth-to-mouth resuscitation on the pitch. Now the time had come, and he didn't hesitate before tilting my head back and blowing air into my mouth. His actions made it clear to every last person in the stadium just how serious the situation was. Tears were streaming down our manager's face. The assistant manager Ian Thompson, once a player known for being absolutely unshakeable and hard as nails, was cowering behind the subs' bench. He couldn't look over at the pitch, he told me later: "I just couldn't."

After a few minutes, a steward came to Anita and her mother Margaret in the stands. They should come down to the pitch, they were told; it could be the last time Anita would see the father of her child alive. Each second seemed to last for hours. "I've got him back," Ray called after what seemed like an eternity. I'd started breathing again. Anita stood there in tears, Margaret holding her tight. "Stay awake, stay awake," she called to me. My eyes were open, but they rolled back. "Are you sure he's alive?" she screamed at Ray. "Are you really sure?" No. A couple of seconds later I stopped breathing again. Ray began mouth-to-mouth again. I began breathing again, but only for a couple of seconds. Luckily for me, Ray's first ever attempt at resuscitation proved successful three times, and the ambulance arrived on the pitch a few minutes later. I have only received mouth to mouth once, but instead of Pamela Anderson giving me the kiss of life I end up with a sweaty smacker from a 60-year-old Yorkshireman. Thanks Ray!

The match had long since been abandoned – something which is about as common in England as the national side winning a penalty shootout. And yet, these things do happen in football; a number of famous professional footballers have died of cardiac arrest or other heart problems on the pitch, like Cameroonian international Marc-Vivien Foé or the Hungarian Miklós Fehér. If someone had told me when I was 20 that my life would one day end on a football pitch, then I'd have accepted it. As melodramatic as it may sound, I live for football, and I would even have died for it. It's an idea I certainly prefer over the thought of drawing my last breath in some hospital, frail and in pain.

But I woke up. As if on a small, blurry television, I could make out the face of a young woman. The television screen went dead again. Shortly afterwards, the woman reappeared, this time a little clearer. "He's waking up," I heard her say in a muffled voice.

A second woman appeared on the screen, which was gradually getting a little wider. Suddenly I came to. I was still lying on the stretcher they'd used to haul me off the grass and into the ambulance. My beloved goalkeeper shirt had been cut open; Apparently this had been necessary for the resuscitation attempts. I tried moving my arms and legs. I couldn't. Was I paralysed? I was terrified. It was then I realised that I was fixed to the stretcher by straps across my arms, legs and even my head.

Where was I? I didn't recognise the room – but the inside of the stadium was large and like a maze. You can't know every room, I thought. A narrow, white doctor's room with a couple of cupboards, beside one of which stood two nurses in green gowns, their backs turned towards me. They look like aliens, I thought in my dazed state. Then I remembered: I must have been substituted. On Boxing Day of all days! The last thing I remembered was smashing into Donaldson. "What the hell is going on?" I called out to one of the nurses. She turned around, the syringe she held in her hand filled with some sedative. I ignored the blinding pain in my chest. "Why did you make me come off?" I tugged at the straps they'd used to fix my legs and arms. "Let me go right now, I have to get back on the pitch." The woman smiled. "You're at Bradford Royal Infirmary. And the match was abandoned more than an hour ago. You should just be thankful to be alive." I didn't believe a word she was saying.

A young doctor came in through the door. "We can unstrap you now," he explained. "We just needed to do an MRI scan to make sure your spinal column wasn't damaged." I still didn't understand what had happened.

Anita and Trevor entered the room. Anita's eyes were red from crying, but now she was just happy to see me alive. Slowly I sat up and hugged her carefully. She told me about the collision and the three resuscitation attempts. "You took a huge blow to your solar plexus. Several of your organs failed. We're extremely lucky you're still with us." The force of the impact had caused the blood vessels in my abdomen to expand, which meant that the pressure of the blood entering my heart had dropped and there hadn't been enough blood supplying my organs. My lungs had completely collapsed, and had it not been for Ray resuscitating me I wouldn't have stood a chance.

I listened to them, but were it not for the blinding pain in my chest I could have sworn they were talking about someone else. I was happy to be taken for some x-rays and to undergo tests to assess how well my organs were functioning. My sternum had suffered a hairline fracture, but my back was intact and the other tests revealed that I had recovered quickly. "You'll have to stay in under observation for three days. Your lungs will need a few days to recover. I'll see you tomorrow," said the doctor and left.

I wanted to go home. Immediately. I could get out of bed, so there was no reason I couldn't go home too. My stubbornness had landed me in trouble a few times in the past, but nobody was going to deter me this time either. After a long discussion, Anita eventually drove me home.

My parents. I'd forgotten my parents. It had never made sense to them why I spent the day after Christmas Day on a football pitch and not at church. I'd promised them that I would phone after the match, just like I always did after a game. It was a habit I'd had since I was very young, but this time they'd been waiting since 5pm and the clock next to my bed showed that it was already 9.30pm. I picked up the phone. My mother answered. "Hello," I said, and suddenly I couldn't hold my tongue. "I just died. Three times. But I'm alive again now." Horrified, my mother listened to my story. Even today she can still describe everything that happened to her on that day, her walk through the snow and the shortness of breath she had suffered during the afternoon. She swears that she had felt what was happening in England. I was never one to make things easy for her.

The days that followed were a nightmare. Not the pain, but the inactivity. Completely listless, I flipped through the TV channels – 45 channels in 45 seconds. I thumbed through a few football magazines, but even that didn't help. Even the countless cards and flowers which poured in for me from across the country did nothing to improve my mood. The doctors had urged me to refrain from any strenuous activity for 10 days. But I have never been able to do that. I need movement. I need to communicate with people.

After two days I got out of bed. The pain wasn't that bad. Anita went on at me for hours, but I paid no attention. For me, football is like an addiction. After five days I attended training. "Hey Lutz," said Trevor as he greeted me. "It's good to see you paying us a visit. Have the doctors already allowed you to get out of bed?" I went and got my kitbag from the boot of the car. "I'm not paying you a visit, Trevor. I'm joining in." He protested, but couldn't stop me from going in goal. From behind the fence I could hear a couple of fans slagging me off for being so reckless with my own health. But I wasn't in any pain, and in any case I couldn't do anything else. And I kept telling myself that I mustn't wait too long before making my comeback. Ski jumpers have to get back to the jump as soon as possible following serious accidents, otherwise they become afraid of their sport. The same went for me. I was afraid of becoming afraid. Afraid of tackles, afraid of throwing myself into the fray.

Bradford's next match was in two days. I insisted on playing, and Trevor eventually agreed after I'd spent an eternity persuading him. Just like before every match, I took all the time in the world to don my kit. I chose a shirt I hadn't yet lost in too often. A green one; after all, the purple-and-black one I'd worn during my last game hadn't brought me much luck at all. It was a cup match, and the fans didn't share Trevor's and my family's concern. In English football, there's little room for thoughts about a person's health. My fellow countryman Bert Trautmann, a former prisoner of war, played for Manchester City and became a legend in the 1960s. He had once played on in an FA Cup Final despite breaking a bone in his neck, and decades later every footballer in England still knew his story.

I don't want to compare myself to Trautmann, but the same mechanisms were at work. As I came onto the pitch the fans stood up – even those of the other team. The stadium announcer exclaimed: "Here's a man who gave his life for Bradford three times."

The stadium erupted in applause, and everyone yelled my name – and they carried on after the game, even though we'd lost. It's been many years since I last played in that city, but whenever I'm in England I always try to see one of that great team's matches. The stadium announcer is still there. Whenever he sees me, he still speaks those same words into his microphone: "Today in the stands we welcome a man who gave his life three times for Bradford Park Avenue."

CHAPTER 9
ROAD TRIP ACROSS AMERICA

absolutely love the cartoon character Popeye. I've always loved the adventures of the spinach-eating sailor with the smoky voice and unbridled strength in his tattooed arms. As a child I used to devour the comics, and my eyes were always glued to the TV screen whenever Popeye was on.

Perhaps that was the reason why I couldn't feel any anger towards the American fans howling behind me. I was standing in goal for the Calgary Mustangs, and behind me in the stands the opposing team's fans were singing that well-known, whistling Popeye theme tune that sounds so much like a sailor's shanty. Only they'd come up with new lyrics. Straight after kick-off, instead of "I'm Popeye the sailor man" they began belting out "He's Lutzie, the jailor man!" Again and again. Toot toot.

By that point Anita and I had left England, since there were simply too many other places we wanted to explore. Whenever I changed clubs we would follow the old rule of professional football which dictates that you should go wherever you can earn the most money. After the birth of our daughter, Georgina, I first moved to Oslo and signed with Bærum SK in the Norwegian First Division. That was perhaps the best season of my career. The country's sports journalists named me their goalkeeper of the year, and at the end of the 2003 season I had lucrative offers from several of Norway's top clubs as well as the Calgary Mustangs, a newly founded Canadian club. For a while there was also talk of me joining AC Milan's reserve team, and I actually completed a six-week training camp with the legendary Italian team. In the end Anita and I opted for Canada.

So there I was playing for my new team at an away game in Portland. The atmosphere had never been so heated playing against other clubs. The fans did everything they could to put me off. This is nothing unusual for a goalkeeper. Over the course of Oliver Kahn's career, he had so many bananas thrown at him that he could quite easily have fed all the monkeys in every zoo in Germany with them. The goalkeeper is one of the most important positions on any team, and he is more dependent on his nerves than any of the other players on the pitch. Anyone who succeeds in making the away team's keeper feel unsure of himself will more than likely help contribute to the hosts securing a home win. I had to hand it to the home fans in Portland; they were certainly imaginative. During the second half they switched to the gospel song "He's got the whole world in his hands" – or, more specifically, they started singing something to the tune of the happy Christian song. They had changed the lyrics. Their voices rang out in chorus, echoing through the stadium: "He's got the whole jail in his ass." Lovely.

I couldn't not notice the singing. As soon as I ran out onto the pitch, a few drunken fans started calling me a Singapore prison whore. But it was just like any time I was provoked: I played out of my skin. It was 1-1 with 10 minutes to go. I had saved around a dozen shots on goal, but the fans' singing continued unabated. "Singapoooore – Prison whooooore." At that point it hit me that I wasn't bothered by it. Of course I was intimidated, but my wounds from Singapore had more or less healed. When the match was interrupted for a substitution, I turned and faced the Portland fans and started dancing to their song. Lots of them began to laugh, and I attempted to conduct my new choir. When someone threw a cup of beer in my direction and a few drops splashed onto my sleeve, I quipped: "That's no German beer!"

In England, Jürgen Klinsmann went from being an unpopular player with a reputation as a diver to a crowd favourite, simply because he celebrated his first goal for Tottenham Hotspur by leaping through the air and simulating a dive. You can be successful in England if you learn not to take yourself too seriously. And the same really is true of North America. The next day, the newspapers praised my little dance routine.

We had arrived in Calgary a few weeks earlier, at the beginning of March 2004. It was 17 degrees, with beautiful sunshine. "I think we can cope with this," I said. But the weather in Canada is incredibly changeable, and during my very first match I experienced conditions similar to those I'd faced in Finland years earlier. It was a balmy 12 degrees at kick-off, and the start of what promised to be a wonderful spring afternoon. But then the wind changed, and an icy storm closed in from the Rocky Mountains, which begin just an hour's drive west of Calgary. The temperature on the pitch dropped to minus five during the second half. We were playing on artificial turf, which was normal in Canada, and the playing surface seemed particularly unforgiving that day. Depending on the quality, astroturf can already be extremely brutal, especially when it is dry. During some of my training sessions the friction was so strong that my tracksuit gave off smoke as I slid on the ground. Some artificial pitches are sprinkled with miniscule rubber balls made of shredded old car tyres so as to reduce the friction. Those things get everywhere, especially into your eyelids and nostrils – nowhere is safe from them. Sometimes it would be a week before I had managed to remove all those little balls from my ears. In Calgary on this occasion it was so slippery that it felt like someone had poured a ton of soapy water across the pitch. To make matters worse, the cold caught me by surprise. I paced up and down the penalty area incessantly in an attempt to keep warm. My Canadian teammates just carried on playing, since they had been accustomed to such temperature fluctuations since childhood.

The brand new team had been founded before the start of the season. Two investors had spent around 200,000 dollars on a professional licence and then put a team together. A couple of Canadians joined us from competing league teams. And the rest were an interesting bunch: Apart from me, the Mustangs signed a striker from the Caribbean island nation of Trinidad and Tobago. If we had training in the morning, he had a habit of sleeping in until well after we had started. Plus there was a Slovenian midfielder, who was an absolute heartthrob but spent hours on the phone every day to his girlfriend back home. We also had a Belgian centre-back – who managed to lose not only all his money during his first training session, but also his passport before our first international flight – as well as a Dutch playmaker called Geert Brusselers, who had already played all over the world just like I had. And finally we had our German manager Thomas Niendorf, a disciplinarian who had learned his trade in East Germany before the Wall fell. The investors must have thought that the more diverse the range of characters the better we would fit together. And they were right.

That year, my life effectively consisted of one long road trip. We played several times a week in the United Soccer League (USL), a professional North American league that ran at the same time as Major League Soccer (MLS) and involved matches in both Canada and the United States. Later it became the second tier of the MLS. The fixtures were regionalised, so that, for instance, there were some weeks when all the matches took place in the western part of North America: On one trip we flew to Vancouver and headed on from there in several small minibuses, with six of us to a bus. It was three hours to Seattle, where we played an evening match before moving on to Portland a day later. In the following week we would then be heading to the US states of Minnesota and Milwaukee. Sometimes we were on the go for 12 days at a time. A life on the road. We felt a little bit like rock stars on tour. There are only two options when six young men spend so many hours crammed into such a small space: Either you fight or you decide to relax and enjoy your time together. We opted for the latter.

On those trips we celebrated birthdays, played cards and shared the craziest anecdotes from our past. I admit most of them were about women. And I realised that I'm not the only professional footballer to have been dealt a few strange hands in life. It's certainly a job that provides excellent conditions for bizarreness to unfold. It uproots you, constantly forcing you to move on to new places and pastures new. Anyone who has ever moved to a new town will know that it can be the most hectic time in your life. But try to imagine what it's like to move on every year, usually to a different country, and be watched by hundreds of thousands of highly emotional spectators whenever you go to work. That should give you a pretty good idea of just how colourful each and every player's past turned out to be as we spent hour after hour telling stories whilst driving along North American back roads.

I was used to that life. One of my greatest strengths had always been my ability to quickly find my form in spite of my new surroundings. Or perhaps it was the other way around, and those new surroundings were what made me find my form. After a while my mind always craves new experiences, and I've always been keen to immerse myself in the unknown. I never could understand teammates who would rather hide behind their PlayStation than explore the foreign country they were playing in – thousands of professionals have that kind of mentality.

North America had a positive effect on me, and I found myself returning to the form I had reached the previous season in Norway. It could be that the seasons of 2003 in Oslo and 2004 in Canada really were the best of my career. The USL was marketed in a similar way to the professional American football and basketball leagues, and there were statistics for everything. I liked that. After a couple of match days I was the player with the most saves, just like years ago in Singapore. We often ended up drawing. In such cases, matches in North America go on into extra time, and as such I was soon also top in terms of the most minutes played in the league. I love all those stats.

Even so, it was strange playing football in Canada and the US. That was where I began to understand how differently the beautiful game is integrated into different regional cultures. In Europe it's an emotional outlet, something people identify with, a science. People absorb even the tiniest of details about football. There are three daily newspapers about football in Italy alone. In Germany, every single fan feels competent enough to pass judgement on the state of the national side. And however little Rudi Völler, Jürgen Klinsmann or Jogi Löw might have thought of the criticism coming from those 80 million wannabe national coaches, not until my time in Canada did I realise just how competent German fans really are.

Sometimes it felt as if the people just came to the stadium to eat. The spectators would sit down in the stands and calmly spread their food out, despite the fact that the atmosphere down on the pitch had long since become heated to say the least. Lots of people would go to a football match where a German might go to a café – to have a bit of a chat. In pubs, unknown bands often struggle for attention while everyone carries on chatting away at the tables, ignoring the artists. Now I know how that feels.

There was one occasion which summed up the position of football in Canada compared to other sports. In the spring of 2004 the Calgary Flames ice hockey team reached the Stanley Cup finals series where they would face the Tampa Bay Lightning. Like in baseball's World Series, the finals involve a seven-game series, and one of the matches was scheduled for the same day (and same kick-off time) as our crunch game against Minnesota. The Mustangs' president tried to get the game moved but the league refused, so he tried to make an event of it. He announced that we would be showing the Stanley Cup on the big screen during the match and we ended up getting a big crowd of about 10,000. It was one of the strangest things I have ever experienced in football. We played our match with the entire crowd staring at the big screen the whole time, watching not just another match but another sport! No one was paying the slightest bit of attention to our game. There were huge cheers when the ball went out for a throw-in because something had happened in the hockey game, and absolute silence when we scored a goal. Ice hockey is so big in Canada that I'm pretty sure that some of the players on our team were playing with one eye on the big screens too.

Calgary's fantastic natural surroundings compensated for the marginal existence football led in comparison to all-American sports like ice hockey and American football. Sometimes after training I would just spend hours driving around. The club had put me up in a house just outside Calgary and given me the use of a huge Jeep, which I used to explore the area in my free time. A lot of people had told me that the city of Calgary was a concrete jungle in the middle of nowhere. You could see it that way, but I liked it all the same. Calgary is clean and, above all, it's people are open which makes up for the crimes against architecture committed by many oil companies with their ugly office buildings. One area of the city is called Kensington, and from its hills you can see the Rocky Mountains on the horizon. I often spent my evenings driving around there. I can't think of many better places to be alone with your thoughts. I'll never forget my drives and hikes out into the forests of the Rocky Mountains. Anita and I would often not see another soul for hours.

Twice on our travels we saw brown bears by the side of the road. They often lose their way and come down out of the mountains towards Calgary, and even though they're not monsters they're certainly not cuddly toys either. Hundreds of bears are shot every year because the residents, most of whom are armed, feel threatened by them. And it's understandable considering how they sometimes make their way into people's homes and raid their food cupboards. Some accidents, however, can only be blamed on people's lack of common sense. I once read a newspaper article about a Japanese couple who had stopped at a car park for a break with their 14-year-old son. A bear approached them and began peacefully rummaging through a bin for scraps of food. The parents sent their son over to take a photo of the animal. He got as close as a few metres away from the bear, which then got nervous and lashed out with its paw, tearing the boy's scalp off. The boy needed emergency surgery. Luckily he survived. That was one of only a few accidents involving people when I was there – although my neighbour's greyhound did fall victim to a bear attack.

Anita and Georgina had come to join me in Canada a few weeks after I arrived. Anita found it hard not being in Bradford, which was why she had only been with me for about half the time I spent in Norway, spending the rest of it in England. She accepted the path I had taken, but wanted nothing more than a normal life in a little house in England with a husband she actually got to see once in a while. But I knew that my time as a professional was limited, so I was unable to fulfil that wish of hers – despite everything she had done for me. Things weren't easy between us.

If Anita was with me then I enjoyed a quiet, secluded family life. But when she was back in England, I spent the evenings partying with the team. We all got VIP tickets from the local clubs and bars, just like the city's other professional athletes. Ice hockey players and we footballers were particularly popular with the ladies in Calgary.

After one match in Minneapolis down in the States, six of us headed into town. There was a lot going on outside one club, so we decided to just go in. But no sooner had we entered than we noticed the strange looks we were receiving from the other patrons. Then we realised that there were almost no women. "This is a gay club," I said to my Dutch teammate Geert Brusselers. "Who cares," he replied, "it's fine as long as no one tries any funny stuff. Let's stay for one beer." But Chris, a tall defender from Italy, looked like he'd just fallen into the lion enclosure at the zoo. "Do we have to?" he asked. "One beer and we'll move on," I reassured him.

Over the years there were a number of occasions when I realised that one of my teammates was gay. I know of twelve homosexual players in Germany's Bundesliga alone. I never had a problem with it, but even in the 21st century so many football players are still extremely homophobic. In the Premier League, so far the only footballer to come out is the former Aston Villa, West Ham and Everton player Thomas Hitzlsperger – and even he only did so after the end of his career. Being a gay footballer is still one of the game's final taboos.

I've never understood it. In my opinion one of the most important rules is that everyone should be allowed to live their life as they see fit. It was no use getting into a discussion, but I felt like provoking my Italian teammate a little. The bar was on the top floor, with a spiral staircase leading upwards. As we made our way to the stairs, Chris kept looking around as if he were about to be jumped by 10 gay guys. I laughed at him, and as he climbed the stairs I reached through the bannister and gave his backside a good pinch. The others were already laughing, but Chris turned around angrily. A stranger was stood behind him, and the panicked Italian didn't waste any time at all before punching him in the face. A huge commotion ensued. The stranger fell down the stairs, and there was a smash as a couple of glasses broke. There was hysterical screaming everywhere. The Italian stood in the middle of it all, looking like an eight-year-old who had got lost and ended up in a nudist bar. To this day, if I'm ever in a bad mood all I have to do is think of that image and I'll be laughing in seconds.

Back then I spent a lot of time with Geert Brusselers and his family in particular. We explored the scenery at leisure and in our own way, although not always exercising brilliant judgement. We visited the Calgary Stampede, one of the biggest outdoor festivals there is. My research on the subject of cowboys and Indians consisted of the stories I had read as a child and movies, but I thought I could make up for any gaps in my knowledge in my own uncomplicated way. I decided to go up to a tall Indian and greet him: "How, my red brother." A Canadian later told me that using that term is considered extremely racist. With a menacing look on his face, the Indian began to come after me and Brusselers.

He was carrying a tomahawk, but the situation didn't turn out to be that dangerous after all. The man was blind drunk.

Alcohol is a major problem among the indigenous peoples of North America. A Canadian woman I knew was a nurse who spent six months of the year working in Yellowknife, which is the capital of the Northwest Territories in northern Canada and has a large Indian population. She spent her days pumping screen wash and spirits out of people's stomachs.

I was enjoying life – but the season didn't go entirely according to plan. As much as I loved leading one or two of the statistics, I would have happily traded it all in for a place in the play-offs. The club tried everything. We even had our very own team priest, Brian Carnduff. He was a big football fan, strong, in his early forties, had a high hairline and accompanied us to all our matches. There was a room next to the dressing room where we would pray together for 10 minutes before home games, and before away matches we did it in the dressing room itself. Right from the start of my professional career I always recited the Lord's Prayer before kick-off. Those few minutes with Carnduff always did me a lot of good. We prayed for good health, but also secretly hoped for a bit of luck with the result. But even ecclesiastical assistance was no use in the end. To qualify for the play-offs we would have had to make the top four. We came fifth.

I had a two-year contract, but I knew that the club desperately needed every dollar it had after missing its target for the season: So I agreed to go on loan back to Dunedin, the New Zealand club where I had felt so comfortable playing in previous years. I didn't mind that the loan agreement included a clause stating I could be called back to Calgary at any moment.

It was the third time I had played for Dunedin, and it took just a couple of days for me to settle into my old routine: training, annoying big Scotty for a bit, and occasionally storming our striker's lectures. My intention was to play there for six months, at the best time of the year to be in New Zealand, and then return to Calgary for the start of the North American season in April 2005. I was certain that this time I'd be winning the title. After all, we were top at the end of the first half of the season.

The club had its best start to a season in its history, with 12 wins and just one match lost.

But 10 days before Christmas a fax arrived at Dunedin that utterly ruined my Christmas spirit. Due to financial problems, there was some doubt as to whether the Calgary Mustangs would still exist next year. They required me to be back there before Christmas to arrange my transfer to another club. There I was once again, standing on the platform in the shunting yard of international football with no idea where the next train was heading.

I only stayed in Calgary for a few days. But that was long enough for me to realise that the Calgary Mustangs' days really were numbered. Some of the Canadian players had already signed preliminary contracts with rival league clubs. It was extremely difficult to reach anyone at the offices by phone, and the club's website hadn't been updated for weeks either. Discouraged by the team's failure to qualify for the play-offs and disappointing average attendance numbers, the investors had withdrawn their financial backing. I met the vice president, Michael Kratky, in his office. As soon as I entered I noticed that most of the files had already disappeared from the shelves behind his desk: "Don't worry," he began. Experience had taught me that such an introduction could only mean bad news. "We've found a club in Ukraine's top division and they can even afford to pay you far more than we do. And they play at a decent level."

I have always been a thoroughly apolitical person. Even so, I had heard a little bit about how Ukraine was going through a complicated period at the time. In the weeks leading up to Christmas 2004, word of the Orange Revolution had spread to New Zealand. But I hadn't realised just how dramatic the situation was until I flew to Kiev together with a Canadian lawyer, who was going to oversee my transfer.

Rumours had been circulating for months that opposition leader Viktor Yushchenko had been poisoned – and this was confirmed by doctors after the election. The dioxin had launched a savage attack on his organs and caused facial disfigurement. He had been out of action for some four weeks during the emotionally charged election campaign. There had been a run-off at the end of November between him and the then Prime Minister Viktor Yanukovych, with the latter declared the official victor. But international election observers protested, alleging serious fraud, and both the European Union and the United States rejected the result. From then on there were daily protests by hundreds of thousands of people in Kiev against the government, which in turn mobilised thousands of troops. By the time the lawyer and I arrived in Kiev that January, the atmosphere was so explosive that serious violent unrest could have broken out at any moment. Just outside our hotel the demonstrators were throwing stones at the police. The taxi drove us through the city to Obolon Kiev's stadium at walking pace. During those weeks I suspected that the two of us were the only people in the city thinking about football.

In fact it was business as usual at the club, which was preparing for the start of the season at the end of February. The officials couldn't understand our scepticism in view of the political crisis. "Things will calm down," the manager said to me. "Times are just slightly more hectic than normal. But it'll be fine." I trained with them twice, but by the third night the demonstrations outside our hotel had lost nothing of their intensity. I hadn't yet signed my contract, so I decided to leave Kiev as quickly as possible.

I informed the club's president of my decision. He said that although they had thought I was going to join the team they could, of course, understand my change of heart. He shook my hand. I was told that my plane ticket to Calgary was in the secretary's office, where an employee needed to make a copy for the accounts. But the woman wouldn't give me the ticket. "There's no ticket here," she said. And the president wasn't available to speak to anymore, apparently. That was his way of getting revenge for me changing my mind and leaving them with an unexpected goalkeeper problem. I spent half an hour getting worked up over it, but then the lawyer and I went to the airport. We decided to just buy a new ticket there.

At least that was the plan. But when we arrived at the airport, it was in a state of utter chaos. "It's unlikely you'll find a flight this week," said the airline worker. Neither to Germany nor to any other airport where we might be able to change and fly back to Canada. "All our flights are fully booked." It was as if the entire population wanted to leave the country. The other people queuing behind us in the hope of purchasing a ticket were beginning to get impatient. "You could try going to Romania or Poland," advised the woman. "The situation won't be changing here for the next few days. You might have more luck there."

We took a taxi straight to the train station. By then it was late afternoon and we had to wait an hour for the night train to Chernivtsi near the Romanian border. Our nerves were somewhat frayed following the stress of the last few days, but it all just melted away as soon as we boarded the ancient night train, which was grey with age, and set off for Romania. We had paid the equivalent of 12 euros for the journey to Chernivtsi, and it was going to take 18 hours. The Canadian lawyer was seriously annoyed at the prospect and hadn't said a word while we were waiting. I, on the other hand, was like an excited little boy during the journey as we rattled through the forests of Ukraine. It had been exactly the same in Finland almost a decade earlier – the rumble of the train beneath me and the monotony of the forest whizzing by have an almost unrivalled calming effect on me. And it's no different up in the far north of Ukraine, even though the trains might be more run-down: I stared out of the window for eight hours, and for eight hours I saw nothing but trees. Then we travelled through one tiny station, which was followed by another seven hours of just trees. A conductor brought us lemon tea every couple of hours. We didn't drink it. In Kiev someone had told us that people often put sleeping pills in the drinks on trains in order to make it easier to get at the passengers' luggage. We both had our laptops and a bit of cash with us so we didn't want to risk it.

We arrived in Chernivtsi the next morning. The train station hadn't been given a makeover since the Soviet Union had come to an end. It was a single grey block covered in crumbling plaster. A couple of decrepit taxis were parked outside. It was another 30 kilometres to the border. The journey cost five dollars, but the Russian-speaking driver wouldn't take us across the border. He just kept saying, "nyet, nyet." In the end we had to walk through an abandoned border checkpoint. A little building with a barrier in the middle of the forest. By that point the Canadian had started communicating with me again, although now he just swore quietly to himself.

The train ride to the capital, Bucharest, took 10 hours. At that point our journey sped up drastically. We flew to Munich, where I wanted to spend a couple of days, and the Canadian flew on to Calgary. My father picked me up from the airport. "How are you?" he asked, his face expressionless. "Fine." He had been following what was going on in Ukraine on the news, but it hadn't been enough to give him any real cause for concern. By then he had become pretty tough when it came to worrying about his son.

And I really had been in more difficult situations than this. My contract in Calgary had more than a year left to go, and nobody could force me to move to another club. In the months that followed, the Mustangs sorted out all of the details to do with the insolvency proceedings – but they didn't find a suitable new club for me. My players' agents were having trouble too, since the season was already well under way in most European leagues. Two uneventful weeks passed before I decided to fly back to Canada. The season began in early April, so as per my contract I flew to Calgary at the beginning of March.

The next morning I went to the club's offices next to the stadium, full kitbag in hand. The door was open and the reception area had already been completely gutted. A photocopier still stood in one corner of the office, and a couple of wires hung down from the ceiling – they'd even taken the lights. I was about to leave when suddenly I heard noises coming from the office of the owner, John Torode. A builder was putting some files away. "There's no one left. If you want to speak to Torode you'll have to go to his office."

Torode had made his money through gigantic real estate projects, and his business headquarters were a few streets away. His secretary was sat in the hallway and I could see Torode studying some paperwork in the room behind her. He was shocked when he saw me: "Hi John, I'm back," I said, greeting him as if nothing had happened. "When does training start?" Torode spoke in a slightly higher voice than usual, which he always did if he was agitated. "Lutz, are you a bit slow or something? The team is history." I smiled. "That's as may be, but my contract isn't, and it doesn't run out for more than a year. I assume you'll be organising a car and a place to live for me in the next couple of days." Torode carried on insulting me but I wasn't about to back down. "Call again tomorrow," he muttered eventually. "We'll sort something out."

But there was no answer when I phoned the next morning, neither at the office nor on his mobile. Nor was there the next day. So I drove back to Torode's office. His secretary was sat at her desk again. The door to the bigger room was ajar, and through the gap I could see John.

"He's not here," the secretary lied.

I pointed towards John.

"But he's sitting there."

"No, he's not here."

I opened the door and pointed at John. "He's sitting there." They both attempted to solve the problem by saying nothing. Rarely have I ever experienced anything so childish, but there's something I enjoy about absurd situations. "If he's not in," I said, raising my voice, "then please tell him that in the next 10 minutes I'll first be calling the league and then I'm meeting my lawyer, who specialises in labour law. Then this whole affair will end up in court, and John can invest as much in legal fees as in my salary. Thanks John!" I left, shaking my head.

But John Torode wanted to chance it. We spoke twice more on the phone, and he was certain that he didn't have to pay me because the club had gone bankrupt. The weeks passed by. I worked as a goalkeeper trainer at clubs in the city, and it looked like things were heading towards a long, drawn-out lawsuit. I couldn't bear the thought of it, especially since I didn't have the time. The market value of professional footballers can plummet if they don't play for a while. The days passed, and I'd probably still be sitting in my hotel room right now were it not for the fact that I happened to meet the club's second major investor, Dr Hanne, in a restaurant.

Just like for John Torode, Hanne's unsuccessful investment in the Mustangs had by no means threatened his very existence; to both of them the club was similar to what Chelsea has been for Russian oligarch Roman Abramovich. It was a toy, a status symbol. Hanne had left Torode in charge of dealing with the bankruptcy proceedings, and had no idea that I was in Canada. "Come to my office tomorrow," he said. Hanne wasn't one to beat around the bush, and clearly had a backbone – a rare quality in his business. The next day we came to an agreement in less than 10 minutes. He paid me my basic salary until the end of the season in cash, and I agreed to waive payments for the car, accommodation and points bonuses – something that would otherwise have been discussed in court. I went home clutching a bulging envelope filled with banknotes.

The money only provided me with the security I needed for a few weeks, since most of it went towards the lawyers' fees I had run up years earlier in Singapore. I was still paying off the huge sum that had accumulated during my trial. But at least I was able to stay in Canada for a month while I looked for a new club.

That search was always the same. Back then I already knew around 30 players' agents all over the world, all of whom had my CV as well as videos with clips from matches I had played in. Whenever I was not signed to a club, I would spend my mornings concentrating on keeping fit. In the afternoons I would then sit at a table with exactly four objects, no matter where I was on the planet: In front of me would be a laptop, and beside that a phone, a notepad and an ancient ring binder containing around 500 telephone numbers. Even now I am lost without that folder. Sometimes there would be a dozen Skype chat windows open on my screen at once, and I would make phone calls at the same time. I gradually collected different offers from all over the world and wrote them down on the notepad. As soon as a transfer was arranged, the agent responsible for it could look forward to up to 20 per cent of my year's salary, which they got from my new club. In my case, of course, we were talking about pathetic amounts compared to other professional footballers around the world. In the 2007/08 Bundesliga season, agents in Germany pocketed 37 million pounds in transfer commission – and it's a growing business. There are hundreds of licensed players' agents in Germany alone.

In this case, a Russian agent's luck was in. He had provided the Mustangs' initial contact in Ukraine. Now he came up with an offer from a First Division club in western Ukraine. Apparently the small town was set in beautiful countryside hundreds of kilometres from Kiev and the focus of the uprising. In any case, that situation had calmed down completely.

Even I knew that much. In the first few months of 2005, the newspapers were filled with encouraging signs from Ukraine. Yushchenko had since been appointed president, and contrary to my fears the Orange Revolution had taken place without widespread bloodshed. What's more, it wasn't easy to find a short-term contract lasting until the beginning of the new season in New Zealand in November. My former team Dunedin, where I had been on loan from Calgary until the latter went bankrupt, had already made me an offer for the new season. However, it wouldn't be starting for another half a year, so this new offer came at just the right moment for me to bridge the gap. Anita had stayed with me during the first season in Calgary, but then she moved back to England. By this point, every time we spoke we ended up having a huge row, and our relationship was as good as destroyed. So I quickly accepted the offer from the Ukrainian club. I got out the plastic wallet where I keep my mobile SIM cards from each country – I now have 25 of them – and I put the Ukrainian one in.

When I arrived in Ukraine there really was no sign of the Orange Revolution. But the agent had transferred me to the most corrupt club I've ever played for and whose name I would rather not share. I was only there for a few weeks, never playing any official matches. It doesn't appear on any of my CVs. I was put up in a hotel and trusted that I would somehow find my way to the club on my own. I was introduced to the club's translator, which I thought was really good of them. He was a really nice guy with nice manners – but not very helpful. It's true he was able to translate, and was actually very good at it, but unfortunately only between Spanish and Russian. There I sat in my Ukrainian hotel room, having just signed with a team where barely anyone spoke English and needing to find my bearings in a town where almost nobody spoke English either.

I needed a translator. Immediately. I spent hours making phone calls straight after my first training session. Nobody in the town was able to help me. I also called four translation agencies in Kiev, but none of them could help either. Annoyed, I phoned a small agency which happened to be the last one on my list. "Unfortunately we can't send anyone to you," said the employee. I was gradually beginning to lose all hope, but then she came up with an idea: "We have a translator who currently just translates documents to do with exploration oil drilling. She sits at her desk all day. We could arrange a telephone service. Whenever you have a problem communicating, call us and we'll pass you on to her." I agreed. From that point on, a woman called Amalia with an elegant, highly educated-sounding voice was my all-purpose personal translator. To be honest I was surprised she didn't cancel the arrangement after just a couple of days, because her phone began ringing every few minutes. When I went out to eat I would give the waiter my phone. Shortly afterwards I needed to give a taxi driver directions. If the coach was giving us instructions in the dressing room, I would hold the phone up and have her translate what he said. Once I even called her at night from the hotel: "I'm hungry. Please can you tell room service to send something up?" The club must have been paying a lot, because even then the translator lost nothing of her professional courtesy.

But even Amalia was unable to help me in some situations. After a couple of days the president, a fairly old man with severely gelled-back hair, gave me my company car, a black BMW X5 with tinted windows. Four-wheel drive, 200 HP, brand new and the finest leather interior. It was the best car I was ever given the use of by a club. But the X5 didn't have a satnav. It was just five minutes from the hotel to the training ground, but I got hopelessly lost on the second day.

After spending a few minutes driving around the town's littered streets, I stopped at a corner and wound the window down. "Do any of you speak English?" I called. A man was sitting on a bench in front of a kiosk, and next to him stood an elderly couple. The three of them stared at me, uncomprehending. But then a young man did come up to me. "At last, thank you," I began when he reached the car. Then I saw that he had pulled out a gun. "Get out slow and nothing happen," he said in broken English, just as calmly as if he really was giving me directions. I was shocked but realised that he was serious. No sooner had I got out than the guy drove off. My kitbag, which had my mobile phone in it, was still on the back seat. I knew that carjackings were a big problem in South Africa, and as such most new cars are now fitted with tracking devices. This means helicopters can pinpoint stolen vehicles on Johannesburg's huge freeways, allowing motorcycle squads to pursue them. I hadn't expected to run into such a problem in Ukraine.

Strangely, the three onlookers didn't seem particularly shocked. The man in front of the little grocery shop slowly got up and waved me over to him. He pointed to his telephone in the corner and said something in Russian, so I assumed I could use the phone. I called my interpreter in Kiev; hers was the only number I knew off by heart. Amalia called the club, and half an hour later I was picked up by one of the staff.

Before training I had to explain to the president how I had managed to lose the club's brand-new car. He caught me at the entrance to the dressing room and made it clear that I should call my interpreter. Amalia explained to him what had happened that morning. Once the president was up to speed he typed something into his mobile, ignoring me. "Go," he said in the end before shooing me away like a little boy. "Go training."

There was a large car park in front of the club's premises. When I walked past it after training, I could hardly believe my eyes. The BMW X5 that had been stolen from me that morning was parked there. Confused, I went to the office. The president was unavailable and nobody was prepared to tell me how the car had reappeared. Not until weeks later did Amalia hear what had happened from club staff.

In the Ukrainian football scene it was common knowledge that the president had plenty of contacts with the criminal underworld and was also feared by the town's petty criminals. All his cars had particular registration numbers that were known in the town's criminal scene. As soon as the thief had seen the number plate after taking my car, he immediately returned the vehicle to the club and formally apologised for the misunderstanding. It's not that he would have had a guilty conscience – after all, as I later discovered, the car had actually originally been stolen in Germany – but was probably more concerned for his own safety.

It began to dawn on me how the club was able to afford my salary. But that wasn't the only reason I didn't like the town or the club. The place was generally run-down, and one night I even got stuck in the hotel lift for half an hour. The emergency telephone was out of order and it wouldn't have surprised me if the air supply had stopped working and I ended up suffocating.

In the end a cantankerous repairman opened the door. The lift was still a metre away from the next floor when it had become stuck. I climbed up. My room was on the seventh floor, but from then on I only ever used the stairs.

There weren't many enjoyable moments during those few weeks. My life consisted primarily of training, and barely anyone spoke English or German. So I was delighted to meet Amalia for coffee after a match in Kiev. By then we had spoken on the phone hundreds of times. It was usually just for a few seconds, but she had become something of a lifeline to me. I had a pretty firm idea in my mind of what she would be like in person. I had often pictured a neatly dressed woman in her late forties wearing glasses as she translated oil drilling reports in a dreary office, with a professional footballer phoning her every once in a while.

I was wrong, at least as far as how she looked was concerned. She was only in her late twenties, slim and had delicate facial features as well as long, long legs. On the phone she always sounded like someone from the tax office, highly professional, but as we sat there enjoying a coffee in the Kiev sunshine she was bursting with a love of life.

Anita and I had recently split up, and it did me good to talk to Amalia. From then on I didn't just phone her when I needed a translation. We thought the same things about life, and our phone calls lasted for hours. She told me about her young daughter and about life in Tashkent back in Uzbekistan, while I gradually shared stories of the highs and lows of my life so far. We slowly fell in love with each other.

But at the same time there was nothing I wanted more than to leave Ukraine as soon as possible. And I wasn't the only person on the team who wanted out. Hardly anyone was paid on time. A player from Senegal who had signed with the club four months earlier still hadn't seen a single penny. Two other players and I lent him the equivalent of a couple of hundred dollars, because otherwise he wouldn't have been able to afford to feed himself. He was booed by the fans during our pre-season matches, simply because of the colour of his skin. They were extremely racist. The past couple of years in Canada, Norway and New Zealand had almost been paradise for me. Now, though, the chaos had finally caught up with me again.

Just before the end of the pre-season, I made a decision: I didn't want to live there. Two months were enough. I requested that my contract be terminated. And then I left.

CHAPTER 10
WANTED: ENTREPRENEURS IN ARMENIA

T he groundsman was late. Yet again. It was a hot August day in Albania, over 35 degrees and not a cloud in the sky. Twenty-two players were standing around outside the dressing room waiting for the man with the key to finally appear. We had spent two hours training. We didn't mind that there was no hot water for the training ground's showers. The problem was that there wasn't even any cold water either unless the man was there to open up his little hut and turn the water on.

Eventually the Albanian turned up, and fired up the generator. It sounded like the engine of a classic car, and rusty water soon began dripping from the Soviet-era pipes. We stood impatiently in front of the showers, waiting as the water gradually got clearer and heated up just enough for a bit of steam to form. We had quickly worked out that after three minutes the liquid turned into something you could just about subject your skin to.

While Germany, busy enjoying the high of hosting the World Cup, was swept up in the football fairy tale that was summer 2006, I had moved to Albania. Out of curiosity. My good friend Uli Schulze, who played for FC Magdeburg in the year they won the 1974 European Cup Winners' Cup, had just signed as manager of the nine-time Albanian champions Vllaznia Shkodër, and had asked me whether I fancied coming along too. Up until then I had heard about pretty much every football league in the world, but I knew barely anything about Albania, which is only about half the size of Scotland. That was reason enough for me to say yes.

Apparently it was almost impossible to find a used car in Albania that wasn't a total write-off, so back in Bavaria I spent 3,000 euros on an old VW Golf 3, and not a BMW like I usually would have – and I set off with my Albanian soon-to-be teammate, Uliks Kottri. The journey took almost three days, winding on for 1,400 kilometres; it felt like we were travelling halfway around the world as we left Germany and passed through Austria, Slovenia, Croatia, Bosnia and Montenegro before finally arriving in Albania.

Schulze had warned me that the country's roads were considered the worst in Europe. The closer we got to Uliks' hometown, the deeper the potholes became. One 80-kilometre stretch of dirt road over a mountain range took no less than four hours. Even so, I was impressed by Albania's rugged landscape. Concrete structures lined the roads like giant mushrooms. Uliks was happy to tell me about the country's eventful past. "We owe it all to Enver Hoxha," he said. The dictator had led the country into absolute isolation in the 1980s. He had thousands of bunkers built, many of them in the border areas. The ones which hadn't since been converted for use as sheep pens usually served as public toilets.

It would be wrong to say I liked the town of Shkodër from the outset. It had been raining for days, meaning the drains were completely overwhelmed. A slightly foul stench hung in the air. But I found the city fascinating. It had a hectic atmosphere, much like Istanbul. Buzzing about all over the place, the cars and mopeds seemed to outnumber the inhabitants. Many of them even went the wrong way around the roundabouts, taking the corners at breakneck speed. Crosses stood inconspicuously by the side of the road, almost lost in the commotion – the Albanians' unconventional driving style clearly cost many lives.

Although the club had made it to the cup final the previous season, their last championship had been far too long ago – back in 2001 – so the fans were demanding change in view of the team's long barren spell. Apart from the new manager Schulze and me, the club had also brought in 15 new players. And the president was still keen to find more fresh faces: Before I had left we had trialled around a dozen players at a three-week training camp held in the German city of Magdeburg. Most of them were no good, and time and again we sent players off to the train station in the team's bus, rucksack in hand. From there they would travel on to their next try-out. Thousands of young men travel around Europe in that way every summer, ever hopeful that they might find a contract – no matter how small the league, or their pay packet. It's a far cry from transfers worth millions involving players like Gareth Bale and Cristiano Ronaldo, but it's just one more side of the reality of the football business.

As different as professional football might be in Albania compared to leagues where the superstars play, the fans are no less passionate in Shkodër than in cities like Manchester or Liverpool, those two great stages of club football. The city was home to a good 100,000 people, and 99,000 of them seemed to be loyal fans. The club's red-and-blue flag flew everywhere. Thirty thousand spectators would attend our home games. Such a mass of people can create an immense, exhilarating and sometimes even terrifying power. Many of them brought rockets and flares into the stadium. If we won they would carry us out of the stadium on their shoulders – even after unimportant league matches. But if we lost, an immense rage would be unleashed.

It had been months since Anita and I had split up. I had worried ever since, wondering how often I would get to see my daughter Georgina. It wasn't an easy time. Luckily, my former translator Amalia had been by my side. We had stayed in touch after I left Ukraine, and became an item not long after Anita and I had gone our separate ways. Amalia is a very decisive woman, and so it was that, from one day to the next, she decided to quit her translation job in Kiev and first came with me to New Zealand – where I played a couple more seasons in Dunedin, although the club was now called Otago United – before coming with me to Albania. All this moving around was new to Amalia, and she slowly had to adapt to a completely new lifestyle. But she was amazing and always adapted straightaway to whatever situation we found ourselves in. We simply went through the phases of a relationship a bit quicker than most, and we married on 22 June 2006 in Tashkent, Uzbekistan. Suddenly Amalia's surname was Pfannenstiel, which is quite a tongue-twister for native speakers of Russian, and at first she couldn't even pronounce her own name.

We could hardly have spent our first few months of married life in more explosive surroundings. The result of a match would determine the fans' mood for days on end. At first I thought that must be a good thing. All it took was one win at the beginning of the season, and people already started to notice me on the street. Total strangers kept offering to buy me cups of tea, and once I even got asked to dinner. Suddenly I saw nothing but beaming faces all day. But our third match, an away game, ended in a shock 3-1 defeat. It was then that I realised why there was such a heavy police presence in the stadium. Once it became apparent that we were going to lose, dozens of fireworks began flying down onto the pitch from both stands; our fans were actually aiming at us players. And also at the referee. He had allowed a controversial penalty kick against us, and now he had to be escorted off the pitch by a dozen security personnel – the fans were throwing stones, tomatoes and eggs in his direction.

Most of the stadiums were in a terrible state. Before one cup match against the third-tier team Sarandë, down near the Greek coast, I spent 20 minutes removing shards of glass from my penalty area. There were hardly any matches where I wasn't hit by lighters or stones. Once, in the middle of the second half, a little boy aged maybe 10 ran past the policemen on duty behind my goal. Once he was about four metres away from me, he threw a plastic bottle at my head, stuck his middle finger up at me and ran back into the crowd. Later on when we wanted to leave the stadium, a few mad fans pelted our bus with rocks the size of a fist. I felt like I was in a radioactive waste transporter surrounded by angry protesters.

Our team were technically brilliant but awful when it came to discipline, and Uli Schulze tried everything he could to keep them on their toes. He introduced two long training sessions every day, and the older players moaned that they'd never had to run so much in their lives.

But while Schulze spent hours lecturing the team on tactics with the help of a translator, the older players and staff turned to other methods to try to guarantee our success. Following our surprising defeat, we were due to play at home against Tirana SK; it promised to be one of the top clashes of the season. During our final training session, the physio brought a sheep to the ground. He came by bike, casually walking the animal along on a lead. Without a care in the world he tied it to a fence and stood next to the pitch where we were warming up. I smiled. Matey over there must be taking his pet sheep for a walk, I thought to myself before remembering the penguin I had tried and failed to keep as a pet years earlier. The physio and the sheep stared at each other stoically while we rehearsed free kicks. The team were in good shape and we had every reason to feel optimistic about the game. But that wasn't enough for the Albanian players.

Once training was over they walked over to the sheep. Suddenly the physio pulled a large knife out of a bag and took a couple of purposeful strides towards the animal. The sheep bucked, apparently sensing its fate, but it didn't stand a chance. With a swift movement, the man slit the sheep's throat. A large pool of blood began to spread across the dry grass. The ground was so hard that it didn't drain away and formed a large puddle. It happened so fast, it was all over before I'd realised what was going on. I turned away in disgust, with the sheep still twitching. The physio just continued, calmly speaking a few words. It didn't sound particularly solemn, and didn't feel like some sort of cult ritual either. It was more like a sober address, with the players standing around him and the sheep while it bled to death. They were so composed that they could have been waiting for a bus. I left the training ground without saying a word. "You'll see, we'll win tomorrow," one of them said to me later on. As it happened, the sheep didn't give its life in vain – well, not entirely. The next day we secured a 1-1 draw against Tirana, and soon afterwards we beat cup winners Elbasani 2-0.

With its 100,000 inhabitants, Shkodër was little bigger than the city of Bath in Gloucestershire, but it had three daily newspapers in heavy competition with each other. Such a situation is disastrous for journalistic quality. In Spain, every now and then players complain about the sports newspapers *Marca* and *AS*, which devote 10 pages of each edition to Real Madrid alone. Regardless of whether you're talking about Real Madrid, Manchester United or the tiny Vllaznia Shkodër in Albania, it's fair to say that the daily lives of 20 or so professional footballers are simply not interesting enough to fill so many pages. However, I have rarely come across tabloid journalism that was as aggressive as it was in Albania. The reporters would resort to the most outlandish methods to get close to the latest news and rumours. They had no respect for the players, and even less for themselves.

Two days after we beat Elbasani, I went to the toilets next to our training ground. Only the players were allowed to use them. There were two cubicles, one of which was locked. When I came back out, there were already three Albanians waiting impatiently outside. I shrugged – I had no idea who was taking so long in the other cubicle. It didn't actually matter, but I felt like taunting the dawdler a bit so I peeked beneath the dividing wall in the hope of recognising whoever it was by their football boots. But they were normal shoes. None of our players used those toilets when we weren't training, so when they did use them they always wore their boots. "Who's there?" asked one of the Albanians. No answer. We knocked on the door. It took a while, but eventually the man came out. He was a reporter from the biggest newspaper. He had spent hours locked in the toilet just on the off chance he might eavesdrop on a conversation between players. His cover blown and utterly humiliated, he frantically dashed past us and ran off. Usually I would have taken the piss and laughed at him – but I was too dumbfounded. I'd never met such a pathetic reporter, and nor have I since.

This particular journalist was friends with the regular goalkeeper before me, a slightly overweight guy called Grimma who was now on the bench. He had kept goal for the team over the past few years, and many people were of the opinion that he was one of the reasons behind the team's mediocre performance in recent seasons. But the dirty fellow we found in the toilets didn't agree. In his articles he consistently stirred up bad feeling against anyone he didn't like, and that certainly included me. Once when we were playing an away match, our opponents were awarded a penalty just before the final whistle. They managed to equalise. The final result was 1-1, and this journo was quick to point the finger. The penalty, which had gone just inside the post, "should clearly have been saved," he wrote the next day. Every single goal we conceded was apparently the result of my own personal failure. He wasn't successful though. Schulze made it quite clear to the press that I was his undisputed regular keeper.

Professional footballers don't have an easy time of it in Albania; they are an outlet for the emotions of the country's highly volatile population. But their lives are paradise compared to those of Albanian referees. Time and time again when I was out there, refs would fall victim to the violent fans – thanks not least to the irresponsible press: The match reports in the newspapers were full of hateful rants about the men dressed in black. Sometimes it was quite exaggerated, but it wasn't always entirely unjustified. The referees were amateurs, earning the equivalent of just a few dollars for each match. Many of them felt that they earned far too little considering the hardships they had to endure, and it had long been an open secret that they were corrupt to the core.

Before one cup match, our club president got onto our team's bus before we left for the game and pointed at eight regular players, including me: "You can stay here. We'll be fine without you." It seemed obvious to me that he had arranged the result with the other club. We got off the bus and no one was even that surprised. Match fixing was part of everyday life in Albania. But I hadn't known that our president was quite so happy to get in on the act.

And yet that was part of how the club was run. And not just our club. A few weeks later we were 1-0 up at half time during an away game; so many fireworks had already been set off that the stands looked as if they were on fire. The atmosphere was heated, but from down on the pitch we were able to get back into the stand undisturbed. We were making our way to the dressing room when suddenly we heard shouting. Around the corner, the president of the home club had intercepted the referee. He was shouting at the man, getting louder and louder. Two policemen arrived, but they didn't restrain the president. Instead, a bizarre scene unfolded before my eyes. The policemen grabbed the referee so he couldn't get away. The president then removed one of his designer shoes and hit the poor ref on the head with it. He struck four times and swore wildly before the policemen finally let go. The ref then hurried into his dressing room. To this day I still don't know whether the president was simply unhappy with his performance or if the referee hadn't stuck to an agreement. Back in the dressing room I had trouble listening to what Schulze was saying – the memory of what I had witnessed was just too weird.

But that was how the league worked in Albania, and that day was no exception. We were ahead until just before the end. Then a harmless long ball came across the edge of the penalty area. The other team's players were nowhere near our defender as he headed the ball out of harm's way. I heard the whistle. The referee pointed at the penalty spot. "What? You have got to be kidding," I yelled, rushing towards him together with my teammates. But it was no use, and the referee placed the ball on the penalty spot. I dived to my left, but the striker hit the ball to his left too and it was 1-1. More flares burned in the stands, but this time the home fans were happy.

After the match it was our turn to corner the referee inside the stadium, although we kept our shoes on. He didn't even try talking his way out of it: "Do you really think I want to have my head kicked in by 3,000 fans?" He had simply been too afraid of what would happen if the home team lost, and presumably called the penalty without even having been bribed. It was the only way he could guarantee getting home unscathed.

Uli Schulze actually did a fantastic job at Vllaznia Shkodër, working night and day to serve this bizarre club. But shortly before the end of the first half of the season we were only third in the table, which was reason enough for the president to let Schulze go. He was replaced by Mirel Josa, who had once coached the Albanian national side. The man was temperamental and blessed with an almighty pair of lungs. Judging by his incessant bellowing across the pitch during our matches, he could probably have been an opera singer. I could only hear it from afar. Josa was a sympathiser of my rival for the no 1 shirt, Grimma. I was dropped and had to watch the next game from the stands. During the winter break he then signed half a dozen new players. He made it quite clear to the guys brought in by his predecessor that their services were no longer required. Josa can't have said more than 10 words to me in total. I got the message.

Slowly but surely, my move to Albania was turning out to have been a big mistake. Once again I picked up the phone and spent hours talking to players' agents all over the world. I wanted to leave. It didn't matter where I went. I wanted to be gone, as soon as possible. I listened to every single offer, even if some sounded absurd. I received a message from an agent in Armenia telling me that two of the country's clubs were interested. Both offers would have been for around 4,000 dollars per month. I wrote back saying I was willing to discuss the offers with him.

The next day I received a call from the Armenian agent. Suddenly there was no more talk of the offers for me to sign as a goalkeeper. He explained that he had told an investor about me. For a while now, apparently, the man had been planning to purchase a first-tier club licence and set up a professional Armenian team from scratch. A table had been reserved at a restaurant in the Armenian capital of Yerevan for the following day, and the investor wanted to explain his concept to me in person.

Josa didn't really care whether I turned up for training or not, so the next morning Amalia and I boarded a flight to Armenia. We met at a swanky restaurant, where the investor was already waiting for us at the table. A polite man in his mid-forties, he wore a dark-grey suit. He seemed genuine. Sentence by sentence, Amalia translated the Armenian's idea. His plan involved getting young players available on free transfers to sign long-term contracts, giving them a year or two to mature in the league and then transferring them to bigger leagues for six-figure sums.

He wanted to use the club to make money. It was as simple as that. He hoped to achieve a clear return on his investment – there were no parallels with the vanity of what Roman Abramovich did, investing around 600 million pounds in Chelsea as if it were some expensive hobby. This man was the opposite. He was offering me a five-year contract and wanted me to be in charge of the project as a goalkeeper, coach and manager, although I imagined that with so much responsibility I would soon end up having to concentrate entirely on working as a coach and manager. So this offer would mean me hanging up my boots, at least for as long as the job lasted. But I sensed that this could be a once-in-a-lifetime opportunity. I discussed it with Amalia briefly before agreeing right there in the restaurant.

Three days later, Amalia and I moved to Armenia. I didn't have any second thoughts about leaving Albania, and didn't even bother saying goodbye to Josa. He had never made any bones about how much he disliked me, but the feeling was mutual. I had a good chuckle when I read something about him a year later. The Albanian Football Association had banned him for six months because he hadn't allowed his team back onto the pitch after the first half of a match. His justification: The referees had been bribed.

In Armenia I found myself doing something that came naturally to me. I think my organisational skills are probably better than my skills as a footballer, which – with the benefit of hindsight – ultimately weren't good enough for me to play in the Bundesliga or the Premier League. Back then I didn't have a problem with the fact that my working day began at 7am and ended at no earlier than 9pm – seven days a week.

Such commitment was unavoidable, since the project I was managing was truly low-budget. The investor and future club president had set aside a budget of just a million dollars for the first year, which doesn't go far if you're starting a brand new club – even in Armenia. Our club was to be based in Ijevan in northern Armenia, and the president registered the name FC Bentonit Ijevan. For the time being, we had nothing other than the name. My job was to create a successful club out of thin air, with the help of Amalia – who was brilliant at negotiating contracts and translated all our meetings and interviews – and my stepdaughter, Amalia Junior. It was a Pfannenstiel family business!

After a few days we left Yerevan and headed for Ijevan. The president insisted on demonstrating his vision by giving me a personal tour of the construction site where the new stadium was being built. I had seen an animation of a small, modern arena with a capacity of 12,000 on his computer. I was excited. As we were driving out to the new stadium grounds in his luxury SUV, the president talked non-stop. He spoke so quickly that Amalia, who was translating, had trouble keeping up. He talked about his two-year plan, which would end with the team competing for the UEFA Cup. And he waxed lyrical about the sold-out stadiums and a football boom in the region that was just waiting to be sparked.

Then the chauffeur stopped. "What's wrong?" I asked Amalia. In front of us there was a large field. We got out, and the investor carried on talking. A couple of diggers were parked on the grass, and the ground had been dug up here and there. Apart from a couple of bits of steel and piles of sand, it was just a field. The investor pointed at the steel ceremoniously: "This is where your office will be."

"Great," I said, trying not to let my doubt show.

But it wasn't much use and I burst out laughing. You needed quite a good imagination if you wanted to share the Armenian man's vision. Still, he believed the city was the perfect place because there weren't any other professional clubs in the region. But that also meant that the infrastructure any professional sport requires was also severely lacking. In reality the city was little more than a village, and the field had about as much in common with a professional stadium as my hometown Zwiesel did with New York. I was glad to hear that, while the stadium was still under construction, he planned to have the club based in the capital city, Yerevan, for the upcoming season. We would play our first year in a plain but functional 6,000-seat stadium on the outskirts of the city.

But before we could play a match, first I had to find some players. I spent hours and hours on the phone making hundreds of calls to agents, clubs and other contacts I had in the game from all over the world. Football is always overflowing with out of contract players who are desperately trying to find a club, especially during the European summer, and I managed to divert some to Armenia. By the time I had put down the phone we had 50 players from all over the world, including Brazil and former Soviet states like Georgia, Uzbekistan and Ukraine, heading to the club for a trial.

I organised a training camp and put the players through their paces to see if they were good enough. "I will have you running up and down the mountains until you hate me," I said as I welcomed them a couple of days after returning from my excursion to Ijevan's phantom stadium. It was the middle of January, minus five degrees, and our breath froze into little clouds. "If you don't like it, that's fine. You can leave now. But if you give it everything, then I'll get you fit enough for the championship and ready for a career in the major leagues." None of them left. In the space of three weeks we filtered out a team of 22 players from 11 countries on four continents, and almost all of them were complete unknowns. Even I didn't know exactly how good the team would be. The highest earner was paid 4,000 dollars each month, while some of the young Armenian players received the princely sum of 200 dollars. I rented a large house on the outskirts of Yerevan, where the whole team lived as if they were at boarding school. I found local doctors and physios willing to work for us on a freelance basis. Unfortunately I did have to get rid of the first doctor after four days. He had treated a defender's injured knee by cutting a fresh onion in half and placing it on the player's knee. He told me that it would draw any infection out of the joint. That was the last thing he told me, and two minutes later we had sent him packing.

Amalia and I moved into an apartment in central Yerevan, although I ended up spending nearly all my time at the big house and often even sleeping there in the bed in my office. Amalia was a great help, supporting me day and night. I don't think I could have done it without her. It was a huge task, and the things I'd learned about sports management on my distance learning degree from Düsseldorf didn't really help me in Armenia. Some of the players didn't even have bank accounts, so I would take my rucksack to the bank on the last day of every month. The Armenian investor had opened an account which I had access to. I withdrew 30,000 dollars and paid everyone involved, from our top strikers to the cleaning lady, in cash; one after the other they came to my office and collected their wages in envelopes. It might sound unbelievable, but I've often been paid like that over the years.

The training ground was situated outside Yerevan at 2,000 metres above sea level, and behind us the beautiful, snow-capped Mount Ararat towered into the sky. It meant we had to get used to permanent high-altitude training. The local players thought the location was a good omen, since it had been claimed that Noah's

Ark was found on the mountain and so many Armenians believe Jesus was Armenian. The Armenian fans also believed that our view of the famous mountain would bring us a good season.

I put together a training programme based on the toughest elements I had experienced under the 30 coaches I had trained with during my career so far. The days consisted of dozens of high-intensity interval runs. It was no problem for the Mexicans, who had often played and trained at similar altitudes. The Brazilians, on the other hand, lagged far behind when I first began testing their stamina. Two Georgian players ended up vomiting several times. Some of them really did begin to hate me, just like I had warned them they would a couple of weeks earlier. I couldn't help but notice it thanks to the looks they gave me and the curses they hissed in their mother tongues.

But that didn't bother me. Our budget was limited and we had barely any time to grow together as a team. Our only option was to be fitter than the other teams. Our doctors had their hands full. The combination of the altitude, the icy cold and the physical exertion left some players with feverish infections. The doctors made them drink hot tea after training. Buckets of the stuff. Players with stomach bugs were given homemade yoghurt to compensate for the salts they lost. Our housekeeper told me that yoghurt was invented in the region. I've no idea whether that's true or not, but it worked.

As the season drew nearer our team caused more and more of a stir. We played 14 pre-season matches and won 13 of them – some of them against hands-down championship favourites like FC Mika. The cup competition commenced before the league did and in the first round we were drawn against FC Gandzasar, who were based in Kapan in southern Armenia, not far from the Iranian border. The first leg would be away, with the return taking place a week later in Yerevan. Their coach, Souren Barseghyan, had been one of the most famous in the country back in the Soviet era and was a brawny man with cropped, greying hair and eyelids that were heavy from regular drinking. He had learned his trade in the 1970s, and he didn't like the fact that our newly assembled squad with its German novice of a coach had already managed to become many people's favourites for the title.

We drove the 1,200 kilometres to Kapan by bus – not only to save on costs, but also because there wasn't a single airport within 300-kilometres of the place. The journey took more than 20 hours, and we arrived with barely a second to spare before the press conference. As in most countries, it was normal in Armenia for both managers to speak to the media on the eve of a match. Barseghyan used the opportunity to launch a scathing tirade against my club. He turned towards me on the podium. "You think you're clever, German," he snarled at me in English. "But tomorrow we'll beat the arrogance out of you and your millionaire club." I couldn't help but laugh, since at the end of the day the conditions we were working under were hardly worthy of such a description. "Good luck with that," was all I said in response before shaking the perplexed coach's hand.

We lost the first leg 1-0, conceding a goal three minutes before the final whistle. Before leaving the pitch, Barseghyan was keen for the reporters waiting with their microphones to hear exactly how he had put the "wannabe club from Yerevan" in its place. He hated me. I just thought he was funny. "That man's brain clearly lacks enough convolutions to remember that we'll be meeting again for the second leg next week," I had Amalia translate. "We'll make it through to the next round – there's no two ways about it."

A week later, Barseghyan was strangely subdued. We won the second leg 2-0, a match even the German Ambassador to Armenia didn't miss. Bentonit had thus knocked one of Armenia's best-established teams out of the cup. By then I was certain that our concept was going to work; we would succeed in the league and then maybe even qualify for the UEFA Cup. It had been just two months, but four fan clubs had already been set up and an Armenian football magazine had tipped us as one of the favourites in its season preview. The newspaper headlines called me "King Lutz".

The people in Armenia had always been incredibly nice to us. Amalia and I were invited to dinner on what felt like a daily basis, even by people who could barely afford to buy their own food. The Armenians are a proud, fantastic people, although sometimes they're a bit sure of themselves. They wear strikingly chic clothing if they can somehow afford it, and are proud of absolutely everything – even the local lemonade, which apparently tastes better than all other lemonades on the planet.

The league season began in the middle of March, and we had got through the worst of the stress back at the end of February. Or so I thought, until one sunny Tuesday. As usual I drove to the bank to withdraw money to cover the month's expenses. I was sitting at the bank clerk's desk when he suddenly began frantically typing something into his keyboard. "What's wrong?" I asked, with Amalia translating. "I don't know what's happened here," the employee answered. "The account has been cleared." I panicked. "That's not possible. Please try again." But it was true. I was no longer able to access any cash.

I called the president on his mobile. His phone was switched off. I finally got hold of him that evening. "One of my business deals has gone down the pan and I needed to shift some cash," he explained. "There'll be money in the account again in a couple of days. Please just be patient." Totally embarrassed, I had to explain to the team what had happened. They had no choice but to wait.

A few days passed but there was still no money in the account. I called the president again and again, and again and again he fobbed me off with his excuses. It took a whole week before he finally spat it out. "I have to file for bankruptcy," he said. "The project's finished. I'm sorry."

I imagine that feeling must be something like how it feels like to be struck by lightning; one of those powerful bolts, capable of splitting a century-old oak tree in half. It was completely normal for Armenian clubs to run out of money and simply disappear. And so was being conned. But I had grown incredibly fond of the project, and the situation was anything but normal for me. The players felt exactly the same. The next morning we didn't go straight to training but instead gathered in the meeting room. Some of the players cried on being confronted with the news, but most just stared dumbly at the floor. What could I say? There were no words that could have made the situation any less dismal.

I spent the next few days trying to find new clubs for the players, who only had a few contacts themselves. If a club goes bankrupt, FIFA allows transfers to take place outside of the normal transfer windows. Only very few of them had any trouble, since over the past few weeks all of them had made an outstanding impression across the region. Even so, every phone call I made only served to reinforce the pain of the situation.

After a couple of days I received an offer of my own; a two-year contract with Bærum SK in the Norwegian Second Division. I had a pretty good reputation up there in Scandinavia ever since being voted goalkeeper of the year in 2003. And they weren't too worried about me perhaps not yet being match fit because of my work managing the club in Armenia. Even so, I just couldn't get excited about the offer. Never before had I ever created a project that was as dear to me as FC Bentonit Ijevan.

The first game of the Armenian league season was to take place shortly before I was due to fly out of the country. Only four players had left our house; the whole team were still in a state of shock following the devastating news about the club's bankruptcy. "You won't be paid a single dollar for this match," I told the players at our last team meeting on the day before the game. "If you play, then it'll only be for yourselves and your teammates. It's entirely up to you whether or not you should come." The room fell silent for a moment. Then our Serbian captain, Damir Dakic, said: "Coach, we won't be playing for Bentonit tomorrow, we'll be playing for you." It was one of the nicest things anyone had ever said to me.

They all came. They played inspiring football. In the end we beat the premier league club FC Shirak 4-0. We were still sitting inside the dressing room hours later, drinking beer and fantastic Armenian brandy the players had brought with them. There was hardly a dry eye in the house as we reminisced sadly about the last couple of months. That match was one of the most painful in my career. It was the last time my beloved Bentonit played.

CHAPTER 11
BRAZIL: SINGING ALL THE WAY HOME

T here comes a point when enough is enough. You start to long for security. I had played in 12 countries, on five continents and at 22 clubs, with fate and my own curiosity always driving me on. For years I had been unable to imagine my life any other way. Perhaps it was because of my burning desire to see even the most far-flung corners of the world with my own two eyes. Then again, perhaps it was the fact that constantly moving on and discovering new people and places meant that I never had the chance to stop and think about the truly important things in life. It was as if I was addicted to new experiences. The longer I spent moving all over the world, the harder it became for me to imagine settling down in one place for good.

But now, at the age of 34 and following the disappointment of Armenia, I was ready. After spending a few months playing in Norway I signed with the Vancouver Whitecaps in the middle of the North American season. I signed a contract until the end of the season with the option of extending it by a year. The club also said that when it ran out I could become their goalkeeping coach – it was a bit like an annuity agreement. Vancouver was one of the nicest cities I'd ever been to and the Whitecaps were an extremely well-managed club.

After a short spell with Bærum SK in Norway, I flew straight from Oslo to the US, where the club were due to play an away match against Charleston Battery in North Carolina. I was supposed to join them, so I had a demanding few days ahead of me. Just the evening before, I had still been in goal for Bærum in a cup match against Lillestroem. I had packed my things afterwards, utterly exhausted. As we approached America, the aeroplane encountered heavy turbulence as a hurricane began to play with us like a child does with a yoyo. Even so, for the first time in my career I was sitting there with the calming, warm feeling that I was flying somewhere I might actually stay for a while.

Feeling unusually calm, I allowed the catastrophic chaos of New York's John F. Kennedy Airport to wash over me. Generally I'd say it's one of the craziest I've ever been to anyway, but as a result of the storm it actually took six hours before I finally got through immigration. Anyway, my connecting flight to Charleston had been cancelled hours earlier. All I could do was wait until the next morning before flying on to North Carolina. I got there just in time for kick-off and immediately became acquainted with the qualities of a certain Bob Lilley, one of the three worst coaches of my entire career. He put me on the bench straight away – they had already sold their second-choice keeper and were expecting me to arrive on time to fill the gap. Exhausted after my marathon trip, I fell asleep in the dugout twice while Lilley hurled abuse at his players from the sidelines. He could have trumpeted as loudly as an elephant but it still wouldn't have roused me.

It's true I had an exhausting start, but afterwards my life in Canada turned into a dream. And I wasn't used to that. The Whitecaps put me and Amalia up in a nice apartment on the sixth floor of a modern residential complex. I was given the use of a new SUV and the club owner even invited us to join him for a round of golf on days when there was no training. I had every reason to be happy. Vancouver was a fantastic city for the family – me and the two Amalias – safe and friendly with a great school.

My life on the football pitch also took a turn for the better, as I played at a good standard in front of 10,000 spectators every week. I even got to play against one of the most famous footballers on the planet when Los Angeles Galaxy signed David Beckham. A dazzling marketing campaign and his marriage to Posh Spice meant that he was one of the few football players that everyone knew, even in Canada. We met Beckham before and after the game, and although he was a football god and fashion icon in America, he seemed a nice, friendly lad to us. It's just a shame he sometimes lets his wife dress him in funny clothes.

A crowd of 70,000 turned up to watch the match. Beckham played a fairly unremarkable game, but the spectators didn't care. A spectacular volley by one of our strikers met with polite applause, as did I when only just reaching a shot destined for the top corner with my fingertips and deflecting it over the bar. On the other hand, a hurricane broke out whenever Beckham so much as took a throw-in, with the crowd getting off of their seats and cheering. If one thing is true about football in North America, it's that it's all show.

Everything was going so well. And yet, as was usually the case when some semblance of calm returned to my life, I began to brood. My career had panned out differently than how I had imagined it would back in 1993. Not worse. Not better. But differently. I had never set foot on the pitch in one of the major leagues, and I hadn't got rich either. Strictly speaking I hadn't properly fulfilled my childhood dream: Unlike they had done with Ratko Svilar, Eurosport didn't broadcast any of my matches, and in Germany there were no little boys secretly switching on their TVs to cheer me on in the dead of night.

Be that as it may, somehow I had still managed to inspire lots of people through my travels. Again and again I would receive post from fans who had managed to get hold of my postal or email address and sent me moving letters and emails. Again and again journalists would write down my story and tell me about the many, many readers' letters they had received after publishing an article about me. Again and again I wondered why that was, since at the end of the day, while it was true I had experienced great football matches, they often hadn't been watched by more than a couple of hundred spectators. Perhaps it was because football simply had the power to consume me. It has a better grip on me than I do myself. Sometimes Amalia used to wake up in the night, frightened, as I lay next to her making saves and deflecting shots in my sleep. Out for the count, I would suddenly turn to her and try to reach a ball in the corner of the goal. I'd knock her head with my hand and wake her up. "It's dangerous sleeping next to you," she often told me.

I am perhaps the antithesis of the media-savvy professionals of the Bundesliga and Premier League, their careers as meticulously planned as they are boring. Of course they win championships and earn millions, but they don't really stir any emotions that last beyond the glittering stages of the Champions League. It's not often that they really make a connection with their fans on a human level. But apparently that's something I did achieve a few times thanks to the lows and highs I experienced.

As I slowly set myself up with a normal life in Canada, I began to realise that I wouldn't swap my career for that of these so-called star players. Time and again I had seen a player's arrogance grow in proportion to his bank balance. I was proud of my career. It had enabled me to get to know some of the most interesting people and places on the planet and experience football in ways that barely anyone had before me. If I lie still, I can hear the vuvuzelas of South Africa as if I were still playing for the Orlando Pirates. Whenever Bradford's stadium announcer introduces me as "the man who died for us", it calls forth emotions within me that no championship title could replace. I have forged deep friendships with the people who got me back on my feet after my difficult time in Singapore, and those friendships will endure until I die. In those few weeks, the true value of my career dawned on me for the very first time.

At the same time I tried to fend off such thoughts. You're sitting here on your terrace and reflecting on life like an old man, I thought to myself. However positively I was able to look back on my past, there was just no shaking the fact that that old seed of discontent, that unrest, was still inside me. It had been with me all those years; it might have been hidden from view temporarily, but it was still in me. Sometimes my desire to experience something new would ebb, becoming less demanding. There were even a few times when I briefly thought it might have disappeared altogether. But in my heart of hearts I knew that it was always there and always would be. It was like a virus that takes hold of the cells of your body, sometimes showing more of itself and sometimes less – without ever leaving. And there was a part of me that liked that disease.

It didn't take much to reactivate the virus in all its former glory. One phone call was enough. During the weeks before I moved to Canada, my German agent Joakim Olsen had kept on and on at me, drumming it into me that I was just one small step away from a world record.

Since 1993 I had played professional football in Europe, Asia, Africa, Oceania and North America – five regions. No player had ever signed with clubs from all six of the continental confederations recognised by the international federation, FIFA, and I was only missing South America. I had never set out to hold that record; my career had been all about the journey and my experiences. It had been about living and suffering for football, which just happened to have taken me all around the globe.

Joakim Olsen worked closely with the German players' agent Peter Vogler, who lived in Rio de Janeiro. "He'd have no trouble finding a club for you," said Olsen in an attempt to entice me.

I had chosen Canada, but as each day passed in the paradise that was Vancouver, I secretly began to regret my choice more and more. It was glaringly obvious to me that, at the age of 34, I didn't have much time left before any professional clubs in Brazil would lose all interest in me.

After four months Vogler came up with a proposition that was too good for me to turn down. He said he had been in touch with Macaé Esporte FC, a recently promoted first-division club from Rio de Janeiro state. The club's owner had heard of me – even Portuguese-language football magazines had run features on me, it seemed. The club was still smarting from a few missed opportunities in recent seasons, which it owed in part to the team's weak goalkeeper. I was in luck: Macaé wanted to sign me immediately. In a month's time, it dawned on me, I could be playing on that one missing continent. My virus was back, that longing to be on the move which was so good at brushing aside any need I had for security. I said I'd try anything.

In Vancouver they were less than pleased to hear of my plans. Ultimately the club had more or less bent over backwards to secure my transfer and I had played a handful of games for them. We discussed it for a long time before they finally consented and gave me their official permission to leave. "Do you realise what you're giving up for this ridiculous idea of yours?" the manager asked me, referring not only to the idyllic Vancouver lifestyle I'd be leaving behind. Amalia was amazingly supportive. Even though we had a great life in the city she understood how important this was to me. She was also quite looking forward to the Brazilian sunshine!

Professional football has a dubious reputation in Brazil. Very few clubs pay their players on time, and professionals have to learn to live without any privacy whatsoever. At the time I made the decision to leave Vancouver, the headlines were dominated by a supposed scandal surrounding former World Player of the Year Ronaldo. He had been drinking at a nightclub in Rio de Janeiro before returning to his hotel room with three beautiful women, who undressed him and took photos with him. They turned out to be transvestites, and I later heard that a newspaper rewarded them handsomely for their little set-up. Even the media back in Germany spent weeks talking of a sex scandal involving Ronaldo. But none of that bothered me since I'd played in worse countries over the years. "Yes, I know what I'm giving up," I replied to the manager, "but I can't not do this."

But in situations like that you don't realise what you're letting yourself in for until you get there. My driver, whose name was André, slowly drove the car the 180 kilometres from Rio to the oil city of Macaé. The roads became narrower and narrower, the little houses more and more tightly packed next to each other. "It's not such a bad area," he said to me. Not that I'd asked him.

He had been given the job of taking me to the accommodation the club had arranged for me.

André stopped outside a small stone building in the middle of one of Macaé's favelas, as the city's poor districts are known. They get their name from the eponymous Brazilian climbing plant – both of them take root somewhere before slowly spreading further and further. Most people live in these poverty-stricken areas illegally, and many of the favelas are controlled by drug lords. Furious, I walked through the house. The kitchen cupboards were missing a few doors and the walls were so poorly insulated that you could hear every single word being spoken on the street outside. The president of Macaé Esporte had promised me a house by the beach. His tactic had obviously been to wait for me to arrive in Brazil before revealing what the conditions there would really be like.

When we first met that afternoon, the president had no recollection of what I had been promised. He was a short man who couldn't read or write – but that didn't stop him from being a fairly influential politician in the city. I was the first foreign player from Europe ever to sign with his club, and he had absolutely no idea how to get the bureaucratic ball rolling for me to be allowed to play there. Usually it worked the other way round. There's huge demand for rising stars from Brazil, and every year clubs from all over the world spend hundreds of millions of pounds on them. They are their country's true ambassadors. Players like Ronaldo, Ronaldinho or Neymar usually wait until they are transferred to a foreign team before adopting the names we all come to know, and these depend on the region where they grew up. The country boasts an endless supply for its domestic professional league. Every year the clubs are turned completely inside out by all the transfers that take place, but still they manage to be as strong as ever when competing – no other country on the planet produces so much raw talent.

There are plenty of examples of Brazilian footballers who have been deceived by clubs or agents. A few years ago, seven young Brazilians had spent several days stranded at Frankfurt Airport.

They had been promised 3,000 euros per month playing in a minor European league, so their parents had sold everything they had in order to buy them each a one-way ticket. But the club had changed its mind at the last minute and didn't even bother meeting the players at the airport. The leagues in Greece and Turkey are considered particularly corrupt in this respect. In the past Brazilian players have been known to give up their whole livelihoods, only to be fobbed off with a fraction of what they were originally promised upon arriving.

Now I had the pleasure of experiencing the same thing in the home country of all those cheated players. I presented a form to the president which I needed for my work permit. The man did know how to write his name, but he hesitated anyway. He told me he was in the middle of an election campaign. "If I sign this now and you cause trouble, I'll be risking my political career." He even refused to pay for my flight, even though he had promised he would do so a week earlier. And things didn't get any better. My preliminary contract had been signed, but before signing my final contract he wanted to discuss my salary again. In Brazil everybody knew that the club, just like many others in the league, paid the majority of its players illegally in cash. The practice has always been tolerated by Brazil's politicians – none of the country's elected officials would dare mess with football.

I spent the night in a hotel. In my anger I had threatened the president that I would lodge a complaint about the club with FIFA. But what was the point? It wouldn't make my situation any better. That one meeting was enough for me to realise that I needed to start looking around for alternatives.

I spent a couple of days at a club called Gama, not far from the capital, Brasilia, but things were no less chaotic there than they had been at Macaé. I simply couldn't have afforded to sign with them anyway, since Gama was barely able to pay its players more than a couple of hundred euros per month – what little savings I had wouldn't have been enough if I were on such a low income, especially as I still hadn't quite finished paying off the mountain of legal fees I had amassed in Singapore.

My search for a new club took several weeks. I spent many hours on the road – I would spend half my day at the office of Vogler, my agent, before quickly heading into Rio, where one of the clubs allowed me to join its players for training. The traffic chaos that reigns in Brazilian cities is an absolute disaster – the only way you can hope to get into town quickly is by taking one of the overcrowded public buses. A lane is reserved for them on the highways heading into the city.

One day I sat by the window at the back of the bus, my kitbag on my lap. The closer we got to the city, the fuller the bus became. A young man clutching a bag of peanuts sat down next to me. After a couple of minutes he started talking to me quietly in Portuguese. Countless people had already tried flogging me all sorts of things in Brazil: drugs, fruit, women, and plenty of peanuts. "No thanks, I don't want anything," I said, as I always did. But the man didn't let up and carried on talking at me. I didn't give in, shaking my head firmly until all of a sudden the bus stopped and he frantically jumped off.

An American woman sitting two rows behind me leaned forward. She looked pale. "He just tried to mug you and you didn't even notice," she said. She had been living in Brazil for years and had understood what the peanut seller was saying. Apparently he had a gun in his jacket pocket and wanted my mobile phone and wallet. Dozens of similar muggings occur in Rio every day. The cramped buses mean the victims have no chance of escaping. The perpetrators speak to their victims in a tone you might use to talk about the weather. Even if other passengers realise what's going on next to them, they're usually too frightened to say anything. I wasn't always lucky in Brazil, but for those few minutes all my guardian angels were on board that bus to Rio with me.

I'm not the kind of person to get upset over an experience like that for long. What really does bother me though is not being signed to a club. Even so, I did my best to enjoy the more positive aspects of life in Brazil. Amalia and I spent Christmas with orphans and homeless people in one of Rio de Janeiro's toughest favelas. We brought chocolate and had a truly enjoyable evening with them. The people there wanted to have fun together, and whether or not they spoke the same language as us was completely irrelevant.

After a while I signed a professional contract with a Rio-based club called America FC, a popular club which has won the State Championship seven times. I trained and played a few pre-season matches for them, but it turned out that they were in financial difficulties and couldn't afford to pay me. It was incredibly frustrating and I began to wonder if I would ever get to play a competitive match in Brazil and break the world record.

Then, out of the blue, I finally received the offer I had been waiting for. Atlético Ibirama, one of the biggest clubs in Santa Catarina in southern Brazil, had heard about me. Many people of German and Italian heritage had settled in this region around the time of the Second World War, making it perhaps the most European region in all of South America. The full name of the club is actually Club Atlético Hermann Aichinger, named after a wealthy Austrian who donated land to the club to build its stadium. In the nearby city of Blumenau there was even an annual Oktoberfest, which attracted people from all over Brazil.

I can judge pretty quickly whether or not a person is being genuine with me. After spending five minutes at the club's ground I was certain that my world record attempt was now going to succeed after all. The club was located in between two patches of forest, its pitch nestled in a sea of green. I accepted their offer there and then, the idyllic isolation of Ibirama making me quickly forget all the trouble back in Rio de Janeiro.

No sooner had I signed a half-year contract taking me up to the end of the regional championship than an unusual commotion began to sweep over the little club. I was about to become the first German to play professional football in Brazil, and news also spread of the world record I was about to lay claim to. The club's peaceful routine vanished. We were visited by TV crews from all over the world every day. Brazil's largest broadcaster, Globo, profiled me in a long documentary and journalists even came all the way from Germany. When interviewed by a reporter from Germany's ARD broadcaster, Genesio Ayres Marchetti, the club's vice president, made it all sound somewhat grander than it was: "Lutz has lifted the curtain on our club for all the world to see." He avoided saying my surname. Nobody in Brazil could pronounce it, so everyone called me "*Goleiro Alemao*" [German Goalkeeper] or "*Alemao Indiano*" [German Indian] because of my long hair.

For the fourth time in my life, journalists began calling me incessantly. There was, however, one major difference compared to my imprisonment in Singapore, my heart stopping in Bradford and the bizarre affair with my stolen goalkeeper shirt in New Zealand: For the first time I was truly proud of my situation.

Unfortunately it was to be several agonising weeks before I was finally able to play my first match. I had managed to sprain one of my fingers during one of my very first training sessions. What's more, Brazilian bureaucracy proved to be more stubborn than expected when it came to processing my application for a work permit. In the end all I could do was watch our first home match from the stands. The stadium had been designed to hold 8,000 spectators, but such details are merely theoretical in Brazil. What matters is how many people fit inside the stadium, and in our case it must have been at least 12,000. The fans would perch on the roof, on the walls, and even sit two to a seat. They didn't need to conceal their flares when entering the stadium; there were no security checks anyway. You could have strolled in with a nuclear bomb and nobody would have batted an eyelid. That mass of people produced a brilliant, deafening noise.

The jungle began directly behind the main stand. The president told me that the noise upset many of the animals, and that sometimes the monkeys responded particularly aggressively. "There's this one really big one which has already come out of the jungle a few times. It sits in a tree behind the stadium and starts screaming. It drowns out everything else." A while ago it had even attacked a spectator, he said, but the person managed to walk away from it relatively unscathed.

A couple of days later I had recovered from my finger injury and was able to begin training again. We spent at least eight hours a day at the training ground, and were it not for the Brazilians and their perpetual good mood it would have been about as enjoyable as a military drill. A little later people really admired Jürgen Klinsmann for introducing eight-hour shifts at Bayern Munich, but they had been an everyday occurrence where I was in Brazil for years – just like they are in most professions around the world. Those training sessions were some of the toughest in my career. Contrary to the cliché that Brazilians are not interested in the player between the sticks, I can't think of any country where more attention is paid to honing the goalkeeper's skills than in Brazil.

It was during one of those gruelling training sessions that I saw the monkey for myself. It came out of the jungle just 100 metres away from the training ground and began to approach us in a frenzied dash. It was muscular and a good two metres tall. "Everyone inside," shouted the coach, and we ran for it. A quarter of an hour later the monkey was gone again. Other than the odd protest against the most popular sport in the world, the creature never did any harm. And since it never actually attacked any of us the authorities decided not to hunt it.

It had been two weeks since I first came to Ibirama. I gradually got to know the other players. Until that point my life hadn't always been easy, but it had been a walk in the park compared to the things those guys had been through. Many had grown up in the favelas, six of them from Rio de Janeiro and four from São Paulo. None of them were from Ibirama. "Without football I would be dead," one player called Douglas once said to me. As a boy in Rio he had done exactly two things: played football and sold drugs. School was out of the question. Football had since transformed him into a well-paid young man, but in the dressing room the scars of his past were still clearly visible. When he was younger a gunfight had left him with several bullets in his abdomen. He didn't talk about it very much but everyone knew that he was still on good terms with Rio's drug lords. He had long been in a position where he could afford to buy his parents a big house in a more affluent part of Rio. "But they don't want to leave," he told me. "And why should they, if they're happy?" Many of the players' families had lived in the same districts for decades, and even if one of their sons manages to become prosperous they choose to stay where they are.

Ever since the start of my career I've had the same pre-match rituals which are designed to make me less nervous. Before kick-off I always step onto the pitch with my left foot first, and I always put my left shin pad on before the right one. I also recite the Lord's Prayer twice before the match begins – that helps too. But on that day I was more nervous than I had been in a long time. We had travelled by bus to Jaraguá do Sul for an away game. Twenty thousand spectators had turned up and were radiating that chaotic vitality for which Brazilian football is famous. They danced up in the stands despite the sweltering Sunday afternoon heat, letting off flares and fireworks. Barely any of them were aware that I was creating a new world record, but I told myself they were celebrating with me.

Our goalkeeper coach fired a few shots at my goal while the outfield players warmed up in front of me. That was my usual routine. I had done it all thousands of times before. But that moment became etched into my memory. Over the past 15 years I had travelled several million kilometres in the name of football. Memories from my childhood came flooding back; there was the afternoon when my friend Tobias Probst and I had sworn that one day we would play in Brazil. And now, a quarter of a century on, I really was doing it.

The game began and I felt an immense sense of pride welling inside me. I had never been interested in what other people said about me or what they thought of my career. At that moment I was happy with what football had given me, despite all the pain and the things I had gone without. And I thought to myself that perhaps, through my eventful career, I had even given something back to football, a sport that is so good at reflecting life.

But I didn't have much time to waste on such thoughts during the next 90 minutes. While it's true that the national side have been practising tactically advanced football for years, the old cliché still applies in Brazil's regional competitions that in South America they're not too worried about having a watertight defence. Shot after shot rolled towards me. I needed to focus as much as possible, since I couldn't afford to make any mistakes during that match. I managed it, although in the end we did lose 1-0. The TV channel broadcasting the game named me man of the match.

Usually if I lose a match I'll be in a bad mood for at least two days – I've been like that ever since childhood. But that day was different, even minutes after the final whistle. I was overcome by a feeling of complete satisfaction and happiness, in the knowledge that I had become the first person to play competitive, professional football in all six FIFA confederations. My team-mates were also aware that that Sunday was a special day for me. On our way back to Ibirama, one of them produced a cool box full of beer. Two of them had drums, and they began to sing. Others provided accompaniment to the music with plastic bottles filled with sand and little stones. A couple of the players got out of their seats and started dancing in the aisle of the bus. They always used to sing, whether in the dressing room, before and after training, or on the bus. Today I still keep a couple of videos of them on my phone, and they're the best remedy if I'm ever in a bad mood. Until then I had usually managed to avoid being forced to pick up a drum and join in with them. But now they wanted me to sing too. "Alemao, Alemao," they shouted again and again until I finally gave in and started dancing with them. I had picked up the odd word in Portuguese – it was hard not to, living in Brazil – and it was just about enough for me to join in with their Brazilian folk songs. We danced and sang all the way back to Ibirama.

If it were possible for me to capture a single moment from my life and put it on repeat again and again in an infinite loop until I died, then I would choose those two hours on the rickety bus, even if it is true that the way I sing is exactly the same as the way I live my life: In my own special way.

EPILOGUE

That emotional day in Brazil when I became the first footballer to play professionally in all six FIFA confederations was back in 2008, but as you can probably guess that's not quite the end of the story. For a start, having played on six of the seven continents, I still had one to go ... Antarctica.

But first things first. I completed the season with Atletico Ibirama and we finished in mid-table, which was round about where the club usually finished. I also played a cup match in the world famous Maracana Stadium against the legendary Botafogo team, which was a very special moment in my life. Brazil was a wonderful experience and a great lifestyle. Amalia loved the sunshine, the beach, the great food and the fact that I was really chilled out. I would just go to training then come home and we'd hang out by the pool. Happy days ... but soon it was time to move on.

After the end of the Brazilian season I was recruited by the manager of the Cuban national team, Reinhold Fanz, and worked as a goalkeeping coach. We took the whole team out of Cuba and created training camps in Germany and Austria, which was financed by a German businessman. Reinhold was a tough coach and we had two or three training sessions every day and plenty of practice matches. The team developed well, but they were still well below European standards.

The camps had state-of-the-art facilities and the players stayed in expensive hotels. You can imagine what 30 Cubans, who would usually have had a glass of milk, one egg and one piece of toast for breakfast, plus some rice and beans or pasta two times a day, thought of eating every meal at the mega buffet of a 5-star restaurant. They were loving it!

In the World Cup qualification campaign we managed to reach the group stages easily, but then we played tough games against Trinidad and Tobago, Guatemala and the USA. When we played the USA in Washington we travelled with a small group of players and lots of Cuban security people. They were very worried that the players would try to flee into America – and this is exactly what happened. Two of our best players escaped the clutches of the security guards before the game and we got beaten 6-1. After the match Reinhold was fired and my time with the team was also cut short. Two years later, when I was in Norway, I got a phone call at 5am from my German agent. He said that there was a black guy standing outside his front door and saying my name. It turned out that it was the goalkeeper from the Cuban national team, Dany Quintero. He had managed to escape from another Cuban training camp in Germany and ended up hiding in my agent's house until the rest of the team had returned home. He is still living in Germany today, studying and playing non-league football.

After my adventure with the Cuban national team ended in 2008, I was lured back to Norway to play for Flekkerøy, which is a beautiful holiday island connected to the mainland by a tunnel. And it was here that I started to think more and more about something that had been bothering me over the years: Global warming and the future of the planet.

It's true that we professional footballers aren't exactly the best custodians of our planet. I myself have flown around the world countless times. Building stadiums and hosting matches places a considerable burden on the natural world. And were it not for us, would gas-guzzlers like Hummer SUVs ever have become so popular? Basically, it's not the most environmentally friendly of professions, and people probably think that we don't really care.

But anyone who spends a bit of time travelling around the world will see what's happening right now. It became particularly apparent to me in Norway, where I played four times during my career and felt more comfortable than anywhere else. The quality of life in Norway is wonderful. In Flekkerøy, apart from a picturesque house by the water, the club even lent me a fishing boat. It takes a lot to really calm me down – but a couple of hours in that little wooden boat made me the calmest, most balanced person on the planet. I've gone back to that place time and again. I can't see myself ever living in the north of the country, where you don't see a ray of sunlight for months on end. But Oslo? Just say the word and I'll happily live there forever. In 2009 I signed another contract in this great country, this time with Manglerud Star in the Norwegian Second Division. I also took on a few coaching and managerial duties.

I must have been a Viking in a past life – in no other country does playing my very best football seem to come so naturally to me. In no other country have I met so many nice people. And in no other country do I enjoy the scenery as much as I do there. Sadly, climatologists predict that the country's 1,600 glaciers could all melt within the next 100 years. This would result in water shortages in the summer and an energy crisis, since the country is heavily reliant on hydroelectricity. Rodent populations are also dwindling, with countless species affected.

The situation is similar in New Zealand, particularly on the South Island where I played. Over the last 30 years, the country's 50 biggest glaciers have lost almost 20 per cent of their volume. Now only around 40 cubic kilometres remain. What's more, they are not only part of the ecology of the area, but they also make up the spectacular scenery of the island. I've rarely seen anything as beautiful as Mount Cook, which rises to almost 4,000 metres.

The effects of this climate catastrophe can be felt in almost all of the countries that I played in. For example, the Aral Sea in Central Asia has shrunk by 90 per cent in the past 50 years and reminds me of a lifeless, lunar landscape. Also, when playing on the Maldives I saw how entire sections of the islands could be submerged during storms. And then there's Canada, which is home to around two thirds of the world's 25,000 polar bears. They are only able to hunt when seals briefly surface for air through holes in the ice. But Hudson Bay is now only frozen over for a few months each year and the period is becoming ever shorter, having decreased by three weeks over the last twenty years. And that means the polar bears are going hungry, causing their population to decline more quickly. The list goes on.

Back in 2007, while I was in Vancouver, I had started an organisation called Global United FC. The idea was that we would use football to highlight the problems facing the world due to climate change, and I would use my contacts in the game to organise matches featuring well-known football stars to raise money and awareness. "We love football. We love our planet" is our catchphrase. In the winter of 2008−09 the first Global United FC event was held, an indoor tournament in Norway, and then we came up with the idea of playing a fundraising match in Antarctica. The added bonus of course would be my chance to play on the last remaining continent, but something like this was going to take a lot of planning.

So, in the meantime I continued to travel the globe in the name of football. In 2009 I was coaching and playing at Manglerud Star, which had big plans and brought in plenty of new expensive players with international experience, such as Namibian international Oliver Risser and former Norwegian international Tommy Stenersen. But the club got into financial difficulties and things turned sour after a big argument about wages. After two months without being paid I decided to leave. It was frustrating because I had had the option to renew my contract in Flekkerøy, which was the most relaxing and peaceful time of my life, and I also had an offer to work as a goalkeeping coach in Sudan for big money. However, I had believed in Mangleruds long-term plan and, in the end, I was one of the few players who got every single penny they were owed before the club went out of business eighteen months later.

In an attempt to find a new club I got in touch with a few people in Africa, and my former teammate Oliver Risser told me good things about Namibia. He said there were lots of Germans living there, it was an English-speaking country and it was close to South Africa. It all sounded good. So just a few days before the transfer window closed, I signed a two-year contract with Ramblers FC in Windhoek. I took over as a sports director, but I was also registered as a player and could play in matches.

Ramblers was one of two teams in the Namibian Premier League which were based in former white areas, had white owners and were referred to as 'white' clubs, even though all their players were black. The two local teams, SK Windhoek and Ramblers, had the best youth academies in the country, but the fewest supporters. The teams from the local township of Katutura had no real infastructure, but had a massive number of fans. So when we played at home we were lucky to have 500 supporters, but whenever there was a big match in Katutura's 10,000-seater Sam Nujoma Stadium, named after Namibia's founding father, the stadium was rocking.

The head coach of Ramblers was a nice guy, a former national player, but he didn't take his job very seriously. There was no structure to his training programme and he had no idea about fitness or tactics. An average training session consisted of a 10-minute warm-up, led by a senior player, and then an hour-long first team versus youth team match. No wonder the team had performed poorly. After a bad start I took over as head coach as well, and the first thing I did was create a clear structure for the team. We decided on a modern 4-2-3-1 formation, and during the week I worked on fitness and tactics. The players already had bags of skill and technique.

Luckily we had a two-week break for some international games and I had some time to change things around. In our first match, away against the current champions African Stars, the tactics worked and we drew 1-1. Overall we played nine games during my time as head coach, winning three, drawing five and losing only one. This took the team away from the foot of the league and put us securely in mid-table.

I was then called up by Belgian coach Tom Sainfiet. Tom was in charge of the Namibian national team, known as the Brave Warriors, and wanted me to assist him as goalkeeping coach. It was a very interesting and rewarding time, especially after my stint with the Cuban national team had been cut short. Kurdish head coach Ali Akan took over at Ramblers and I concentrated on my job as a sports director and national team goalkeeping coach. I was also preparing for the 2010 World Cup in South Africa because German TV station ZDF, one of the biggest channels in the world, had hired me to work as an expert presenter during the tournament.

The highlight of my time with Namibia was the match we played against South Africa, exactly 100 days before the start of the World Cup. It was a sell-out crowd with many important football people in attendance, and Namibia played one of the best games in its young history. We drew 1-1 after being 1-0 down, and the South Africa manager, Carlos Alberto Perreira, was visibly angry after the final whistle. Prior to the game he had made disrespectful comments about our world ranking. But we had the last laugh, and it's still one of my proudest moments.

Another great memory I have is working with Namibian goalkeeper Athiel Mbaha, who played in the South African league with many teams, including the Orlando Pirates, as well as representing his country in the Africa Cup of Nations. The most amazing thing is that he achieved all this despite being deaf since the age of seven — he was unable to hear or speak during matches. Playing at such a high level with this handicap is unique, and he did suffer during his career as it's very easy to blame mistakes or poor results on a player who can't speak up for himself. But my methods really worked on him and he was brilliant during my time with the team. I remain close friends with Athiel; he plays for the Global United FC team and has trained to be a goalkeeping coach with me as his instructor. In 2013 I gave Athiel a present via Global United FC, a top-class hearing aid. Athiel is now able to hear again and he has also dramatically improved his speech. I am so happy for him and I hope that this small donation will make his life as a coach a bit easier. For me he is a real hero of modern sport.

My years in Africa were inspiring, fascinating and often funny. This is mainly because Africans are the most superstitious people in the world, and I witnessed many bizarre incidents during my time with the team. Eggs were buried near the goalposts for good luck. Witch doctors sprinkled players with all kinds of weird-smelling liquids. Players with bad injuries carried on like there was nothing wrong with them after a visit from the juju man. Some of my players were even afraid of their girlfriends putting a spell on them, and most players had more than one girlfriend!

On a less amusing note, at one point when I was in charge of Ramblers I decided I wanted my players to take a health check, including all the normal blood tests that you would give to European players. But the whole team refused and I was called into the president's office. He informed me that if I insisted on a blood sample I might have no players left. Plenty of my players were HIV positive, but it was a topic you didn't discuss. Not just HIV, but also alcohol misuse and domestic violence, both of which are massive problems in Namibia. One of my players was murdered because he looked "too intensely" at his former girlfriend. But despite these problems the country and its natural surroundings, from the deserts in the south to the Etosha National park in the north, are incredible. It has an unbelievable range of wildlife and the people are friendly and welcoming.

However, I did find the behaviour of some white people disgusting. Once when I was standing at some traffic lights, a fat white farmer in a pick-up truck stopped next to me. It was cold and raining, and in the back of the truck, out in the open, a black woman was sitting with her baby, while the farmer's dog was sat in the front. When I see something like that I lose it. I asked the guy to put his dog in the back and let the shivering lady and her baby sit on the front seat. The answer shocked me: I don't let a "kaffer" in my car. I called him a racist c**t and we nearly had a fight in the street.

The white Namibians I dealt with on a daily basis were very liberal and friendly – the Ramblers' president, Harald Hecht, a born and bred Namibian who was very tall and had red hair, was a top guy – but most of the other white people I met were assholes. I think it's genetic. I really admire the black people who have forgiven the former regime and are trying their best to live a normal life.

Just before the 2010 World Cup we held a massive Global United FC event in Windhoek. I invited 30 international players, including Sunday Oliseh (Nigeria), Fredi Bobic (Germany), Tony Sanneh (USA), Wynton Rufer (New Zealand), Sean Dundee (South Africa and Liverpool), Phil Masinga (South Africa and Leeds), Lucas Radebe (South Africa and Leeds), Jens Nowotny (Germany), Stig Tøfting (Denmark), Stig Inge Bjornebye (Norway and Liverpool) and many more. It was the biggest football event in the history of the country and, as Namibia unfortunately missed out on any involvement in the World Cup, it gave them two days of World Cup fever.

Then the World Cup arrived and I suddenly found myself in a completely different world. I was a pundit for German channel ZDF, together with Oliver Kahn, and I was responsible for reporting on all the African teams, as well as Australia and New Zealand. I worked really hard to prepare for every assignment, as I was now starring alongside football legends like Zinedine Zidane, Edgar Davids, Jay Jay Okocha and Zico. Once word got around of my knowledge of African football in particular, and the crazy story of my life all over the world, I was interviewed by many other channels and made to feel like a celebrity. It turned out that my move to Africa was one of the best I ever made. I spent the whole tournament in South Africa travelling between our studio in Johannesburg and all the other host cities, and I came across pretty well on screen.

One night during the tournament I was invited to a function in one of Johannesburg's top nightclubs, Taboo. I was there with South African legends like Mark Fish and Phil Masinga, and some other big international names. Also in the club that night was the American/Senegalese rapper Akon and his entourage of around 25 people. The big Hummers were parked outside. It just so happened that I decided to leave the club, along with my colleagues, at exactly the same time as Akon and his crew. But when we got to the door it turned out that the four bouncers were all Orlando Pirates fans and recognised me as the German keeper who had played for them not so long ago. They all wanted to have a chat and get their picture taken with me. Unfortunately for Akon this blocked his path, much to the annoyance of his gang. It nearly ended in a fight. During the exchanges I heard one of the bouncers utter the classic line: "I don't give a fuck who this Akon is, I'm making a picture with my favourite keeper." That raised me to another level in the eyes of my TV colleagues.

Early in 2011 I had to decide if I still wanted to continue coaching in Namibia or return to Europe and push my coaching, managing and media career. I was also a coaching instructor for the German FA and was sent abroad on short-term projects to educate coaches all over the world. I was given the job title of 'Foreign Expert' and held courses in Mali, India, Namibia, South Africa, Brazil, Burundi, Azerbaijan and many other countries. It was a job I loved.

I was considering a few head coaching positions in Africa when an old friend, Alex Rosen, called and informed me that he was now the head of youth at 1899 Hoffenheim, which is a really well-run Bundesliga club. Hoffenheim is famous for being based in a small town and having a wealthy owner, Dietmar Hopp, who loves the club and has financed its development. The club is therefore relatively rich and this has always attracted negative attention. But the project at Hoffenheim – the club rose from the fifth tier of German football to the Bundesliga in eight years – is something special. It focuses on an inventive, modern playing style, and also on bringing players through its brilliant youth academy.

Alex told me that he thought a guy with my international experience would fit in very well with what the club was trying to do and he arranged an appointment with the sports director, Ernst Tanner. Tanner was a special guy. Formerly the boss of the youth of 1860 Munich, he became well known for his skill at scouting players in Germany. We had never met before, but after just a few minutes I knew that this was the club I wanted to work for. A few days later I got an offer and I was very proud to be working with such highly qualified and hardworking people like Ernst Tanner and Alex Rosen.

As I write this during the run up to the 2014 World Cup in Brazil, I am still working at Hoffenheim. That's four years in one place! Things have changed slightly, as Ernst Tanner has moved to Red Bull Salzburg to take charge of the youth system, and in 2013 the club made the brilliant decision to make Alex Rosen the sports director and sign Markus Gisdol as head coach. This saved the club after former Bayern Munich and Liverpool player Markus Babbel's disastrous 10 months in charge.

So now I work with Alex Rosen in his new position as sports director, and it has been great to team up with a person who loves football just as much as I do. I am responsible for international relations and scouting, which is a very wide-ranging job, but basically I help the sports director to sell players and find suitable new players for the team. I use my wide network of contacts, and of course I still get to travel all over the world and scratch my itchy feet! I love my job and I can imagine working here for many more years. I also really look up to the club's owner, Dietmar Hopp, and the way he supports the work we are trying to do. On top of that, I have never met a guy who puts so much of his private wealth into charity projects without talking about it. Global United FC and 1899 Hoffenheim work together on various charity projects in Africa and the organisation is doing great.

Amalia are I are still going strong. We had some lovely, calm and peaceful years in Norway, and then when I finished playing we moved back to Germany and we have a very settled life with Amalia Junior and our beloved Labrador, Dana. It has not been easy for her to live with a guy like me. When we first met I was moving from club to club, country to country, always chasing a new opportunity, sometimes not earning very much, sometimes going months without earning anything at all. It was not exactly the glamorous, fingernail-painting life of a WAG that you read about in the gossip magazines. But she always stood by me, in the good times and the bad times, and I owe all the success I have achieved in recent years to her. Even now it is tough for her when I am travelling the world looking at players or doing TV work, but like the old saying goes, behind every successful man stands a great woman, and this is certainly true in my case.

And of course when I am away from home she still gets to see me on TV! When I appeared on ESPN in Singapore in 1999, people told me that I was quite cool and knowledgeable and came across very well. But after my prison stint I thought I would never get another chance. As it turned out, the 2010 World Cup opened up many doors for me and now my media career is really taking off. I regularly appear as a pundit for the Europa League on German channel Sat 1, and I covered the 2013 Africa Cup of Nations for Eurosport.

At the 2012 Africa Cup of Nations in Gabon and Equatorial Guinea, John Bennett from BBC World was looking for a pundit with good knowledge of African football and approached me. During the tournament we did a few interviews and I was also a guest on a number of shows. I must have performed quite well as I'm now a regular pundit for BBC World. I did a lot of stuff for them during the 2013 Africa Cup of Nations in South Africa and the Olympic football tournament at London 2012, but I am especially proud of my work during Euro 2012 in Poland and Ukraine, and two Champions League Finals in Munich (2012) and London (2013).

And as I write this, 2014 is turning into an even crazier year for me, as I am fully involved in the ZDF coverage of the 2014 World Cup in Brazil. I have been making a documentary series with one of Germany's best filmmakers, Albert Knechtel, about the 12 host cities for German TV, and also creating clips to be shown before the matches, which has involved travelling all over the country and interviewing Brazilian football legends like Zico, Rivaldo, Ze Roberto, Paulo Sergio and many more. During the tournament I will be working as an expert for ZDF, along with Oliver Kahn, as well as doing reports and interviews for BBC World.

During filming I also tried to make more friends in the animal kingdom. While I was in the Amazon rainforest, near the World Cup venue in Manaus, I got the chance to swim with some rare pink river dolphins. They're very strange and beautiful creatures and I thought about what it would be like to have one as a pet. But when I was swimming I got too close and the dolphin bit my finger. It must have mistaken it for a fish! There was lots of blood and it was very painful, but I just couldn't stop laughing. I still needed to finish the filming of me playing and swimming with the dolphins, so I held the one who bit me between my legs and patted him, praying that he wouldn't bite me in the downstairs department. The boat to the hospital took three hours, and when I got there they gave me three injections – one in my backside – but no painkillers as they stitched my finger up. As Mario Balotelli would say, "Why always me?"

I'm enjoying working in the media, but I still have things I want to achieve in football. I would like to be coach again, hopefully with a national team, and I also want to carry on working as a coaching instructor for the German FA. To pass my international experience and knowledge to others is a passion I want to continue.

And, of course, Global United FC continues to go from strength to strength. We started to make plans for the match in Antarctica way back in 2009. By the time I presented the project to Greenpeace with my former teammate and Norwegian national player Tommy Stenersen, I was well past caring if people laughed at me. My experiences from the previous months had taught me that a lot of clichés about footballers were simply untrue. I had contacted countless professional football players. Some of them I knew, some I didn't. I got hold of the phone numbers of players like Maradona and Beckham, even if the idea of getting them involved still sounded unrealistic. And amazingly one player after another said they were willing to join in: Solskjaer (Norway), Balakov (Bulgaria), Soldo (Croatia), Tøfting (Denmark), Oliseh (Nigeria), Cafu (Brazil) and even the legendary Argentinian goalkeeper Ubaldo Fillol. From Germany, former national players like Fredi Bobic, Jörg Heinrich and Marko Rehmer also got on board.

I've tried every trick in the book to secure the biggest names for the project. For instance, I was surprised how easy it was to arrange a meeting with Maradona in Buenos Aires. I just needed to call a few of his former Argentinian teammates. But our negotiations came to a halt as soon as they started. He had apparently hoped there would be money in it for him. But we don't want to pay anyone any money, not even Zinedine Zidane or David Beckham, who we are also trying to secure. The players have to really want to do it. I then used my Cuban contacts – I remembered that Maradona had been to the island a few times in the past for rehab as a guest of Castro – and had a few Cuban officials approach Maradona again. This time it worked! As it stands he has promised to participate in at least one Global United FC match.

We have played a number of charity matches over the last few years in Germany, Switzerland and Namibia to raise money and awareness for the project. And I even spent five days being filmed live inside an igloo! It was another crazy idea, but we raised 20,000 euros and received plenty of media coverage for Global United FC.

But the match we are planning to play on King George Island will probably attract the most attention. It's the largest of the South Shetland Isles and is only 120 kilometres away from the Antarctic coast. The game has to be held in December during the Antarctic summer, where temperatures can climb to between two and seven degrees. And we'll play at the airport of a research station there, as the runway is about as wide as a football pitch. There won't be any spectators, but the game will be recorded and used to make a 90-minute film highlighting the threat of climate change. The major football stars who take part in the film will address the problems that exist in these places, such as the impact of the melting ice, its implications for wildlife, and how countries like the Maldives will ultimately be affected by rising sea levels.

We want to use a sport that brings the entire world together to draw attention to the greatest problem on the planet. A lot of professional footballers have more of an influence on most ordinary people than politicians do. Your average football fan in Newcastle would rather drink a pint at the pub while watching football than worry about global warming. In Brazil I noticed how people would turn the volume down on the TV whenever politicians began talking about the issue. But if Romário or Bebeto talked about the most trivial of subjects, then the nation would hang on their every word. In Ivory Coast, more people listen to star striker Didier Drogba than any politician.

Ultimately, through the actions of iconic football players, it might be possible to make a considerable number of people aware of the massive problem that is affecting us all. At least it's worth a try. I want nothing more than to tap into new audiences for organisations that have already been fighting to raise people's awareness of this issue for years. And with the help of my dear friend Rainer Hahn, we have managed to set up a well-structured organisation which will hopefully continue to have success after we're gone.

It's a passion which has accompanied me over the years. After my tough time in prison in Singapore, and certainly after my resuscitation in England, it became clear that there's more to life than globetrotting and professional football. Together those two events became a turning point in my life. And so I intend to keep pursuing this problem – with at least the same doggedness as I've pursued my football career, which I don't intend to end before I turn 40. And my contacts, from Bolivia to Burundi, will help me, just as I hope they will help me to build a future in the football business later on.

As a child my powers of imagination could reach no further into the future than my mid- to late thirties, the age when you usually stop playing professional football. Even in my early twenties I could still hardly imagine what might come afterwards. Now I've reached that age, and I suspect that the truly important tasks in my life are only just beginning.

LUTZ PFANNENSTIEL: LIST OF CLUBS

1991–93	1. FC Bad Kötzting (Germany)
1993–94	Penang FA (Malaysia)
1994–95	Wimbledon (England)
1995–96	Nottingham Forest (England)
1996–97 (loan)	Orlando Pirates (South Africa)
1997	Sembawang Rangers (Singapore)
1997–98	TPV (Finland)
1998	FC Haka (Finland)
1998–99	SV Wacker Burghausen (Germany)
1999–2000	Geylang United (Singapore)
2001	Dunedin Technical (New Zealand)
2001–02 (loan)	Bradford Park Avenue (England)
2001–02	Huddersfield Town (England)
2002	ASV Cham (Germany)
2002–03	Bradford Park Avenue
2002	Dunedin Technical (New Zealand)
2003	Bærum SK (Norway)
2003	Dunedin Technical (New Zealand)
2004	Calgary Mustangs (Canada)
2004–06	Otago United (formerly Dunedin Technical) (New Zealand)
2006–07	KS Vllaznia Shkodër (Albania)
2007 FC	FC Bentonit Ijevan (Armenia)
2007	Bærum SK (Norway)
2007	Vancouver Whitecaps (Canada)
2008	America FC (Brazil)
2008	Clube Atlético Hermann Aichinger (Brazil)
2008–09	Flekkerøy (Norway)
2009	Manglerud Star (Norway)
2009–10	Ramblers (Namibia)
2003	Dunedin Technical (player-coach)
2007	FC Bentonit Ijevan (manager)
2008	Flekkerøy (goalkeeping coach)
2009	Manglerud Star (player-coach)
2009	Cuba (goalkeeping coach)
2009–10	Ramblers FC (head coach and technical director)
2009–10	Namibia (assistant and goalkeeping coach)
2011–	1899 Hoffenheim (Head of International Relations and Scouting)